THE ARMED ROVERS

THE ARMED ROVERS

Beauforts & Beaufighters over the Mediterranean

ROY C. NESBIT

Airlife
CLASSIC

Jacket Painting

The painting by Charles Thompson depicts the attack by Beauforts and Beaufighters on 26 October 1942 against the tanker *Prosperina*, known as 'Rommel's Last Tanker'. The sinking of the vessel outside Tobruk was considered by the Germans to be the deciding factor in the Battle of El Alamein.

Copyright © 1995 Roy C Nesbit

First published in the UK in 1995
by **Airlife Publishing Ltd**

This edition published 2002

British Library Cataloguing-in-Publication Data
A catalogue record for this book
is available from the British Library

ISBN 1 84037 369 5

Printed in England by Livesey Ltd., Shrewsbury (01743) 235651

Distributed in North America by
STACKPOLE BOOKS
5067 Ritter Road, Mechanicsburg, PA 17055
www.stackpolebooks.com

For a complete list of all Airlife titles please contact:

Airlife Publishing Ltd
101 Longden Road, Shrewsbury, SY3 9EB, England
E-mail: sales@airlifebooks.com
Website: www.airlifebooks.com

This book is dedicated to those who served in the maritime squadrons of the RAF and the Commonwealth Air Forces in the Mediterranean during the Second World War.

ACKNOWLEDGEMENTS

My thanks are due to officials and staff in the following organisations for help in researching the contents of this book: *Aeroplane Monthly*, London; Commonwealth War Graves Commission, Maidenhead; Deutsche Dienststelle, Berlin; Imperial War Museum, Lambeth; Ministry of Defence, Air Historical Branch, London; Ministry of Defence, Naval Historical Branch, London; National Maritime Museum, Greenwich; Public Record Office, Kew. I am also grateful for help with research, photographs, or checking of narrative to: Aviation Bookshop, London; Mr Rick Chapman, Germany; Squadron Leader J. Dudley F. Cowderoy, RAFVR; Mr Roger Hayward; Mr Karl Kössler, Germany; Mr Philip N. Owen; Mr Peter Petrick, Germany; Flight Lieutenant Andrew S. Thomas, RAF; 47 Squadron Archives, Lyneham.

I should also like to offer my sincere thanks to Charles J. Thompson, GAvA AFAA for his generosity in painting the picture on which the cover of this book is based.

This book includes accounts of some of the activities of maritime squadrons of the RAF in the Mediterranean, and could not have been written without the help and encouragement of some of those who served in these squadrons: Wing Commander A.H. Aldridge DFC* RAFVR; Flight Lieutenant T. Armstrong DFC RAFVR; Flight Lieutenant C M. Bounevialle DFC RAFVR; Flight Sergeant F.A. Brinton RAFVR; Wing Commander D.O. Butler DFC RAF (ret'd); Flight Lieutenant E.F. Carlisle-Brown RAFVR; Flight Lieutenant E.R.R. Cerely MM RAFVR; Warrant Officer A.J. Coles RAFVR; Flight Lieutenant The Rev. L.W. Daffurn DFC RAFVR; Group Captain M.L. Gaine DSO AFC RAF (ret'd); Flight Lieutenant D.N. Gates RAFVR; Squadron Leader E. Gillies DFC* RAF (ret'd); Flying Officer C.M. Grant RAFVR; Flying Officer D.E. Hamar RAFVR; the late Wing Commander D.E. Hammond DSO DFC* RNZAF; Wing Commander N.B. Harvey DSO RAF (ret'd); the late Squadron Leader N. Hearn-Phillips AFC DFM RAF (ret'd); Flight Lieutenant W.A.G. Hook DFC RAFVR; Flight Lieutenant S.J. Kernaghan AFC DFM RCAF; Flight Lieutenant R.C. Kitching RAFVR; the late Wing Commander J.A. Lee-Evans DFC RAF (ret'd); the late Wing Commander R.V. Manning DFC CD RCAF (ret'd); Group Captain C.A. Masterman OBE DFC RAF (ret'd); Flight Lieutenant T.A. McGarry DFC RAFVR; Flight Lieutenant J.G. Miller DFM RAFVR; Flight Lieutenant T.F.P. Nisbet AFC RAFVR; Warrant Officer S.G. Philpott RAAF; Flight Lieutenant E.P.A.I. Roberts RAFVR; Flight Lieutenant D.W. Schmidt DFC* RCAF; Flight Sergeant J. Sercombe RAF (ret'd); Flight Lieutenant N.G. Spark RAFVR; Wing Commander L.H. Tester DFM RAF (ret'd); Flight Lieutenant G.G. Tuffin RCAF; Flight Lieutenant H.F. Watlington DFM RCAF; Flight Lieutenant E.G. Whiston RAFVR.

FOREWORD
by
Air Chief Marshal Sir Christopher Foxley-Norris,
GCB, OBE, DSO, MA, RAF (Ret'd)

This book is of particular interest because it details the critical part played by
the RAF's anti-shipping squadrons in defeating Rommel, by interdicting his
essential sea supplies; a fact which he was the first to acknowledge. I did not
come on the scene until late in 1943, but was thereafter a Flight Commander
listed in one of the Beaufighter squadrons on page 14 (252) and finally
Commanding Officer of 603 Squadron.

The anti-shipping squadrons involved were equipped successively with
Blenheims Mk IV, Beauforts and Beaufighters, and torpedo-carrying Wellingtons at night. All suffered heavy casualties, largely attributable to one
inherent defect in armament, i.e. that the aircraft had to point directly at, and
usually overfly, their heavily defended targets at low level. This applied
particularly to the torpedo-carrier, which had to fly straight and level to
launch. At one stage, the Beaufighter squadrons were suffering fifty per cent
casualties. The two versions of rockets proved the most effective armament but
were introduced deplorably late into the Mediterranean squadrons.

Well-earned credit for the successful campaign is given to the all-important
flow of intelligence originating from the central decoding unit at Bletchley.
The Axis never woke up to this fact and attributed the vulnerability
erroneously to all sorts of other sources.

A detailed account is given of the calamitous Cos-Leros operation but the
blame for it (largely Churchill's initiative) was never directed at the right
heads. The basic defect lay in the attempt to conduct a major amphibious
assault and occupation without being able to ensure air superiority. A lot of
lives were lost in consequence.

The book fills a major gap in contemporary accounts of World War II. The
crews concerned performed with skill and courage unsurpassed in any other
theatre of war, and they played a vital part in the ultimate victory.

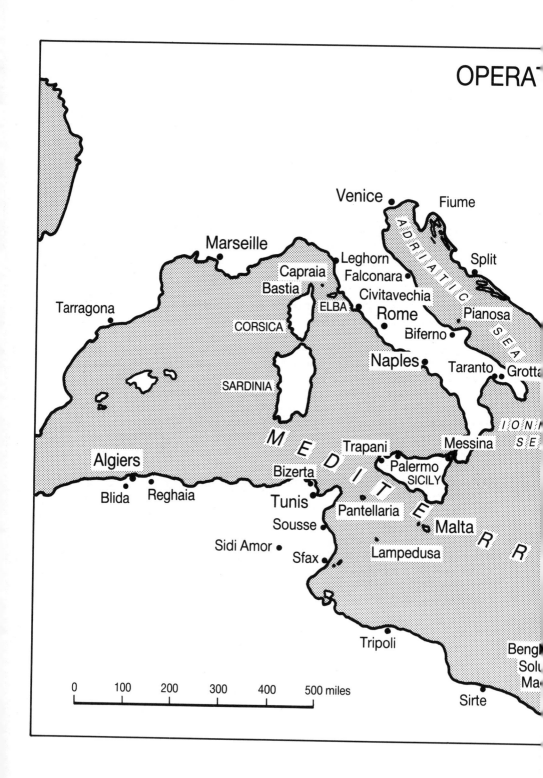

OPERAT

Venice · Fiume

Marseille · ADRIATIC

Leghorn Split
Capraia Falconara
Bastia Civitavechia Pianosa
Tarragona ELBA Rome
CORSICA Biferno SEA

Naples Taranto Grotta
SARDINIA

ION
SE

MEDITER Trapani Messina
Algiers Bizerta Palermo
Blida Reghaia Tunis SICILY
Pantellaria
Sousse Malta
Sidi Amor Lampedusa
Sfax

Tripoli Beng
Solu
Ma

| 0 | 100 | 200 | 300 | 400 | 500 miles |

Sirte

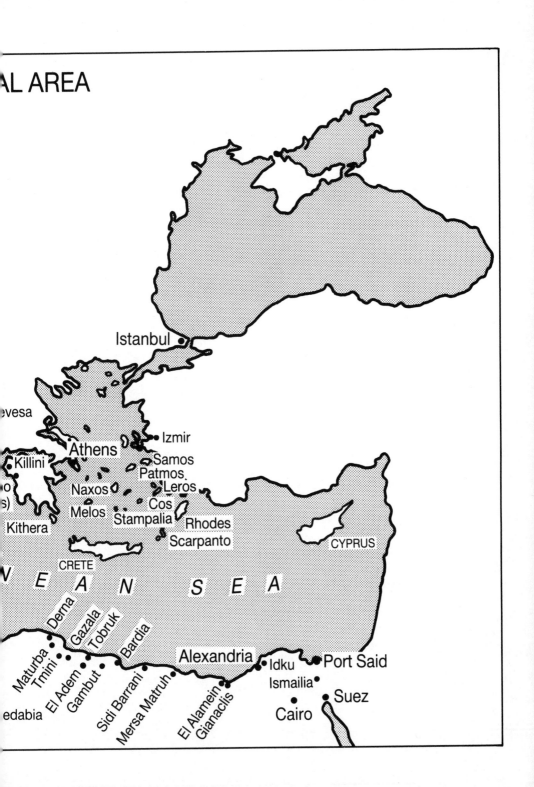

AL AREA

Istanbul

evesa

Izmir

Athens

Killini

Samos

Patmos

(o

Naxos

Leros

s)

Cos

Kithera

Melos

Stampalia

Rhodes

Scarpanto

CYPRUS

CRETE

M E A N   S E A

Derna

Gazala

Tobruk

Maturba

Bardia

Tmini

El Adem

Alexandria

Idku

Port Said

edabia

Gambut

Ismailia

Sidi Barrani

Suez

Mersa Matruh

El Alamein

Cairo

Gianaclis

CONTENTS

Foreword by Air Chief Marshal Sir Christopher
Foxley-Norris GCB OBE DSO MA RAF (ret'd).

1

THE STRIKE AIRCREWS

On 16 November 1942, the Air Member for Training, Air Marshal Sir A. Guy R. Garrod, sent a table of RAF operational casualties to the Air Member for Personnel, Air Marshal Sir Bertine E. Sutton. Rearranging this table in decreasing percentage of danger to the aircrews, it reads:

	Percentage Chance of Survival	
	One Tour	Two Tours
1. Torpedo bomber	17½	3
2. Light bomber	25½	6½
3. Fighter reconnaissance	31	9½
4. Night fighter	39	15
5. Bomber reconnaissance	42	17½
6. Day fighter	43	18½
7. Heavy and medium bombers	44	19½
8. Light general reconnaissance landplane	45	20
9. Medium general reconnaissance landplane	56	31½
10. Long-range fighter	59½	35½
11. Sunderland flying boat	66	43½
12. Heavy general reconnaissance landplane	71	50½
13. Catalina flying boat	77	60

These figures were not made known publicly at the time, nor were they circulated within the RAF. It was left to the aircrews on the squadrons to guess the statistical odds against them, if they chose to brood on that subject. The letter containing the figures is now available for scrutiny at the Public Record Office at Kew, and verifies that the average chance of survival on an operational tour in the RAF was appallingly low.

Of course, not every airman who failed to complete an operational tour was killed. Some were injured and forced to drop out. Some were shot down and became prisoners of war, sometimes after ditching in the sea. A very small number were taken off because they could not stand the strain, with the stigma of 'lacking moral fibre' to dog them for the remainder of their period of RAF service. But most of those who 'failed to return' from operational flights lost their lives.

Nevertheless, there were wide differences in the chances of survival, depending on the types of aircraft and the work on which each squadron was engaged. These figures demonstrate that the aircrews of the torpedo bomber and light bomber squadrons were more at risk than any others in the RAF. Although there were some light bomber squadrons in Bomber Command during the early stages of the war, such as those equipped with Battles and Blenheims, many of the squadrons in the dangerous top two categories formed part of Coastal Command in the UK or were maritime squadrons in the Mediterranean or the Far East. The men in these squadrons were known in the RAF as 'strike crews' and were engaged primarily on anti-shipping work.

One of the purposes of the memorandum was to try to establish a 'datum line' in operational flying hours for each category of aircraft, so that the airmen would have at least a fifty per cent chance of surviving their tours. It was calculated that the torpedo and light bomber aircrews reached this line after eighty hours of operational flying, whereas they were expected to fly for 200 operational hours, but the suggestion that it should be reduced was not acted upon. Instead, the tours remained at 200 hours, but training and tactics were improved. This book is concerned mainly with the men in eight such squadrons, during the periods when they were equipped with Bristol Beauforts or Bristol Beaufighters and flew in the Mediterranean between 1941 and 1945. These were 39, 42, 47, 144, 227, 252, 272 and 603 Squadrons.

At the outbreak of war, there were only two strike squadrons based in the UK – 22 and 42 Squadrons – with two more based in Singapore – 36 and 100 Squadrons. All these were equipped with the Vickers Vildebeest IV torpedo bomber, an obsolete biplane with open cockpits. The two-man crews were highly trained but handicapped by their slow, short-range machine and the absence of suitable fighter escort. They were easy prey for enemy fighters and defensive flak from warships.

Following the catastrophe of the fall of France in June 1940 and the entry of Italy into the war, there was an immediate need for more strike squadrons and trained aircrews. The anti-shipping squadrons were then required to cover most of the north-west coastline of Europe as well as the whole of the Mediterranean. At the same time the threat of the Japanese in the Far East was becoming even more menacing.

By early 1940, the two squadrons based in the UK had been equipped with the Bristol Beaufort, a twin-engined monoplane which was hailed as the fastest torpedo bomber in the world. It carried a crew of four. But it soon became apparent that the machine was subject to engine failure and that it was difficult to fly on one engine. Moreover, it was so poorly armed that it was at the mercy of enemy single-engined fighters, and it sank so quickly after a ditching that there was little time for the crew to scramble into their dinghy. The problems with the engine were largely overcome and the armament was increased, but the work on which the squadrons were engaged – mainly daylight attacks on enemy warships or armed merchant ships – was so hazardous that the machine topped the list compiled by the Air Member for Training in 1942. Another purpose of these statistics was to gauge the replacement rate for the aircrews, for on average the men survived only about two months of operational flying.

In late 1940 and early 1941, the training of strike aircrews for replacement and expansion was woefully inadequate. For instance, in January 1941 the author was sent straight to a Beaufort squadron, after having completed his training as an air observer at Navigation School and then Bombing and Gunnery School. The additional processes of School of General Reconnaissance and Operational Training Unit were omitted entirely, for the need for air observers in squadrons was so urgent. At this stage, the function of air navigation was usually performed by second pilots in Beauforts, and the arrival of air observers enabled these men to be released. This was the quickest method of increasing the numbers of aircrews. The other two crew members were wireless operator/air gunners, who were often drawn from volunteer ground staff at this stage, and they could be trained fairly quickly.

By the autumn of 1941, however, crews with more adequate training during wartime began to arrive in the Beaufort squadrons. Some of the pilots and navigators had received part of their training abroad, under the Empire Air Training Scheme, but the wireless operator/air gunners were trained almost entirely in the UK at this stage.

The development of flying training generally constitutes one of the most remarkable successes of World War Two. In 1934, the RAF as a whole had trained only about 300 new pilots and no other crew members. In 1936 the Royal Air Force Volunteer Reserve was created, a means by which pilots, observers and wireless operators were able from April 1937 onwards to train in their spare time, as a form of 'Citizens' Air Force'. By the time war broke out, the RAFVR stood at over 10,000 men in these three categories, mostly pilots at various stages of training. These were the men who shared with the regular RAF aircrews the brunt of the fighting in the first year of the war. Once war was declared, there was no shortage of additional volunteers for flying duties, but the facilities for training fell far short of requirements. But in December 1939, Canada, Australia and New Zealand agreed to set up flying training schools, partly staffed with RAF instructors. Southern Rhodesia also set up a training group, largely staffed and run by the RAF, while other facilities were provided by South Africa. The first school was opened in Canada in April 1940, and RAF entrants were trained in this country as well as in South Africa and Southern Rhodesia. In addition, all these Commonwealth countries trained their own nationals. The success may be gauged by the figures of mid-1942, when the British Commonwealth was producing 11,000 pilots and 17,000 other aircrew members each year. Other RAF pilots were trained in the USA under the scheme inaugurated by General H.H. 'Hap' Arnold. The Germans and the Italians could not match this output, and indeed were seriously handicapped by shortage of petrol in training their aircrews as the war progressed.

The main problem besetting the expansion of flying training in the UK and the Commonwealth during the early stages of the war was the shortage of flying instructors. The Operational Training Units especially needed to to be staffed with operationally experienced pilots, but the maritime strike squadrons were suffering such heavy casualties that only a trickle of men were completing their tours. Naturally, commanding officers of squadrons were reluctant to part with their most experienced men before they had squeezed the last vestiges of service from them.

Meanwhile, the shortage of flying and ground instructors in the stages before operational training was met by a form of compromise in the RAF generally. Some of the best pupil pilots, air observers and wireless operator/air gunners were 'creamed off' as soon as they had obtained their wings or brevets and 'ploughed back' into the training system as flying or ground instructors, after they had taken suitable courses. Many of these men were resentful when they were told that they had been selected to become instructors, since they felt that they had joined the RAF to fight and not to teach. Nevertheless, about half the wartime flying instructors were found in this way, and a greater proportion of the ground instructors. The remainder of the instructors were pre-war or 'tour-expired' men.

All those who joined the aircrew branch of the RAF in the UK during wartime first entered Flying Training Command. Every man was a volunteer for flying duties, even though he might have been conscripted into military service generally. Most of these volunteers went first to a Receiving Centre for two weeks. The pilots and air observers (who were later called navigators, when the various functions were split up into specialist categories) then passed on to an Initial Training Wing (ITW) for about two months, where they were called 'cadets'. Here the instruction consisted of a general introduction to service life and training in drill and discipline, together with elementary work on technical subjects such as navigation, armaments and signals. Some entrants were excused this initial training, however; these were the cadets who had passed through equivalent courses at one of the University Air Squadrons.

The pupil pilots then moved on to Elementary Flying Training School (EFTS), where they continued learning ground subjects and underwent basic training on single-engined aircraft for about six weeks. Those who went solo and then completed their course were sent to Service Flying Training School (SFTS), where there was further ground training coupled with flying more advanced aircraft, either single – or twin-engined. Those who qualified were awarded their wings, which were usually received with intense pride. The pilots who trained abroad and then arrived in the UK were usually sent to Advanced Flying Unit (AFU) for about a month, in order to improve their skills and familiarise them with flying in the conditions of a wartime and blacked-out Britain.

Meanwhile, the pupil air observers went to Air Observers Navigation School (AONS), where they received detailed instruction on the ground as well as navigation instruction in the air. Then they moved on to Bombing and Gunnery Schools (B & GS), where they learned the theories of bombing and air gunnery, and practised in the air. They also became adept with the Morse code key. After qualification, they were awarded their brevets. The wireless operator/air gunners did not pass through ITW but were sent to Wireless School and then on to Bombing and Gunnery School, where they also received their brevets.

After qualification, all aircrew were either commissioned or given the rank of sergeant. Those who were selected as strike aircrew for the maritime squadrons left Flying Training Command as soon as they received their wings or brevets and then came under the direction of Coastal Command for further training. The next course was at a School of General Reconnaissance (S of GR). At the outbreak of war there was only one of these schools, at Thorney Island in Sussex, and this was soon moved to Squires Gate in Lancashire. Pressure was relieved by the creation of two schools abroad, one at George in South Africa's Cape Province and the other at Charlottetown in Canada's Prince Edward Island. The course, which lasted about three months, concentrated on practice in long-range navigation over the sea, using such methods as astro-navigation.

The next stage for the strike aircrews was Operational Training Unit (OTU). It was here that the pilots, air observers and wireless operator/air gunners met each other, often for the first time, and formed their crews. They were also introduced to their operational aircraft and began to fly in them, while receiving some instruction in the operational conditions to expect on the squadrons. Casualties began to mount at this stage, even before the crews began operations. It is estimated that about fifteen per cent of RAF aircrew losses occurred during training. The majority of these were at OTUs, when the men were training on aircraft which were more difficult to fly, especially at night, and were faster than the machines on which they had trained previously. Accidents occurred when practising take-offs, when flying or landing on one engine, or perhaps crashing into cloud-covered hills as a result of navigational errors. There was also over-intensive use of aircraft at OTUs, resulting in engine failure.

In May 1940 there was only one OTU available for the landplanes of Coastal Command, at Silloth in Cumberland. Throughout the war, Coastal Command's OTUs opened and closed with surprising rapidity. In the spring of 1942 the situation was as follows:

1 OTU	Silloth, Cumberland	Hudsons
2 OTU	Catfoss, Yorkshire	Blenheims and Beaufighters
3 OTU	Cranwell, Lincolnshire	Whitleys and Wellingtons
4 OTU	Invergordon, Ross & Cromarty	Flying boats
5 OTU	Turnberry, Ayrshire	Beauforts
6 OTU	Thornaby, Yorkshire	Hudsons
7 OTU	Limavady, Londonderry	Wellingtons
8 OTU	Fraserburgh, Aberdeen	Spitfires (for photo reconnaisance)

Most aircrews of the maritime strike squadrons received their operational training in the UK but, in late 1941, attempts were made to create additional OTUs abroad. This was partly in response to the need for strike squadrons in the eastern Mediterranean to help counter the Italians, and for similar squadrons in the Indian Ocean as defence against the advancing Japanese. Debert in Nova Scotia was formed for Hudson aircrews, but there were insufficient instructors and output remained small until late 1942. Patricia Bay in British Columbia was selected to train Beaufort aircrews, but lack of equipment and instructors resulted in delays. Indeed, this unit was converted into No. 32 Operational Squadron for several months from December 1941 after the alarming successes of the Japanese in the Pacific, and all training was halted. Nicosia in Cyprus was opened in February 1944, mainly for Beaufighter aircrews.

After OTU, some strike aircrews passed directly to operational squadrons; others had to qualify on yet another course. This was the Torpedo Training Unit (TTU), where the pilot learnt the difficult art of dropping torpedoes against fixed and moving targets, having first studied the theory of the subject. In May 1940 there was only one TTU in the UK, at Abbotsinch in Ayrshire, which trained both Coastal Command and the Fleet Air Arm, although torpedo development took place at Gosport in Hampshire.

Abroad, Patricia Bay in Canada developed a torpedo training course as part of its OTU. In addition, another unit was set up in Egypt, and this assumes particular importance in this narrative. This was Shallufa on the Bitter Lakes, near Suez. At the end of 1940, Shallufa was formed as a headquarters for maritime Wellingtons in the Mediterranean. It became a Wellington OTU in early 1941, and Beauforts began to appear later that year. By March 1943, Shallufa became No. 5 Middle East Training School and thereafter was the main training centre for maritime strike crews in the Mediterranean and the Indian Ocean. The pilots, who were already experienced in their aircraft, were taught tactical approaches at low level on target ships, when flying in various formations. They learnt how to evade enemy fire by side-slipping, diving under the bows of their target, and then skidding away with flat turns over the surface of the sea. They also trained in work at night, guided on to targets by their air-to-surface vessel radar, as well as by homing devices installed in Wellingtons which then dropped flares to silhouette the enemy ships against the skyline for torpedo attacks.

The crews who reached this stage were at last allowed to join an operational strike squadron, but training did not cease. Squadron training was very patchy and inadequate during the latter part of 1940 and much of 1941, but thereafter became steadily more intensive. In fact, the learning and training processes never stopped, except when the men flew on operational flights, and even then the pilot's performance was assessed and the navigator's log analysed if the aircraft returned safely.

A typical syllabus for training on a strike squadron in late 1943 included night flying, formation flying, single-engined flying, practice with air-to-surface vessel radar, controlled approaches using various homing methods, torpedo dropping, air-to-air gunnery, mock combat with single-engined fighters, rocket firing, and long-range navigation exercises. On the ground there was the Link Trainer and continued lectures on a multitude of subjects such as navigation, photography, meteorology, bombing, gunnery, pyrotechnics, ship recognition, wireless and signals, first aid, and intelligence concerning the enemy. Some subjects were covered again and again, but there was a constant stream of new information which was eagerly assimilated by the aircrews. Excellent journals were issued monthly by the Air Ministry, giving details and photographs of actions undertaken by maritime squadrons and containing well-informed articles on technical subjects.

By 1944 the performance of each man in his squadron training programme was listed monthly on standard forms, and each was expected to satisfy Wing or Group Headquarters. Such measures may have seemed irksome when the men were risking their lives in some of the most dangerous flying activities in the RAF, but there is little doubt that the emphasis on continued training improved chances of survival as well as effectiveness against the enemy.

As the training of strike aircrews intensified, new aircraft were provided, although at first these were not ideal for such dangerous operations. At the outbreak of war, Coastal Command squadrons were being equipped with Lockheed Hudsons as replacements for their Avro Ansons. This American aircraft proved excellent when employed on short-range reconnaissance and anti-submarine work, but some of the Hudson squadrons were pressed into service for daylight and night bombing attacks against shipping, tasks to which the machines were not well suited. Other aircraft used by the strike squadrons were those which the other Commands no longer wanted. In the summer of 1940, three squadrons of Bristol Blenheim IVs were transferred to Coastal Command and used for bombing enemy shipping, while other squadrons at home and overseas were equipped with these machines and employed on the same work. In the summer of 1942, Handley Page Hampdens were converted into torpedo bombers and handed over to Coastal Command, being employed mainly along the Norwegian coastline. Beauforts, Hudsons, Blenheims and Hampdens were too lightly armed for anti-shipping work and suffered very heavy casualties, especially when they were not escorted by long-distance fighters. They were remarkable, not for their performance, but because the crews achieved so much with such inadequate machines.

In December 1940, the Bristol Beaufighter IC began to replace the Blenheim VIF as a long-range fighter in Coastal Command, but it was a year before this new aircraft began to enter service with maritime squadrons in the Mediterranean, where it was first employed in the Western Desert. The machine was an adaptation of the Beaufort, but far more heavily armed, and with the crew reduced to two, the navigator performed the additional function of wireless operator. It was followed by the Beaufighter VIC. The combination of Beaufighters with torpedo-carrying Beauforts began to transform the effectiveness of daylight attacks against Axis shipping in the late summer of 1942. Then the Beaufighter TFX, specially designed as a combination fighter and torpedo bomber, began to enter service in the early summer of 1943, both in the UK and the Mediterranean. It was a most effective anti-shipping weapon, and became even more devastating when fitted with rockets a few months later. The ubiquitous Vickers Wellington was also adapted for anti-shipping work. In December 1941, some Wellington ICs were converted to carry two torpedoes and engaged on anti-shipping work in the Mediterranean. They operated primarily at night, equipped with air-to-surface vessel radar and homing radar, and achieved considerable success.

The men who flew in these anti-shipping aircraft considered that they were above average in both intelligence and enterprise. All wanted to acquit themselves well, even though they clearly understood the risks that they faced, and their awareness of danger was sometimes covered by a veneer of humour and cynicism. Although all were volunteers and most had joined the service for only the duration of the war, they could be regarded as tough and highly skilled fighting men. Each man knew that it was not only his own life that he risked, for every crew member depended on the high standard of skill and judgement of others. Indeed, the sense of comradeship was a major factor in continuing to face danger. The men believed, with some justification, that they were the best crews in the Allied air forces.

The tasks that the strike squadrons performed in the Mediterranean were multifarious, although little has been written about them. The Beaufort and Beaufighter squadrons included in their collective repertoires such sorties as torpedo attacks, anti-shipping bombing attacks, cannon and machine gun attacks on escort vessels, rocket attacks, mine laying, fighter escorts, long-range fighter attacks against enemy air transports, bombing of ports, and even strafing of enemy ground troops and transports. Their role was almost always aggressive rather than defensive. A large number of the aggressive sorties were called 'Armed Rovers' and entered as such in the Operations Record books. The operations were guided by an astonishingly effective combination of British Intelligence and photographs taken by reconnaissance aircraft. In spite of the heavy losses suffered by the squadrons, the damage they inflicted on the enemy was enormous.

Nowadays, most of the men who survived their tours in the anti-shipping squadrons or their experiences as prisoners-of-war have retired from their post-war occupations. Some of them have joined squadron or other associations and meet regularly to discuss their experiences or hear news about former comrades. Although they are patriotic to a man, they are not jingoistic nor do they seek to glorify war. What they remember is something which some of those without experience of war find difficult to believe or accept: a heroism, trust and comradeship in their RAF careers which the days of peace have seldom provided with such intensity. This book relates only a few of the actions which these men undertook, but they are representative of the work of the 'Armed Rovers'.

2

An Electrical Storm

Beaufort I serial N1091 of 39 Squadron had been in the air for about five hours when the crew saw the line squall ahead. They had taken off at 0805 hours on 2 November 1941 from Baggush Satellite, near Mersa Matruh in Egypt, with orders to carry out an 'Armed Rover' on one of a new series of operations codenamed 'Plug', with the object of attacking enemy shipping off the coast of south-west Greece. It was known that supply vessels were slipping down this coast before making their dash across the Mediterranean with fuel and war materials for the Axis forces in North Africa.

The Bristol Beaufort, a twin-engined monoplane with a crew of four, was carrying only two 500lb general purpose bombs. Although the aircraft could carry another 1,000lb, the bomb load had been reduced in order to extend the range, since the flight was expected to last for nearly seven hours. This was near the limit of the range, even when nursing the aircraft along at its economical airspeed of 135 knots. Although the Beaufort had been designed as a torpedo bomber, the crews had not been trained on such work, nor were torpedo racks available for the aircraft at Baggush. In fact, the squadron was in the course of converting on to new Beauforts from the Martin Marylands which the crews had flown on reconnaissance and bombing attacks from bases in Egypt since the previous January.

By November 1941, 39 Squadron was the principal anti-shipping strike squadron operating from Egypt. It formed part of 234 Wing, which consisted of three squadrons. Of the other two, 203 Squadron was equipped with Blenheim IVs and engaged primarily on photo-reconnaissance (although the aircraft were sometimes used for anti-shipping work), while 230 Squadron flew Sunderlands on anti-submarine patrols and was also equipped with some Dornier 22 floatplanes flown by Yugoslavian aircrews. This Wing was the main element of 201 (Naval Co-operation) Group, based at Alexandria in the same building as the Naval C-in-C's headquarters.

The Beaufort was flown by Flight Lieutenant Reggie A. Lenton, a twenty-seven-year-old pilot from Reading who had joined the RAF with a short service commission in May 1939. His navigator was

Sergeant Edgar R.R. Cerely, a twenty-year-old from Sanderstead in Surrey; he had also applied for a short service commission as a pilot shortly before the war but had been told to reapply as an air observer, which he did the day after war was declared. The other two men were also wartime volunteers: Sergeant H. John Langley from Brighton sat in the wireless operator's seat, while Sergeant W.J. MacConnachie from Leith occupied the mid-upper turret. It was a scratch crew, for they had not flown together before, although Lenton had been in 39 Squadron since August 1940 and Cerely since March 1941. Indeed, Cerely had been taken off flying two months before, when he found that flying at 30,000 feet on reconnaissance missions in unpressurised Marylands pained his ears and even affected his eyesight. It was not until he complained of inactivity to his commanding officer, Wing Commander R.B. Cox, that he was given the opportunity of a low-level sortie in the Beaufort.

The crew had seen nothing on their flight and were returning with their bombs. Ahead was a long black cloud, low and almost straight. They had no option but to fly through it, for it barred their route home and fuel was running low. Base was over two hours' flying time away, to the south-east. When they entered the line squall, rain and hail lashed down and the Beaufort bounced unpleasantly in the turbulence. The wind strengthened considerably and there was dense black cloud above, with a succession of violent flashes from forked lightning. The thunder was so loud that they could hear the crashes above the roar of the two 1,130hp Taurus engines. But this unnerving experience lasted for only about five minutes and the sturdy Beaufort flew through the squall into clearer air. The crew continued their course for home, or so they thought, but with cloud above and poor visibility below.

After a few minutes, Cerely noticed that the magnetic compass of the 'course setting' bombsight in his nose compartment showed the wrong course. He thought at first that Lenton must have set the wrong course on his P.4 pilot's compass, and clambered back to check. There was a discrepancy of nearly sixty degrees between the two compasses. He went back into the nose and checked the hand-held bearing compass, and this showed yet another course. It was evident that electrical discharges from the storm had affected the magnetism of the aircraft itself, resulting in enormous deviations of the compass needles. This was a very serious matter, for the magnetic compasses provided the only method of steering a course. Lenton had continuously adjusted his gyro to agree with his magnetic compass. They had no sun compass and in any event the sun was not visible. They were outside the range of radio direction finding. Now they were not sure of their heading.

After about an hour and a half of worrying uncertainty, mountains loomed ahead. Cerely could only guess that it must be Crete, well to the east of their intended track. Lenton had no option. One engine was starting to give trouble. There was a lot of sea between them and base, and the fuel tanks were almost empty. They had been in the air for seven hours and could not get home. 'I'll have to put it down,' he told the crew, and turned slightly towards a bay they could see on the shore ahead.

Cerely came out of the nose and strapped himself into the seat beside Lenton. Langley left the wireless operator's seat and sat on the floor of the fuselage against the main bulwark, facing backwards. MacConnachie backed out of the turret and sat on the Elsan pan by the entrance hatch on the port side, also facing backwards.

'We've still got our bombs,' Lenton said suddenly, when they were on the final approach. Cerely unstrapped himself and went back into the nose. He made sure that the bombs were not armed and released them into the sea. Then he scrambled back and stood beside Lenton. There were only a few seconds left and he did not have time to strap himself back into the seat. All he could do was to hold on to the panel on the starboard side and hope for the best, although it seemed unlikely that he could survive.

The mountains towered above but Lenton flew straight towards them, low over the sea. The beach of the bay was curved and quite narrow, only about thirty yards wide. Lenton put the Beaufort down into the sea, about 300 yards from the shore. The aircraft smacked the water, shuddered and rose again. Then it came down for the last time and skidded over the surf to the beach. But the beach was not sand. Instead, it consisted of smooth pebbles, with some stones as big as ostrich eggs. The Beaufort slid over them, with flying sparks coming from its belly. It ground to a violent stop and the nose broke away. Cerely shot through the opening while Lenton jerked forward against his Sutton harness and smashed his forehead against the edge of the instrument panel.

Fortunately, the aircraft did not catch fire. Langley and MacConnachie, who were not harmed, helped Lenton from his seat and away from the wreckage. Blood was pouring from the pilot's scalp. They went forward to look at Cerely, who was lying sprawled on his back, arched over a piece of wreckage. His trousers had been torn off and his eyes were closed.

'C's had it,' said MacConnachie, almost nonchalantly. The navigator was known to his fellow sergeants merely by the initial of his surname. MacConnachie was a tough and resourceful Scotsman, who was to demonstrate his almost indestructible qualities in the months ahead.

But Cerely was not dead. His thighs and buttocks were badly lacerated and he had been knocked out. He heard the air gunner's announcement perfectly clearly at the moment he regained conscious-ness, and looked up at the three men. Then he saw the mask of blood on Lenton's face and laughed with relief, for the pilot was standing steadily on his feet.

The Beaufort had landed on the stone beach of the Bay of Stomiou, on the south-west tip of Crete. Not far to the north was a German observation post, but apparently those manning it failed to notice the arrival of the strange aircraft on the shore. Perched over the sea to the south was the almost deserted monastery of Chrissoskalitissa. But after flying for seven hours without a landfall, the RAF men did not know where they were. Their one thought was to get away from the wreck and avoid capture. Cerely found his missing trousers as well as his Smith and Wesson .38 revolver. They all took their parachutes and began to climb inland, but both Lenton and Cerely had hurt their legs and were soon exhausted. The group found an apparently safe spot in the mountains, wrapped themselves in the silk of their parachutes, and went to sleep.

In the morning, they went back to their crashed aircraft, to gather up some supplies. There was nobody in the vicinity. Lenton pulled the release handle of the 'H-type' dinghy stored in the port wing and became furious when the handle broke away, for the wire had corroded. The men managed to tear open the wing and took the emergency rations from the dinghy, including the Horlicks tablets. They also took a can of water from within the aircraft, unaware that there was plenty of water on the island. Surprisingly, they were not seen by the Germans. Carrying their supplies and the parachutes, they began to climb back inland once more.

The going was tough. There were some rough tracks but there were also jagged limestone rocks which cut their shoes and sometimes it was difficult to find places to put their feet. The men were young, fit and determined, but they were in the unfamiliar circumstances of a strange country.

The mountains seemed interminable. While the others rested for a spell, Cerely climbed a ridge to see ahead. He saw another ridge and climbed that. Ahead was yet another ridge, presumably concealing a whole succession of these obstacles. It was most discouraging, and the navigator made his way back to his companions. The three men were sitting on rocks with a strange man, eating oranges.

The newcomer proved to be the local postman, Antonis Kalitsou-nakis. His manner was extremely friendly but he spoke no English and the four RAF men spoke no Greek. Their first attempts to communicate were little short of comedy. One word all understood was 'Germani'. Lenton pointed in different directions to determine the whereabouts of the Germans. Antonis replied faithfully, saying either 'nai' or 'oxi', dependent on the direction. The RAF men thought that 'nai' meant 'no' and thus that 'oxi' meant 'yes'. In fact, the reverse is true. When the four men headed off in precisely the wrong direction, Antonis rushed after them and turned them round. He indicated that they must follow him, to his house.

The walk was an extremely gruelling experience for the RAF men. Cerely's wounds were troubling him, and Lenton and Langley also began to flag. Only MacConnachie seemed unaffected by the long scramble over the mountains. Like many Scotsmen, he was a 'hill walker', and also he had an iron constitution. Cerely was reeling with fatigue and pain when, late in the day, they arrived at the village of Tzitzifia in the mountains, where Antonis lived. This was only about seven miles inland from the site of their forced landing, but they had walked several times that distance over the rough limestone.

Crete is about 150 miles long and has an average width of about thirty miles, although it narrows to about eight miles at its 'waist'. The majority of this elongated island is mountainous, with peaks rising to over 8,000 feet. There are excellent harbours on the indented north coast, but along the south coast the mountains rise sheer from the sea.

The island had been the scene of desperate battles when General Kurt Student's airborne soldiers descended on it during the previous May. Almost all the defenders were Commonwealth troops who had been evacuated from Greece when the Germans swept through that country. The men had left most of their equipment behind, but they were aided by Cretan irregulars. For air cover, they had only the remnants of three RAF squadrons and one FAA squadron, comprising twenty-four Hurricanes, Gladiators and Fulmars. The Luftwaffe mustered about 650 aircraft for the attack, as well as over 700 air transports and gliders to carry the assault force of 15,000 men. Although the defending troops were numerically superior to the attackers, the weight of air power and better equipment prevailed. Crete was outside the range of the few fighter squadrons in Egypt. No more of these RAF fighters could be sacrificed for the defence of the island, where there were only two airfields and one landing strip, all vulnerable to bombing and strafing raids from Greece.

Nevertheless, the outcome of the battle hung in the balance for several days. The early airborne attackers were almost wiped out by the defenders and it was only by ignoring casualties when pouring in new troops that Student won the Battle of Crete. As so often happened in Britain's history, the Royal Navy prevented a complete disaster by destroying the invading seaborne enemy forces and then evacuating over half the defenders. This was at the cost of three cruisers and six destroyers sunk.

Not all those defenders who remained behind were captured. Some managed to find small boats and made perilous journeys to Turkey or the North African coast. Others slipped away from beaches or prison compounds and hid in the mountains. At first, these evaders were able to live off the country or to use supplies from abandoned dumps. But by autumn many were in rags and wholly dependant on the Cretans for food and shelter. It was estimated that over 500 Commonwealth troops were still at large on the island in November 1941, when the Beaufort crew arrived.

The Germans had insufficient strength to police the whole of the large and rugged island. However, they brought in the Gestapo and used methods of extreme brutality to terrorise the Cretans and to find the Commonwealth 'deserters', as they called them. Any Cretans suspected of sheltering troops were tortured or shot. Sometimes under-cover Germans posed as Commonwealth troops on the run and asked villagers to be taken to their 'comrades' in their hideouts. If they found evaders by this method, the Germans turned round and shot the Cretans, before offering cigarettes and PoW status to the Common-wealth soldiers. Yet betrayal by the Cretans was almost unknown. The islanders loathed the occupying forces and held the British in the highest respect, almost to the point of idolatry.

Thus Lenton and his crew had found the best allies they could wish for in their quest to evade capture and return to their squadron. They spent two days in the house of their new friend, a short period which gave their wounds a chance to begin healing. Then they were moved to the village of Elos, about four miles to the north in direct line over the mountains. Here they were split into two homes. Lenton and Cerely hid in the house of Michalis and Theodora Skalides and their four children. Michalis spoke English, for he had worked as a miner in Utah for several years. The household was poor, with few amenities, but the evaders were given shelter and fed each day. Not a single person in the village betrayed them, although almost everyone knew of their pre-sence.

Meanwhile, the families of the four RAF men were notified that they were 'missing on operations'. It was to be a long-drawn-out and agonising experience for these relatives.

After a fortnight in Elos, the Beaufort crew learnt of a boat which was being prepared for an attempt to escape to North Africa, from the little port of Sfinari on the west coast. They were led to this spot at night and joined a party of about fifteen other evaders who crowded into a Greek caique, a single-masted sailing vessel which was also fitted with an engine. Most of the other evaders were Australians and a few had contrived stupidly to get drunk. Lenton became furious and even talked of shooting one of them with Cerely's revolver. But after the caique had progressed for only a few yards, the engine broke down and they were forced to return to the shore. The ill-fated attempt was abandoned and the Beaufort crew returned to Elos.

On Christmas Eve, the Skalides family saw a stranger approaching their house. Lenton and Cerely hid in the chimney, but the visitor proved to be a friend. By then, there were two British officers of the Special Operations Executive (SOE) on the island, where they were helping to evacuate the last of the Commonwealth troops and encouraging guerilla activity among the Cretans. One of these officers had sent the runner to the Skalides home with a message in English. It read. 'Congratulations. I hear that you are alive and well and in the west of the island. Follow this man and we will have you off in ten days.'

The four RAF men set off on Christmas Day, together with their Cretan guide. They were joined by Sergeant John Medley of the Hussars, who also had been sheltering in Elos. Medley's tank had been knocked out in Greece and he had made his way to Crete in a rowing boat, only to be trapped once more. They trudged over the mountain paths, following a guide who went over the terrain like a mountain goat. The evaders wore hooded cloaks made from blankets, while shoes made from old motor tyres were strapped to their feet. At nights, they slept in little round huts called speitachi, which the Cretan shepherds build from stones in the mountains. Their destination was a mystery to them, but they knew they were travelling in an easterly direction, along the centre-line of the island.

By now, the RAF men spoke a few words of Greek. Each time they asked their guide how much further they had to go, he replied 'Not far, not far' in Greek and continued his remorseless pace. On the second night out, they clambered down the side of the Samaria Gorge, which runs in a north–south direction through the mountains, and then scrambled up the other side. The winter temperature in Crete is higher than that of the mainland, but snow covers the higher reaches and the wind is far stronger. When they passed over the saddle of the Lefka Ori mountains, the wind reached gale force and they had to crawl on their hands and knees for about 150 yards. Little slivers of ice were lifted off the ground and hurled into their faces, cutting the skin.

After four days, Langley was in an extremely bad way. One heel had become so raw and inflamed that eventually he could not stand on it. The men had agreed that anyone who could not continue would have to be left behind. The wireless operator was left in the next hut, with only the consolation of a good fire. The Germans found him and he spent the rest of the war as a PoW. In June 1942, he was gazetted with a Mention in Despatches. At the same time, Cerely began to develop nephritis, an inflammation of the kidneys which was probably caused by drinking contaminated water, although he did not know the medical name for his condition at the time. His hands, knees and face began to swell, and the pain increased.

On the fifth day, the remaining men reached a house in Asi Gonia, about fifty miles in a direct line from their starting point, the village of Elos. Here they met one of the British officers of the SOE, who told them that they had come halfway and must continue their journey to the coast, with all speed.

By now, Cerely was becoming dazed. His face and knees were swollen grotesquely, like balloons, but he still plodded on with the other three men. On the seventh day, he walked for two hours and then keeled over.

Cerely was a man who attracted disasters but somehow recovered from them. His training had been at AONS at Prestwick, followed by B & G School at Everton and OTU at Bicester. From there he joined 21 Squadron at Watton in Norfolk, equipped with Blenheims as a squadron of Bomber Command. His crew made only one sortie, on 7 November 1940 over Belgium, and then volunteered for an overseas posting. Later that month, they left Liverpool on the liner *Dunnottar Castle*. The vessel collided with another ship in fog and limped into Belfast.

On 19 December, the Blenheim crew left Liverpool once more, on board the aircraft carrier HMS *Furious*, which was carrying forty Hurricanes in crates, in addition to her own aircraft. The destination was Takoradi on the Gold Coast, as part of the troop convoy WSA5A, consisting of twenty ships. The cruisers *Berwick*, *Bonadventure* and *Dunedin* were also part of the escort. This convoy was shadowed by the German cruiser *Hipper*, which approached on Christmas Day, unaware of the strength of the escort. There was an exchange of gunfire, in which both *Hipper* and *Berwick* were hit, and the German cruiser made off for Brest. But the convoy was ordered to scatter and *Furious* put into Gibraltar to refuel. The RAF men were transferred to the cruiser *Delhi* and arrived safely in Takoradi.

The Blenheim crew hoped to be posted to a squadron in the Western Desert but instead became part of the ferry pool supplying assembled aircraft to Egypt. On two occasions they flew Blenheim IVs to Cairo, with Hurricanes formatting on them, and came back as passengers on Bristol Bombays. Then a consignment of crated Martin Marylands arrived, some of which were destined for 39 Squadron to replace their outdated Blenheim Is. In February 1941 the crews of this squadron arrived in Takoradi to collect them and Cerely managed to persuade the commanding officer, Wing Commander Alan M. Bowman, to allow him to join the squadron. Bowman was an Australian in the RAF, who had already received the DFC and bar, and was held in the highest respect by his crews. In September 1941, he was posted to Air Headquarters, Western Desert, where unfortunately he was to meet his death.

When Cerely collapsed on the mountain trail in Crete, luck was once again on his side. Within a few minutes another Cretan arrived, collecting firewood with his donkey. The evaders borrowed the donkey and tied Cerely to one side, balancing him with a pile of wood on the other. So the little procession set off again, by then headed in a south-easterly direction. They crossed the Plain of Mesara at night, to avoid the many Germans in this area. Cerely was still unconscious.

On the ninth day, they approached a little inlet on the south coast. This was Tris Eklisiès (Three Churches). On the path, they met a party of Australians who were out looking for firewood. MacConnachie, who by then was barefoot, actually offered to help them. The extraordinary spirit and stamina of this Scotsman may be judged from the fact that he had walked without rest for thirty-six hours, over rock and in bitter weather, following an endurance test of eight days which would have defeated most men. The purpose of the march to this locality was to join evaders who were scheduled to be taken off by a submarine of the Royal Navy, which was expected to arrive on the fourth or fifth of January. The RAF men had arrived only just in time for this appointment, joining about a hundred Commonwealth soldiers who were already waiting.

The three churches were deserted and there were no other buildings. Cerely was only partly conscious when he was taken into one of the churches which served as a makeshift hospital. There he was tended by Major Arnold Gourevitch of the RAMC and Captain K. 'Skip' Dorney of the Royal Australian Medical Corps, both of whom had given devoted service to evaders on the island. There was little medication or food available. The two remaining Beaufort men thought that their navigator was dying and at one stage were told that they should dig a grave for him. But Cerely hung on, somehow recovering on a diet which consisted mainly of beans full of weevils.

The submarine arrived but a storm blew up and the crew was unable to send dinghies ashore. Signals were exchanged by lamp and an arrangement was made for the submarine to return four days later. It did so but the storm did not abate and the operation was cancelled. Meanwhile, the SOE officer supervising the operation, Captain the Hon. C. 'Monty' Woodhouse, received the disburbing news that the Germans had become aware that something was afoot. The RAF men did not understand how the SOE gathered their intelligence, but they realized that the Cretan shepherds seemed to know everything. These people had a method of communicating over the mountains, making strange staccato shouts.

It was imperative to disperse the gathering without delay. A despatch rider from Glasgow, Driver Charlie Craig, told Cerely that he knew of a rowing boat at Kefalas, on the other side of the island. Two of his friends in that area were anxious to escape in it, but they needed a navigator to occupy the remaining seat. Cerely had a small pocket compass, although he had disposed of his revolver. He could walk once more, albeit rather shakily and only with the aid of a stick. Lenton and MacConnachie decided to return to the western end of the island. In fact, they did not believe that Cerely was capable of making such a journey. But the navigator was quite determined and set off with Craig on 10 January 1942.

It was another very long haul, but on this occasion the men were not marching against time. They climbed up and down the mountain ridges in the bitter cold, sleeping at night in the shepherds' huts and invariably receiving food from the staunch Cretans. On one occasion, they found two vats of liquid inside a hut. One contained olive oil but the other was full of alcohol which, although the two men did not realize it at the time, was the fiery drink known as sicouthia in Crete or grappa in Italy. Cerely poured some into an old cigarette tin, took a few mouthfuls, and then went outside to relieve himself. In his weakened state, he fell down in a drunken stupor and Craig dragged him back inside. Then Craig drank the remainder of the tin, went outside and also passed out. But Cerely did not wake up until the morning and Craig remained asleep in the open all night, fortunately without developing frostbite.

Nearing Kefalas on the western side of the north coast, after twelve days, the two men were joined by Trooper Fred Marlow of the Royal Armoured Corps and Private Stan Harlen of the New Zealanders. The four men hid in a cave about a mile and a half east of the village of Kefalas, overlooking the Gulf of Almirou. As usual, the evaders were sustained by the villagers. Every night, two girls or a boy brought food and water to them, clambering for two miles over the sharp limestone rocks out of sight of the Germans. They were Smaragda Xipolitakis, Elefteria Saridakis and Stylianos Sergakis. The food consisted mainly of bread, raisins, olive oil, snails and oranges. It must be remembered that if any of these three helpers had been caught by the Germans, they faced execution.

The evaders stored some of this food to provide rations for their sea journey. After a while they were joined by a Cretan lad, Mitchel, who was being hunted by the Germans and was also determined to escape. The five men remained in the cave for nearly two months, until they felt that their accumulated rations and the improvement in the weather justified the attempt. They finally set off on 19 March 1942, in a twelve-foot boat without a rudder but with oars. At the outset, Cerely had agreed to participate only if he could command the venture, and the others accepted his leadership.

The navigator set course on 034 degrees, which he calculated would bring them to one of the myriad islands of the Cyclades, about 120 miles distant. From there, they hoped to hop from island to island until they reached the Dodecanese islands and thence to Turkey. They believed, with some justification, that the Turkish authorities would quietly hand them over to the British after a short period of internment. A rota of duties at the oars had been written out in an exercise book, as well as a careful allotment of daily rations and water.

The first two days went well. The men kept strictly to their duties and seemed to be making progress, both by day and night. It can be calculated that they had travelled about fifty miles in this period. But at 1845 hours on the third night they ran into a storm, accompanied by thunder and lightning, which intensified until it became terrifying, far worse than anything the men had experienced in their lives. The seas seemed mountainous, one moment towering above them like a wobbling, dark green jelly, and then disappearing into a deep trough. The little boat continually rose and smashed down again, with the danger of breaking up, swamping or overturning. Cerely made a decision and turned back in a southerly direction towards the coast of Crete.

Marlow and Cerely were at the oars when the storm began and it proved impossible for the others to take their places, for they would have been swept overboard in the changeover. Instead, they bailed continuously, clung on and yelled instructions to the oarsmen to keep the boat heading into the waves. To add to their terror, the sounds of gunfire rolled over the sea, which was lit up by brilliant flashes of explosions. They thought that a naval battle was in progress, but it was an attack by the RAF in Egypt on the aerodrome near Heraklion. Six Wellingtons from 37 Squadron at Baggush and 148 Squadron at Kabrit bombed at different times during the night. Their primary target had been the port of Piraeus in Greece, but the weather was so stormy that the six could not find the harbour and turned to the secondary target in Crete.

After some hours with their back-breaking task, the palms of the two oarsmen were rubbed raw, sticking to the oars with congealed blood. Yet there was nothing they could do but continue. They rowed throughout the night and providentially saw the coast at dawn. It proved extremely difficult to find a landing place but at last they grounded the boat, which was leaking badly. Craig jumped into the shallow water and the others were surprised to see that he almost disappeared. When the men also tried to put their feet on the sea bottom, their legs buckled underneath them. They crawled ashore and were unable to stand for several hours.

They had landed at Bali Bay, about twenty miles to the west of Heraklion. In an attempt to conceal themselves, they climbed inland.

Finding a shepherd's stone hut, they installed themselves for a short stay, while Mitchel went off to find some food. Everyone was intent on putting the boat back in trim and resuming their attempt to escape from the island. They had a piece of tin which they hoped would stop the leak, but there was no method of fastening this to the hull. Then they came across an old wooden door and spent their time trying to pull the nails out of it, without tools.

Early the next morning, Cerely woke up and went outside the hut. There were seven uniformed soldiers ranged around the door, one on a mule and the others on foot. All were armed with rifles. They appeared to be second-line troops of the Wehrmacht, possibly not of German nationality. None could speak English, apart from 'Come on!'

Cerely went back into the hut. 'We've got company,' he told the other three, resignedly. It was a bitter disappointment after all their efforts.

The prisoners and guards were formed into a single file and marched off. The walk lasted all morning over hilly country in the direction of Heraklion, until they came to the village of Fodele. Here each was presented with an egg, which was a luxury at that time. Then, to their surprise, the four prisoners were given their first haircuts for months. Perhaps the guards were offended by their unkempt appearance, but it is more likely that they were worried about lice.

The march eastwards continued, until they came to the monastery of Savathianou. After drinking some milk, they began climbing steeply over the mountains towards Heraklion. It was very hard and hot work, but the guards were not harsh and the prisoners were allowed to talk or shout to each other. Marlow walked near the front of the file, while Cerely was the last prisoner, with one guard bringing up the rear. These two prisoners realised that the guards did not understand English, and they began to shout plans of escape to each other. They developed the idea that they should wait until dusk and leap off the track at some suitable bend, then race down the mountain.

As the light began to fade, Cerely shouted several times to Marlow 'How about this place?', but each time the answer came back 'Not yet!' Eventually Cerely lost patience and decided to make a break on his own, at a spot where the track wound round the mountain to the right. He stopped and bent down to adjust the strapping on his home-made shoes, having done this several times before so that the guard behind was familiar with this apparent difficulty. As he hoped, the guard came close and stood beside him, while the file disappeared round the curve of the mountain.

Cerely straightened up suddenly and, with all his strength, struck the guard in the face. The soldier staggered back and his rifle clattered to the ground, while the navigator spun round and leapt down the slope to the left. The escapee bounded recklessly and desperately down the mountainside, half expecting a bullet in the back. But no shots followed him. Instead, there was only the plaintive sound of a whistle. He kept up the pace, covering the ground in great leaps and trying to put as much distance between himself and the soldiers. It was highly dangerous but he did not stop until the inevitable happened and he crashed over with a broken ankle.

By then it was dark, and the escapee crawled into some rocks to hide for the night. In the morning, he was astonished to see that he had bounded down the mountain as far as the monastery, but he dared not approach this refuge.

As usual, it was the Cretans who came to the rescue. Cerely was discovered by a young shepherd boy, Thomas Maris, who was strong enough to lift him on his back and carry him to a more concealed place on a mountain ledge. The navigator was a tall young man who normally weighed about eleven stone, but he had lost almost three stone during his stay on the island. From this vantage point, he could see German search parties combing the area, but his hiding place was not discovered. After a couple of days, the soldiers seemed to have given up the hunt.

The navigator remained on the ledge for another week, while his broken ankle bone began to heal itself. (The broken bone was discovered many years later during a routine medical and X-ray examination, to the surprise of the English doctor.) During this period, Thomas visited him every night, but he was able to bring little food save goat's milk. Although his ankle healed quite rapidly, Cerely developed scabies, primarily in his hands, which became covered with suppurating and stinking sores. Then he was taken by Thomas to a mandra, high above the village of Fodele. This was a pen made of stones, topped with thorn bushes, used to pen goats at night. Here he worked for two weeks with the shepherds, George Penderis and his young sons, sharing their simple life and helping to herd and milk the goats. He had learnt enough Greek to tell his benefactors that he wanted to move on, but the shepherds insisted that it was still too dangerous.

Eventually he accompanied the group when they moved to new pastures, where he remained for two days before taking leave of his stalwart friends. There was only one direction he could take, over the mountains to the west, where he thought that some of the evaders might be still in hiding.

He walked alone for three days. Then he saw a man walking towards him on the same path, and something about the solitary figure looked familiar. As they neared each other, Cerely could hardly believe his eyes, for it was his pilot, Reggie Lenton. In turn, Lenton thought that his navigator must have died after leaving Tris Eklisies on the south coast. Lenton, who had been out foraging for food, led his navigator back to a group of evaders in the mountain. MacConnachie was there, as well as John Medley, 'Skip' Dorney and several old friends.

When escape came, it was surprisingly easy. By then, the SOE had organised a form of shuttle service to and from Crete, using three caiques based at Bardia in Libya. They landed saboteurs and picked up any remaining escapees or evaders. The group was told to go to a little bay on the south coast. A caique arrived on schedule and three days later the men were landed at Bardia. It was the end of May 1942 and the Beaufort men had been on Crete for nearly seven months. During the previous month, their families had been notified that they were probably alive, and this could be confirmed.

Much had changed in 201 Group in the period they had been away. In particular, it had been strengthened by the arrival of 47 Squadron, equipped with Vickers Wellesleys and engaged mainly on reconnaissance, as well as 252 and 272 Squadrons, which were equipped with cannon-firing Beaufighter Is.

On 6 June, the three Beaufort men made a triumphant return to 39 Squadron. Not many of their old comrades remained, and the squadron had also changed. It was now commanded by Wing Commander Arthur J. Mason and the crews were fully fledged on the dangerous work of torpedo attacks in their Beauforts, as we shall see in later chapters. The men learnt of the death of their old commanding officer, Wing Commander Alan Bowman. He had been unable to settle down in a desk job and yearned to continue flying. During the previous September he had made a foray into the desert with another RAF officer and found a Ju 87 which had been abandoned after running out of fuel. After many adventures, they flew the Stuka successfully back to base. Soon afterwards, he was shot down and killed near the Italian fortress of Jalo in Libya, when piloting a Blenheim.

John Medley joined the SOE, after his rescue by that unit. Cerely's three companions in the unsuccessful attempt to reach Turkey – Charlie Craig, Stan Harlen and Fred Marlow ended the war as PoWs in Germany. The three Beaufort men were posted back to the UK. In December 1942, Lenton and Cerely were awarded the Military Cross and Military Medal respectively. By one of the quirks which govern such matters, MacConnachie received no award, although in many ways he had been the strongest member of the crew; however, he was commissioned in November 1942, took a pilot's course, qualified successfully, and remained in the RAF after the war.

Cerely went back into Bomber Command and completed a tour in the Wellington Xs of 196 Squadron, based at Leconfield in Yorkshire. Almost inevitably, he survived another near disaster. On 5 March 1943 he was acting as a bomb aimer in a raid over Essen when, near the Dutch coast, there was an enormous crash underneath the aircraft. Nevertheless, the crew continued to the target and released their load, 3,520 lb of bombs and incendiaries. On their return they discovered that the bomb doors had been torn off and the underside had been severely damaged. They had been in a collision with a Wellington of 466 (RAAF) Squadron, based at the same station, which also managed to limp home. Cerely was commissioned later that month while his pilot, Pilot Officer J.A. Hope, was awarded a DFC.

Lenton joined 540 Squadron, one of the famous PRU squadrons, and became a flight commander. He was awarded a DFC on 1 October 1943 but lost his life over Trondheim fjord on the twenty-sixth of that month, on the last sortie of his tour. One of the appendices to the Operations Record book of his squadron is bound in maroon leather and embossed with gold lettering: 'In Honour of S/Ldr R.A. Lenton, MC, DFC.' This is most unusual, and can only have been done in wartime by his comrades. It can be seen at the Public Record Office at Kew under reference AIR 27/2010.

Elefteria Saridakis continued to support the partisan movement in Crete by supplying information to British Intelligence. She and two other women were arrested by the Germans and sentenced to death. Elefteria and one other women managed to escape, although the other woman was shot. The Cretan heroine was arrested again, but the Germans did not carry out the death sentence since it was near the end of the war.

In May 1978, the Royal Air Forces Escaping Society arranged a reception for twenty-eight Greek 'helpers', fourteen from Crete and nine from the mainland. Ed Cerely acted as courier on a whirlwind tour of the RAF Club in Piccadilly, the RAF Museum in Hendon, RAF Odiham, the Runnymede Memorial and RAF Biggin Hill, as well as other places of interest during the four-day period. At the Guest Night at RAF Odiham, Smaragda Xipolitakis sat in the place of honour between two beefy and smiling group captains. Cerely looked across the tables at her. She was nut-brown, tiny, wrinkled and unable to speak a word of English. It was a sight which filled him with emotion, for he remembered the months when she and her friends scrambled over the limestone rocks, night after night, to bring help to him and his companions.

(**Above**) Beaufort Mark II, serial AW362, of 86 Squadron, flying over the Mediterranean in 1942. (*Roger Hayward*) (**Below left**) Ed Cerely (*left*) talking to the Cretan 'helper' Antonis Kalitsounakis in 1970. Antonis was the postman who found the Beaufort crew the day after their force-landing in Crete in November 1941. Unhappily, he was killed in an air crash a few weeks after this photograph was taken. (*E.R.R. Cerely*) (**Below right**) Squadron Leader Reggie A. Lenton, MC, DFC, after his escape from Crete at the end of May 1942 and before his death in 540 (PRU) Squadron on 26 October 1943. (*E.R.R. Cerely*)

A heroine of the Cretan resistance, Smaragda Xipolitakis, photographed outside her house in Kefalas in 1982. In early 1942, this 'helper' was one of those who brought food nightly to Ed Cerely and three army 'evaders' while they were sheltering in a cave near Kefalas. (*E.R.R. Cerely*)

Flight Sergeant W.J. McConnachie, the air gunner in Beaufort N1091 of 39 Squadron, who also escaped from Crete in May 1942. (*E.R.R. Cerely*)

Flying Officer Derek Hammond being chaired by members of his squadron after the award of his DFC, which was gazetted on 7 April 1942. (*Wing Commander Derek Hammond, DSO, DFC**)

3

THE SCOURGE OF GOD

The arrival of the Deutsches Afrika Korps in the Western Desert during February 1941 came as a most unpleasant shock to the hitherto victorious British and Commonwealth forces, which had chased the Italians all the way from the Egyptian border to the Gulf of Sirte in Libya. The Germans fought in a style which outwitted and alarmed their opponents, in spite of their lack of experience of North Africa and the conditions of desert warfare. They were led, of course, by the dynamic General Erwin Rommel, whose originality and initiative, coupled with a mastery of tactics and battle skill, proved his superiority over the British High Command. Moreover, the Germans brought with them Panzers and artillery which outclassed those of the British. The lightning speed of the German thrusts, coupled with the smooth co-ordination of the elements in their force – Panzers, artillery, infantry, anti-tank units and air force – dismayed and confused their enemy. The British and Commonwealth forces were subjected to a form of blitzkrieg which sent them reeling back across the desert. By April 1941, they were back behind the Egyptian border, leaving only the strongly fortified and manned positions around the port of Tobruk.

But the Axis forces in North Africa suffered from a weakness which ultimately would prove fatal. Almost all their supplies had to be brought in from Europe: arms, ammunition, equipment, fuel and even food. The desert yielded nothing save the occasional oasis and insignificant items of food, or any British supply dumps which could be captured. The problems of the British in this respect, although difficult, could be solved. Egypt was not without resources and water could be pumped to the front line. A railway line stretched from Cairo to the port of Mersa Matruh and then on to Misheifa, south of Sidi Barrani. War material could be carried round the Cape, instead of at tragic cost through the Mediterranean. Aircraft could be crated and shipped to Takoradi on the Gold Coast, where they were assembled and then flown to Egypt.

The Axis forces could bring in some personnel and small supplies by air, but the great bulk of their war materials was carried across the Mediterranean in supply ships and tankers. There were excellent ports in Italy for this purpose, such as Naples, Brindisi, Taranto and Bari. The major problems began during the sea passage, for the vessels were subjected to determined attacks by British submarines, surface warships and aircraft.

Moreover, their difficulties in supply did not end if the vessels reached North Africa. In some ways, they intensified. There were only three ports of any consequence in Libya. By far the largest was Tripoli which, under normal conditions, could handle up to five merchant ships a day. But conditions were seldom normal, for the port received the regular attention of long-distance bombers of the RAF. In practice, the port proved capable of off-loading only 50,000 tons a month. In November 1941 the Axis forces, which consisted of two German and five Italian divisions, required an average of 70,000 tons a month. The port of Benghazi was capable theoretically of coping with the shortfall, but this was only 300 miles from the Egyptian border and was thus subjected to even heavier attacks by the RAF. The third port was Tobruk, but this was in the hands of the stubborn Australians, who proved a match for the encircling Axis forces.

Thus most supplies were sent to Tripoli but these were seldom adequate to meet requirements. Even then, there remained the formidable problem of transporting the supplies eastwards to the front line. The few coastal vessels available for this task could carry only 15,000 tons a month and were prime targets for the RAF's anti-shipping squadrons. There was no railway line running eastwards from Tripoli, and the only alternative was to transport the supplies by truck across 1,000 miles of inhospitable desert. These vehicles were mostly two-tonners and used the only road, which was named the *Via Balbia* and ran along the coast.

The units which consumed the most fuel, arms and other supplies were the two German armoured divisions, which required 20,000 tons a month. It was estimated that the number of trucks employed to supply these divisions in their advanced positions was twenty times the number needed in Russia for an equivalent force, after Germany invaded that country in June 1941. The trucks themselves required fuel. They broke down, or were shot up by RAF aircraft and long-distance desert groups. It was calculated that as much as half the fuel landed at Tripoli was used up between the port and the Axis front line.

Thus, if Rommel obeyed his instincts and launched another attack against an enemy he believed he could defeat, he would soon run out of supplies. He railed against his quartermasters, but they could not solve the problem; other German generals called him 'that mad soldier'. Hitler saw the difficulties of supply quite clearly, for at first he required Rommel to act merely as a blocking force and not to advance beyond his means of support. The supply line to the Axis divisions was likened to a piece of elastic. The further Rommel advanced, the greater the force requiring it to contract.

Of course, the British were fully aware of the handicap suffered by their formidable enemy. When General Sir Claude Auchinleck launched his Eighth Army on the 'Crusader' offensive on 18 November, he did so in the knowledge that the Axis supply situation was even worse than usual. The Axis had lost nineteen supply vessels during the previous month. Of these, twelve had been sunk by the RAF, five by submarines, and two by sea mines. Following these losses, a serious blow was struck by the Royal Navy against an Italian convoy, in the early hours of 9 November. Operating from Malta under the codename of 'Force K', the cruisers *Aurora* and *Penelope*, supported by the destroyers *Lance* and *Lively*, intercepted the convoy about 200 miles east of Malta. The Italian force consisted of seven merchant ships escorted by the cruisers *Trieste* and *Trento*, together with nine destroyers. The British warships attacked this superior force and, in a brilliantly executed night action, sank all the merchant vessels as well as the destroyer *Fulmine*. They also damaged two other destroyers. The supply ships were the German cargo ships *Duisburg* and *San Marco*, the Italian tankers *Minatitlan* and *Conte di Misurata*, and the Italian cargo ships *Rina Corrado*, *Sagitta* and *Maria*. These seven vessels totalled 34,773 tons, while their total cargo was 34,473 tons, including 15,527 tons of fuel. To make matters worse for the Axis, the British submarine *Upholder* sank the destroyer *Libeccio* the following morning. 'Force K' returned to Malta unscathed, in spite of attacks by Italian torpedo bombers during the journey.

At the opening of 'Crusader', the opposing air forces were roughly equal numerically. In March 1941, the Luftwaffe in the Mediterranean had been split into three commands: Fliegerkorps X, based in Sicily, was the command responsible for the air assault on Malta and the attacks on British convoys trying to reach the island; Fliegerführer Afrika was the command which supported Rommel in Libya; and Luftflotte 4 was the command which backed the German invasion of Greece and its islands, including Crete. But the invasion of Russia in June 1941 necessitated the withdrawal of Luftflotte 4. Then Fliegerkorps X was broken up and its units distributed either to Libya or to bases in southern Greece, Crete and Rhodes. These moves resulted in a total of about 180 German aircraft in Greece and about 240 in Libya, where there were also about 300 Italian aircraft. To oppose these forces, totalling 720 aircraft, the RAF could muster 660 aircraft in Egypt and the Western Desert, with another 120 in Malta. However, the rate of serviceability in the RAF was higher than that of its opponents and it is true to say that the crews of the RAF were more aggressive than those of the Regia Aeronautica.

Among the squadrons in the Western Desert was a detachment equipped with the new Beaufighter IC. This detachment consisted of the majority of 272 Squadron, temporarily transferred from 201 (Naval Co-operation) Group. It had moved from its base at Idku, east of Alexandria, to Landing Ground (LG) 10 at Gerawla, near Mersa Matruh.

The crews of 272 Squadron had converted from the Blenheim IVF to the more powerful IC during the previous April, when they were based at Chivenor in north Devon as part of Coastal Command. Under the command of Squadron Leader Andrew W. Fletcher, they then flew their new aircraft to the Middle East. Here they were joined by the crews of 252 Squadron, another maritime Beaufighter unit, which was temporarily disbanded.

At first, 272 Squadron began flying fighter escorts to the supply ships trying to reach Malta. But an additional role was soon devised for the versatile Beaufighter, that of ground strafing. A detachment was sent to Cyprus and, on 3 June, strafed the oil tanks at Beirut, which was under Axis control. Then a detachment was sent to Malta and, led by Fletcher, attacked airfields in Sicily and Sardinia. It was estimated that forty-nine enemy aircraft were destroyed in these attacks, which took place at the end of July.

In October, Fletcher finished his long tour of operations and was posted away, by then wearing the ribbon of a DFC and bar. He was replaced by Squadron Leader R. Gordon Yaxley, who had previously commanded 252 Squadron. Yaxley was a rather unusual pilot, for he had first joined the RAF in 1929 as an aircraft apprentice. However, he won a cadetship in 1932 and qualified as both a pilot and an engineer. Operations which involved RAF armoured cars in Palestine during 1936 resulted in an award to him of the MC. Under his leadership, morale in 272 Squadron continued at a very high level, especially when he was awarded a DFC soon after taking command.

The aircrews of the squadron formed a cosmopolitan gathering. Of the pilots, there were three Australians, three Belgians and two New Zealanders, while most of the remainder were South Africans, Canadians or Scotsmen. On one occasion, Yaxley looked around at his officers in the mess and remarked: 'There isn't a bloody Englishman among the lot of you!' But he knew that his crews formed one of the most effective units of the maritime squadrons in the Middle East.

In many ways the robust Beaufighter was ideal for ground strafing. It had enormous firepower, four Hispano-Suiza 20mm cannons firing through the nose, together with four .303 inch Browning machine guns mounted in the port wing and two more in the starboard wing. The cannons were drum-fed in the Beaufighter IC, each drum containing sixty rounds. There were a dozen spare drums stored further aft, and it was one of the unenviable jobs of the hard-pressed navigator/wireless operator, separated from his pilot by a set of hinged and armoured doors, to heave these heavy drums off their racks and reload the four cannons while the Beaufighter was in action.

The effect of this firepower on the unfortunate target – maybe an aircraft sitting on an airfield or a truck cruising along a coastal road – could be shattering. The Axis troops soon learnt to fear the Beaufighter. With their strongly developed sense of the dramatic, the Italians named the aircraft *il flagello di Dio*, the scourge of God.

The Beaufighter IC was fitted with two 1,425hp Hercules radial engines. These were less powerful than those fitted to later Beaufighters, but the aircraft was capable of an endurance of over six hours, about 1,200 miles. It could fly, with some difficulty, on one engine. This early Beaufighter had a straight tailplane and was more manoeuvrable than the versions which followed. These were fitted with a dihedral tailplane and were thus more stable, a quality which was considered necessary for an aircraft with engines rated to fly at low level.

Like most RAF aircraft, the Beaufighter IC had its foibles. There was a tendency to swing to the right on take-off, a not uncommon fault in many RAF aircraft. If the pilot flew in a 'negative G' attitude when firing the cannons, these jammed immediately. When the cannons were fired, the change in the aircraft's magnetism usually upset the compasses, so that the pilot had to fly due north or south afterwards and give them another burst, which usually cured the fault.

The main problem with the Beaufighter, however, was common to all aircraft in the Western Desert – the extreme difficulty of keeping up standards of servicing. The all-pervasive sand entered the engines, getting into the cylinders and affecting the bearings. White metal was often found in filters, resulting in the need for an engine change. The average life of an engine was only about sixty hours of flying in these conditions, until the new Vokes sand filters were introduced in 1942. The pilots were always worried about engine failure, since the propellers were not fully feathering in this early Beaufighter. Nevertheless, the ground crews of 272 Squadron somehow managed to work miracles in conditions of extreme discomfort and heat, with inadequate replacement of parts. Aircraft which made belly landings were sometimes in the air again within twenty-four hours.

A detachment of twelve Beaufighters from 272 Squadron, together with three spare crews, flew from Idku to LG10 on 9 November 1941. An advance party had driven across the desert to the landing ground two days earlier. The men found that living conditions were somewhat spartan. The messes were Nissen huts in which forty-gallon drums were used as stoves for cooking. Meals usually consisted of Spam, cooked in various ways. Accommodation was in tents, camouflaged with paint and oil. As they were to find out later, these tents were highly inflammable.

Most of the men who flew in the sorties which followed were killed during the war. One of those who survived, later to command 489 (NZ) Squadron in the UK, was Pilot Officer Derek Hammond, a New Zealander from Auckland. After training in Tiger Moths and Oxfords in New Zealand, Hammond arrived in the UK by troopship and passed his GR course at Squires Gate. During this course he flew the Blackburn Botha, an operational trainer with one of the most unhappy reputations in the RAF, for it was considered by pilots to handle and dive like a brick. Surviving this experience, he converted on to Beaufighters at Catfoss and was then posted to 143 Squadron at Dyce, near Edinburgh. This was one of the Coastal Command strike squadrons, engaged in flying over the North Sea in hunts for Ju 88s and U-boats. An unofficial but memorable flight Hammond made was when he 'shot up' Balmoral Castle, at a time when the Royal Family was in residence. Fortunately for him, no complaints were made. Shortly after this, he volunteered for the Middle East and flew out from Redruth in Cornwall via Gibraltar and Malta, arriving at 272 Squadron on 6 October 1941.

Operations from LG10 began on 15 November, three days before the opening of 'Crusader'. Soon after midday, Yaxley led a patrol of three Beaufighters on a strafing raid along the *Via Balbia*, in which a convoy of about twenty trucks was attacked. Some of these ran off the road while others turned over.

During the following morning, a patrol of four Beaufighters found a lone Ju 87 over the sea north of Derna and shot bits off it before it escaped into cloud. A few hours later, three Beaufighters took off for an attack on Tmimi aerodrome, about 120 miles inside the Axis lines. Among the pilots was Hammond, together with his navigator, Sergeant John Bryson. The pilots flew in Coastal Command style, at about twenty feet, but it was the desert beneath them and not the sea.

A few minutes before reaching the aerodrome, they rose to 200 feet to make a diving attack. The Axis soldiers and airmen at Tmimi, unfamiliar with the sight of this new RAF fighter, might have mistaken them for Ju 88s. Surprise was an essential element in such a daylight attack. Tmimi was partly obscured by a sandstorm, but the three Beaufighters formed into line abreast and went into shallow dives. The pilots opened up at long range with their machine guns and watched the spurts of dust 'walk' across the airfield towards several Ju 87s. At about 800 yards, each pilot pressed the firing button of his four cannons. Two Ju 87s and a mobile W/T truck disappeared in a cloud of dust and gunfire.

The three Beaufighters then roared straight over the airfield, towards an access road which led to the *Via Balbia*. A long line of trucks was driving down this road and received the same treatment. Trucks burst into flames while soldiers were seen to jump out and fall, either hit by gunfire or trying to burrow themselves into the sand. But Hammond was too enthusiastic, for his starboard wing hit a telegraph pole. A less robust aircraft might have spun round and crashed, but the sturdy Beaufighter flew on, with two and a half feet shorn from its wingtip.

Hammond turned for home, trailing lengths of telegraph wire and bits of insulation, which were examined with interest when he made a successful landing back at LG10. Meanwhile, the other two aircraft hunted further along the approach road and made two more attacks. In all, the Beaufighters destroyed or damaged about thirty Axis trucks on that day.

The ground crews could not replace the missing wingtip, but they worked out an alternative. They removed an equivalent length from the port wing, so that the Beaufighter was transformed into an aircraft with square wingtips. The men commented at the time that the aero-engineers in the Bristol factory at Filton would have been horrified. But one of the pilots, Sergeant Lowes, braved the high stalling speed of the redesigned Beaufighters and successfully flew it back to Edku for repair.

On the following morning, three more Beaufighters paid another visit to the road at Tmimi and attacked a convoy of six trucks, leaving two on fire. In the afternoon, three other Beaufighters attacked the aerodrome at Gadd el Ahmar, about twenty-five miles south-east of Tmimi, where they destroyed two Savoia-Marchetti SM79 bombers on the ground and knocked over many personnel. So far, the Beaufighter detachment had lost no aircraft in these surprise attacks.

During the night of 17/18 November, violent electrical storms broke over LG10. The flying crews were woken up at 0400 hours, for their allotted task in the opening of 'Crusader' was to deliver a crushing attack on Tmimi aerodrome with all twelve Beaufighters. But torrents of water had rushed down the wadi (watercourse) between their lines and the airfield, so that the area became impassable for transport. Within the landing ground, dug-outs and the armoury were flooded.

Throughout the morning, the weather was a mixture of low cloud and heavy rain, interspersed with blinding sandstorms. It was not until midday that six Beaufighters were able to take off for their target, but their attack was to prove one of the most devastating of the campaign. They arrived over Tmimi at 1415 hours, in time to meet five Ju52s which were climbing shortly after taking off. Within a few minutes all the German transports had crashed in flames. A Henschel 126, used by the Germans for spotting, was also shot down. Then three Beaufighters turned their attention to the airfield where, in spite of concentrated defensive fire, they left four SM79s in flames on the ground. Even then, the six Beaufighters were not finished. They flew south-east and arrived over the aerodrome at Gadd el Ahmar, where a number of Italian soldiers were killed or wounded from their fire. Finally, on the return journey, they met an unlucky Feiseler Storch spotter plane and shot it down.

In the late afternoon, three more Beaufighters took off from LG10 and headed for Barce, a hundred miles deeper into enemy territory than Tmimi. Just south of the town, they found two Ju 52s and shot down both. Then the aerodrome was attacked and the tents shot up. Lastly, they left four petrol trucks in flames.

In one respect, the Beaufighter crews were lucky, for the fighters of the Luftwaffe were even more seriously affected by the storms. Their airfields were situated on softer ground and very few aircraft were able to take off. Only one Me 109 was seen during these attacks. It chased one of the Beaufighters, which managed to elude it. Every Beaufighter returned on this memorable day. It happened to be the first anniversary of the formation of the squadron, giving an extra reason for celebration. Morale was already high when a telegram was received from Air Headquarters, congratulating the squadron on its success.

Tmimi was again the target for the following day. At 0640 hours, Yaxley led six Beaufighters to the enemy aerodrome, arriving two hours later. The first pair of Beaufighters attacked in line abreast and left four Ju 87s and an Me 109 blazing fiercely. They followed through and raked the tents with cannon fire. But the four Beaufighters which followed them received the full blast of the awakened defences. Although they despatched another Ju 87, two Beaufighters were hit. Flight Lieutenant G.L. 'Punch' Campbell flew back on one engine, with his hydraulics also shot away, to make a belly landing at LG10. Sergeant Robert A. Haylock was hit in the foot but he flew all the way to Idku, where he made a good belly landing and was taken straight to hospital.

Later in the afternoon, five more Beaufighters took off. These included Hammond, who so far had not flown since 'Crusader' began. But he soon made up for the omission. The five aircraft also headed for Tmimi, following an urgent intelligence report to the effect that a number of German aircraft had landed there during the morning. Two hours later, the attackers arrived over the aerodrome. Three Beaufighters flew in line abreast, with the remaining two close behind in line astern. The newly-arrived German aircraft were lined up conveniently. Fourteen Ju 87s and one Me 109 went up in flames, while a petrol dump exploded. The fires from the attack could be seen thirty miles away on the return journey. One Beaufighter was hit but, in spite of damage to an aileron control, the pilot joined the other four in a successful landing at LG10.

There was no relaxation of effort on the following day. Four Beau-fighters flew beyond Tmimi to attack the airfield at Maturba, where three Ju 87s, one Ju 88 and a spotter aircraft were destroyed on the ground. Then the attackers flew along the *Via Balbia* and shot up a line of trucks. An Me 109 pursued one of the Beaufighters and caused some damage, but eventually the pilot managed to draw away from the German fighter. On the return journey, another Beaufighter was peppered with holes from ground troops, wounding the navigator in the thigh.

The next day, 22 November, was somewhat less successful. Yaxley led eight Beaufighters all the way to Benina aerodrome, near Benghazi, but found a swarm of enemy fighters circling the locality. He turned the formation away and headed for the *Via Balbia*, where they destroyed seven trucks. But then the weather closed in and they were forced to return to LG10.

The target was changed to Barce aerodrome on the following day, and a line of five SM79s was shot up by four Beaufighters. This day saw the first complete loss of a Beaufighter, when Pilot Officer Norman K. Lee crash-landed on the return journey, after his aircraft had been hit by accurate ground fire. Another Beaufighter, flown by Flying Officer Albert Salter, crashed on landing back at LG10. On the following day, three Beaufighters left fifteen trucks on fire or smoking, on the roads leading to Barce.

The next day – 25 November – Yaxley led five Beaufighters on their longest sortie of the campaign. They took off at 0630 hours and penetrated over 400 miles into enemy territory to the aerodrome at Agedabia, south of Soluch, where they damaged two Fiat CR42s and a Caproni Ca 310 on the ground. They also blew up a petrol tanker on the airfield and attacked a convoy of eight trucks on the approach road. Flight Lieutenant Maurice Bartlett, who had been at the forefront of several of these low-level attacks, hit a telegraph pole and returned to base with three feet missing from his starboard wing. His navigator, Sergeant George Forrest, helped him with the controls on the long and difficult return journey. In the afternoon, Pilot Officer Norman K. Lee and his navigator, Sergeant William H. Gowing, returned to the squadron from their force-landing in the desert two days before. Their Beaufighter had burnt out after landing with one engine on fire, but they were unharmed apart from a few cuts. They had managed to walk to the British lines.

The pressure of operations continued on the following day, when six Beaufighters attacked Agedabia aerodrome once more. They shot down a Ca 311 and then destroyed four CR42s and a Ju 87 on the ground. Sergeant Norman Price and his navigator, Sergeant Frank Southern, were shot down by the defences but survived to become PoWs.

On 27 November, Gordon Yaxley learnt that he had been awarded the DSO, his squadron having been credited with the destruction of forty-six enemy aircraft within six days. But flying was then hampered by more storms and bad visibility. Only four Beaufighters took off on that day, heading for Tmimi but arriving over Maturba, twenty-five miles away. They saw no aircraft but shot up some tents, one Beaufighter being slightly damaged by return fire.

The following day was occupied with collecting new aircraft and practice flying. The storms continued to restrict operations and on 29 November four Beaufighters failed to locate Maturba and instead attacked vehicles on the *Via Balbia*. However, on the last day of the month four Beaufighters attacked Maturba once again, damaging eight enemy aircraft on the airfield. Maurice Bartlett returned with damage to an elevator and most of the rudder shot away.

Four Beaufighters also went out on 2 December, attacking Barce aerodrome and damaging seven Fiat BR20 heavy bombers. Flying Officer Albert A. Salter was shot down and taken prisoner, together with his navigator, Sergeant Albert E. Glover.

The next sortie was on 6 December, when four Beaufighters took off at 0950 hours. The attacked fourteen trucks on the *Via Balbia* between Derna and Tobruk and left two on fire. Then they turned towards Tmimi but had a very hot reception. Two Beaufighters were hit by flak and one of these, flown by Flying Officer Charles Roman, was attacked by an Me 109. The Belgian pilot managed to avoid the German fighter, which made four passes at him. But Pilot Officer William G. Snow was less fortunate. He was shot down by an Me 109 flown by Oberleutnant Gustav Rödel of II/Jagdgeschwader 27, based at Gazala, and crash-landed two miles north of Tmimi. Snow and his navigator, Sergeant John K. Dutton, survived to become PoWs.

Four more Beaufighters took off for the same target at 1115 hours. They damaged five Ju 87s on the airfield as well as six trucks on the *Via Balbia*. Flak over Tmimi was again intense and Flight Lieutenant 'Punch' Campbell's Beaufighter was hit. He managed to keep the aircraft in the air until he was about forty miles from Tmimi and then came down in the desert. Derek Hammond, who had been escorting the damaged Beaufighter, landed nearby. But the ground was rocky and uneven, and his tail wheel collapsed into the fuselage, becoming a sort of skid. Campbell decided to try again and succeeded in taking off, followed by Hammond, but he could not maintain height and landed once more. Hammond landed beside him, although he was worried about his tail wheel. Then an enemy aircraft was seen overhead at about 2,000 feet and the four men rushed to find whatever cover they could, the best being a bush of about twelve inches in height. Fortunately they were not spotted. They all scrambled into Hammond's Beaufighter and made a hazardous take-off. Once in the air, Hammond turned and gave Campbell's Beaufighter a long squirt of cannon fire, before heading back to LG10. At the landing ground, it was found that the bolts holding the tailplane unit had sheared.

Another Beaufighter on this attack was hit. It was flown by an Australian, Pilot Officer Arthur P. Stevenson, who was wounded in both legs. His navigator, Sergeant John E. Olive was hit in the head. In spite of his wounds, Stevenson flew the Beaufighter all the way back to Edku, where both men were taken to hospital. Unfortunately, John Olive died shortly afterwards.

The pace slackened a little after these episodes. On the following day, Flight Lieutenant Bartlett led one other Beaufighter in a strafing raid along the *Via Balbia*, where they damaged twelve trucks. But Bartlett's machine was badly hit by flak near Barce aerodrome and he had difficulty keeping up with his companion on the return flight to LG10.

Two Beaufighters on an 'Armed Rover' over the sea on 11 December attacked two four-engined machines, possibly Ju 90s, but neither of the transports was seen to go down. On the following day, two Beaufighters attacked three Ju 52s heading for Derna, and all the German machines were damaged. Another pair of Beaufighters encountered five Ju 52s heading towards Crete; they damaged all of them, shooting the undercarriage off one transport. On a third sortie, two Beaufighters flown by Yaxley and Hammond met five Ju 52s and attacked. Hammond sent one of the German transports down in flames and all the remaining four were damaged. But both Beaufighters were hit by return fire. Hammond's hydraulics were shot away, and he flew the long journey back to Idku, where he belly-landed safely. In the CO's aircraft, Sergeant George Sproates was wounded in both legs. Yaxley landed at LG10 and the navigator was flown on to Idku, where his wounds were tended in hospital.

The squadron continued to take casualties. On 13 December, Flying Officer Graham W. Morris and his navigator, Sergeant Harry W. Hilton, failed to return from a patrol; the reason was not known, but both men lost their lives. On the same day Flying Officer Charles Roman damaged a Do 24 and an Me 110, returning with a large hole in the tailplane of his Beaufighter. Two days later, Sergeant John Ross was wounded after having attacked a large convoy on the *Via Balbia*, and then damaged a Ju 52. Nevertheless, he flew back to LG10 and made a belly-landing with severed hydraulics.

An unusual episode occurred on 19 December, when two Beaufighters flown by Flight Lieutenant Maurice Bartlett and a New Zealander, Pilot Officer H.H. 'Heck' Crawford, strafed the *Via Balbia* near Barce. Crawford's starboard engine was hit by flak and he turned for home. He managed to nurse the aircraft for about eighty miles south-east of

Barce and then came down in the desert. He and his navigator, Sergeant Keith McL. Taylor, were unhurt and set fire to their machine. Then they saw Bartlett landing near them and ran towards his Beaufighter. When about 400 yards away, they heard the rattle of machine gun fire and dived for cover. Bartlett saw two German tanks and two armoured cars approaching. There was no possibility of picking up the other two men and he took off hastily, with his aircraft badly hit in the tailplane and rudder. Crawford and Taylor tried to hide but they were picked up by the armoured cars. The Germans took away their revolvers and watches, and then drove them to a long convoy heading towards Benghazi, for at this time the Deutsches Afrika Korps was in retreat.

The two prisoners were separated and the convoy moved off. During the night, the RAF men slept under armed guard. The retreat continued throughout the next day, with hourly stops. While it was still dark during the next morning, Crawford was taken to one of the trucks where the troops were preparing for the day's trek. He was left unwatched for a few moments and bolted towards the nearest skyline, which he managed to reach before his escape was noticed. He ran headlong over the rocky desert until dawn broke and he was forced to find a hiding place, which was a rather insignificant thorn bush. Here he remained, nursing a bruised foot, until he felt it was safe to move.

The pilot began to hobble eastwards, but his foot became too painful by the afternoon. He was found by some Bedouins, who fortunately treated him well, although it was thirty-six hours before he could continue. The Arabs decided to head for El Abiar, on the railway line from Benghazi to Derna, which they understood had been evacuated by the Axis forces. They reached this place on 25 December but found it was deserted. Then they continued eastwards, heading for Barce, about thirty miles away, and came to the British lines at midday on 27 December. Crawford returned to 272 Squadron at LG10 on New Year's Eve.

Meanwhile, the Beaufighter detachment continued its strafing operations. The raids spread westwards as the Axis forces retreated, and the road to Agedabia became a prime target. But the Germans were still full of fight. On 22 December, Pilot Officer Kenneth B. Orr and his navigator, Sergeant Kenneth T. Jackson, failed to return from one of these operations and were later reported to be PoWs. Two more Beaufighters were lost in the same area, near El Agheila, during the following day. Both were shot down by an Me 109 flown by Oberleutnant Gerhart Homuth. The Beaufighters were flown by Pilot Officer Norman K. Lee and Pilot Officer James H. Baker. These two men lost their lives, as did their navigators, Sergeant Arthur S. Greaves and Sergeant Edwin S. Fender. On the same day, the Belgian pilot Sergeant René Demoulin shot down a Ju 52.

On Christmas Eve, Flying Officer Charles Roman scored a remarkable success by shooting down an Me 109, one of two which attacked him after he and another pilot had shot up fifteen trucks on the *Via Balbia* near El Agheila. After this, there was a break for Christmas Day, the day when the Eighth Army entered Benghazi.

New crews and aircraft arrived on 27 December, sorely needed to replenish the losses suffered by the detachment. One of the pilots, Flight Sergeant C.A. Ream, had taken rather a long time to arrive. He was one of those who had flown with 272 Squadron in the UK but, after leaving Cornwall on 24 May 1941, ran out of fuel on the flight to Gibraltar and landed in a cornfield near Cadiz. He and his navigator, Sergeant D.S. Gallimore, blew up their IFF (Identification Friend or Foe) radar and burned their papers before being captured by the Spanish Air Force. They were handed over to the British Consul in Seville, who eventually managed to smuggle them on the British ship SS *Aldergrove*, which took them to Gibraltar.

On the last day of the year, four Beaufighters, including Hammond and Roman, destroyed two trucks on the *Via Balbia*, damaged six others, hit a house used as a barracks, attacked a tug and shot down a Feiseler Storch. The final six weeks of the year had been extremely eventful: this maritime squadron had been singled out for special praise for its part in operation 'Crusader'. The low-flying techniques and determination of the crews in their powerful Beaufighters had proved invaluable. They were considered to have achieved an extremely high ratio of successes against losses in the operation.

The intention of operation 'Crusader' had been to destroy the armoured divisions of the Deutsches Afrika Korps, to relieve Tobruk and then drive the Axis forces out of Libya. The first part of the plan went well. After the sea and land supply lines of the Axis forces had been severely disrupted by the Royal Navy and the RAF, the armoured divisions of the Eighth Army moved to outflank the enemy and drive towards Tobruk. Meanwhile, the garrison of the beleaguered port stood ready to break out and form one arm of a pincer movement. The Commonwealth troops were in good spirits and full of confidence, having been assured of their superiority in numbers and quality of equipment, as well as command of the air.

But events did not unfold exactly in accordance with the next part of the plan. The Axis forces recovered quickly from their initial surprise and, after a fierce two-day battle on the ridge at Sidi Rezegh, the British armour was forced back. Rommel then began a lightning thrust into Egypt, causing a somewhat disorderly retreat by some elements of the Eighth Army as well as dismay in their command. But then the troops in Tobruk began to break out and New Zealand divisions moved to meet them. This pincer movement gave Rommel cause for thought.

He turned back his armoured units and bitter fighting followed.

On 5 December, Rommel was made aware of some unpalatable facts. Fourteen of the twenty-two supply ships sent from Italy to North Africa during November had been sunk, taking with them sixty-two per cent of his supplies. He had no option but to retreat, for many of his Panzers were out of action for lack of spares, while ammunition and fuel were almost exhausted. He fell back and formed a new line at Gazala, about thirty miles west of Tobruk. The eight month siege of the port was at an end.

On 13 December, the Eighth Army attacked these new defensive positions and the Axis forces were sent further back to the west, losing many troops but still intact as fighting units. The advancing Commonwealth troops found ample evidence of the attacks made by the RAF and the Long Range Desert Group. They counted 458 enemy aircraft destroyed on airfields, while hundreds more had crashed in the desert or were gathered in graveyard dumps.

By the end of the year, Rommel had formed another line at Agedabia. However, the Eighth Army was unable to keep up the pressure, for its own supply lines were stretched to the limit. Moreover, the men had developed a great respect for Rommel and had to some extent lost confidence in the quality of their own equipment.

Then the fortunes of war swung heavily in favour of Rommel. Successes in the Mediterranean had begun some weeks before, when nineteen German U-boats slipped past Gibraltar from the Atlantic. On 13 November U-81 sank the aircraft carrier *Ark Royal* and twelve days later U-331 sank the battleship *Barham*. Then, on 19 December, three midget submarines manned by audacious Italians entered Alexandria harbour and put out of action the battleships *Queen Elizabeth* and *Valiant*. Thus, while 'Crusader' was in progress, the effectiveness of the Royal Navy's Mediterranean Fleet was seriously impaired.

On 16 December, four merchant ships left Taranto with supplies for the Axis forces in North Africa. These were the German *Ankara* and the Italian *Pisani*, *Monginevro* and *Napoli*. An enormous force escorted these vessels, consisting of four battleships, five cruisers, nineteen destroyers and one torpedo boat. This naval force was split into close escort and distant support groups. During the following night *Napoli* was hit by aircraft bombs, but destroyers and a tug from Tripoli went to her aid. 'Force K' from Malta attempted to intercept the convoy, but on 19 December ran into a minefield east of Tripoli. The cruiser *Neptune* and the destroyer *Kandahar* were sunk, while the cruiser *Aurora* and the destroyer *Penelope* were badly damaged and forced to put back to Malta.

At 0930 hours on 19 December, *Ankara* docked successfully at Benghazi, which at the time was still held by Axis troops. She off-loaded over 4,000 tons of ammunition, fuel and armoured vehicles. This included forty-five Panzers, which enabled the Germans to stave off the armoured attack by the British. The remaining three merchant vessels arrived at Tripoli, bringing almost 11,000 tons of vital supplies to the Axis forces.

This success was repeated under operation 'M-43', seventeen days later. Five merchant ships – *Nino Bixio*, *Monginevro*, *Lerici*, *Gino Allegri* and *Monviso* – left the Italian ports of Messina, Brindisi and Taranto on 3 January 1942. Joining up with another enormous naval escort, they crossed the Mediterranean unharmed and entered Tripoli two days later, where they off-loaded over 12,500 tons of ammunition, over 15,000 tons of fuel, about 650 vehicles and 900 troops.

The safe passage of the second convoy was supported by the arrival of about 400 German aircraft based in Sicily. These formed Luftflotte 2, commanded by Generalfeldmarschall Albert Kesselring, the aircraft having being withdrawn from western Europe and the Russian front. They arrived in early January, their main tasks being to neutralise Malta and to ensure that Rommel would receive uninterrupted supplies in future. The employment of Italian capital ships was proving extremely expensive with fuel, which was in very short supply, although the operations of the fleet had been successful. It was at this time that the great air assault on Malta began.

The arrival of these two large convoys was all that Rommel needed. His troops were still in good heart, having fought a skilful retreat, while be believed that those of the Eighth Army were in a state of uncertainty. His supply lines were now shorter, whereas those of his opponents were correspondingly longer. It was a question of choosing the right moment. Under cover of gales and sandstorms he brought forward his armoured units, by then rechristened Panzerarmee Afrika, and attacked on 21 January 1942. The Eighth Army was taken by surprise and before long the familiar pattern of retreat developed. By 6 February a withdrawal as far as Gazala had been completed. Operation 'Crusader' had ended, not in a defeat, but without achieving its objectives.

All the available records testify to the success of 272 Squadron in this campaign. Awards followed this success. Among these, 'Punch' Campbell received the DFC during January; he left the squadron at the end of his tour, but was killed later in the war. Derek Hammond and Maurice Bartlett were awarded DFCs during April, while George Forrest received the DFM. But Bartlett's DFC was posthumous, for by then he had been accidentally killed in a fire in his tent on New Year's Eve. This may have been caused by a lighted cigarette, but perhaps it was the result of a loose round fired by the exuberant troops nearby, for they used their weapons as alternatives to fireworks.

Gordon Yaxley was also killed, a year after leaving the squadron, in a Sunderland in the Bay of Biscay. 'Heck' Crawford, who had returned to the squadron on New Year's Eve after escaping from the Germans, was killed on 6 February 1942. The port engine of his Beaufighter was hit by flak near Barce, and the starboard engine failed fifteen minutes later. His aircraft caught fire when crash-landing and only his navigator, Sergeant John E. Patterson, managed to stagger away from the flames and exploding ammunition. Fortunately he was befriended by some Arabs who hid him in their tents and tended his wounds until he was fit enough to walk towards the British lines. On 19 February, he fell in with ten British soldiers who had been cut off in the fighting with the advancing Panzerarmee. They ambushed a truck containing a German sergeant and corporal, took them prisoner, drove past Tmimi and arrived in the British lines on 21 February.

The detachment from 272 Squadron continued to fly over the Western Desert until March 1942, when it returned to its more accustomed maritime role.

(**Above**) The attack on 9 October 1942 by four Beaufighters of 252 Squadron and three Bisleys of 15 (SAAF) Squadron on an Axis train, which was completely destroyed by bombs and cannon fire. (*Flt Lt T. Armstrong, DFC*) (**Below**) Living conditions for the aircrews of 252 Squadron in the Western Desert. *Left to right:* Sergeant Gordon Nettleship of the RAAF, Sergeant Stan Kernaghan of the RCAF and Sergeant Archie Powell of the RAF. (*Flt Lt S.J. Kernaghan, AFC, DFM*)

(**Above**) The Italian merchant vessel *Rosolino Pilo* of 8,326 tons on fire after the attack by Beauforts of 86 Squadron from Malta on 17 August 1942. She was finished off by the submarine HMS *United* in the evening of the same day. (*Roger Hayward*) (**Below**) Axis troops surprised on a beach by a Beaufighter of 252 Squadron flown by Sergeant Stan Kernaghan when returning from the attack of 6 October 1942 against Bomba seaplane base. (*Flt Lt S.J. Kernaghan, AFC, DFM*)

4

FIGHTERS FROM EGYPT

D uring the first four months of 1942, a period of stalemate existed between the exhausted armies in the Western Desert. Protected by their minefields, the Axis forces and the Eighth Army faced each other along the line from Gazala, while their respective air forces continued to bombard ground positions and meet in aerial combat.

Meanwhile, the air attacks on Malta intensified from bases in Sicily, the main targets being the airfields at Luqa, Hal Far and Takali. These attacks reached such a pitch that, in spite of the arrival of a handful of Spitfires on the island, the air defences became steadily worn down. Only a few serviceable fighters remained by March, while the bomber force of Blenheims, Wellingtons and Fleet Air Arm Albacores was reduced to a handful. Towards the end of that month, a heavily escorted convoy of four merchant ships attempted to bring relief. One was sunk but three reached Grand Harbour. Then all three were destroyed by air attack, after only 5,000 tons of their precious cargoes had been unloaded. The situation deteriorated even further in April, until at one stage the number of fighters was reduced to only six while ammunition for the anti-aircraft guns had to be severely rationed. On the sixteenth of that month King George VI granted the remarkable award of the George Cross to the entire island.

On 20 April a consignment of forty-seven Spitfires was flown from the US carrier *Wasp*, but these were reduced by air attack to seventeen by the evening of the following day. Even more threatening, it became apparent that plans were being prepared to invade the islands from Sicily, employing a combination of airborne and seaborne troops similar to those which had conquered Crete so dramatically during the previous spring. Fortunately for the Eighth Army in Egypt this plan, code named operation 'Hercules', was given lower priority than a renewed attack in the Western Desert by the Axis forces. It was eventually abandoned following pressure of events on the Russian front and the diversion of German resources to combat the massive attacks by Bomber Command on cities and towns in the Reich. With hindsight, it is probable that operation 'Hercules' would have succeeded, since Malta's defences had been badly worn down and the population was close to starvation.

In the Western Desert during this critical period, another Beaufighter squadron became an effective fighting unit within 201 (Naval Co-operation) Group. This was 252 Squadron, which was formed at Idku in January 1942. It was the third incarnation for the squadron, which had first been formed in 1918 and employed on naval patrol duties for the remainder of World War One. After disbandment in 1919, it was formed again in November 1940 as part of Coastal Command, becoming operational at Chivenor at the end of March 1941, equipped with Blenheims and the new Beaufighter ICs. The commanding officer was Squadron Leader R. Gordon Yaxley, who later commanded 272 Squadron. Within a few weeks the squadron moved to Northern Ireland, from where it was engaged on convoy escort duties. About half the squadron flew in Beaufighters to Malta in June 1941, while the part that remained was absorbed by the newly formed 143 Squadron of Coastal Command. In turn, about half 143 Squadron's Beaufighters flew out during July to join 252 Squadron.

The detachments at Luqa were mainly employed on convoy escort duties, but also made some attacks on airfields in Sicily and Greece. The existence of the squadron was short-lived, however, for the crews and their aircraft were soon transferred to 272 Squadron in Egypt. Even when 252 Squadron was re-formed in January 1942, under the command of Squadron Leader Arthur G. Wincott, its fortunes continued to be intertwined with 272 Squadron. They were the only two long-range fighter squadrons of 201 Group in early 1942; both were equipped with Beaufighter Is, although a few Mark VIs arrived as the year progressed. The two squadrons occasionally operated in concert but for the most part their sorties took place separately. During the first half of 1942, the crews of both squadrons flew mainly from advanced bases in the Western Desert, with occasional detachments to Malta.

One of the pilots who joined the new 252 Squadron was Flying Officer T.F. Paul Nisbet, from Pyrford in Surrey. He was twenty-six years of age and had joined the RAFVR as a part-timer before the war, but was not called up for training until May 1940. He flew Magisters at EFTS in Derby and then Oxfords at SFTS in Cranwell, where he was commissioned in December. He broke his wrist at GR School at Squires Gate, which delayed his OTU training on Blenheims at Catfoss. Then he was posted to 143 Squadron in Northern Ireland during June 1943, when it was equipped with the new Beaufighter IC. Here he crewed up with Sergeant Leslie S. Lewis, a twenty-one-year-old navigator from Dartford in Kent.

The squadron was moved to various aerodromes and the crews flew on long-range patrols over the Western Approaches. In December

1941, when the squadron was based at Sumburgh in the Shetlands, Nisbet and Lewis were ordered to Portreath, where they collected a new Beaufighter. On 2 January 1942 they took off for Gibraltar, flying across the Iberian peninsula down the border between Spain and Portugal, without formal permission from those two countries. From Gibraltar the next leg was to Luqa in Malta, evading an attack by an Me 110 on the final approach. The last leg was to Cairo and Idku, where they joined 252 Squadron.

Living conditions at Idku were quite basic, quarters for all ranks being tents partially dug into the ground, with messes in larger tents. Those at the advanced landing grounds were much the same, except that the food was poorer and water was very limited. Each man was allowed only a gallon of water a day, but the cookhouse took seven pints, so that only a pint was available for washing. Hot tea was the usual drink but this was gritty with sand and the men used some of it for shaving.

After a stint at one of the landing grounds, the crews were sent back to Idku periodically for aircraft maintenance. Their greatest pleasure was a trip to the Hotel Cecil in Alexandria, where a bathroom could be hired by the hour. After the luxury of a bath and a shave, the crews usually gathered for drinks and a meal, the 'kitty' being held by someone such as the squadron medical officer. In spite of these conditions and losses of Beaufighters on operations, morale was remarkably high while the relations between aircrews and ground crews were very good.

In the early months of 1942, 252 Squadron was engaged primarily on long-range fighter patrols escorting naval convoys from Alexandria to Tobruk. One such patrol took place on 15 February 1942 from LG10, near Mersa Matruh, when Nisbet carried a war correspondent. This was a Mr Jan H. Yindrich, and the subsequent report which the war correspondent sent in a long series of cables to the United Press in London makes vivid reading. He described how he perched behind Nisbet, who was a 'six-foot-three fighter pilot', while the sun blazed down, turning the blue Mediterranean Sea into molten silver at times. He spent much of his time peering anxiously through the top hatch towards the sun, for he was aware that enemy aircraft often attacked from that direction.

When they arrived over the convoy, it proved to be the biggest that Yindrich had ever seen. Suddenly, Nisbet jabbed him in the ribs with his elbow and shouted, 'They're bombing the convoy!' The war correspondent reported that the pilot's face lit up at the prospect of combat but that his own stomach turned over when he saw Nisbet turn the firing button on his control column from 'safe' to 'fire'. He turned his attention back to the dazzling sun, imagining deadly Me 109Fs diving down on their tail. But all he saw was a biplane trundling along, which Nisbet identified as a Fleet Air Arm Swordfish on reconnaissance.

There was no sign of enemy aircraft while they circled the convoy, but suddenly a dozen black puffs appeared in the sky as the ships' gunners fired at bombers high above. A series of geysers rose from the the sea, screening two merchant ships from their view. Then two more gouts surrounded two more ships at the rear of the convoy and smoke poured from the funnels of one of the vessels. Yindrich thought she had been hit, but the smoke was probably the result of increased speed to avoid action, for the merchant vessel steamed ahead.

Yindrich was so fascinated by this spectacle that he failed to notice a black tri-motored bomber on their port bow. But Nisbet had spotted it and turned to attack. It was an SM79 and the Italian dived down to sea level in an attempt to escape, with the Beaufighter closing rapidly on its tail. Yindrich felt a terrific vibration under his buttocks as four cannons and six machine guns opened up, accompanied by a yell from Nisbet. 'Take that, you black bastard!' The outline of the bomber was difficult to pick out against the dark blue sea, but there were flecks of spray surrounding it. Then Nisbet pulled up the nose of the Beaufighter and fired another burst. According to the war correspondent, Nisbet shouted 'Get down into the well, you blighter!', except that he did not say 'blighter'. Five bursts were fired altogether and much of the fire seemed to strike the SM79. But the Italian kept flying, and the ammunition drums of the cannons had run out.

Lewis struggled to replace the drums but then the four cannons refused to fire. Another Beaufighter of 252 Squadron, flown by Sergeant W. Smith, swept past to finish off the SM79, which was considered to have been destroyed. Nisbet's Beaufighter had been damaged by return fire and he set course for LG10, where he found another aircraft and flew back to the convoy to resume his patrol.

Jan Yindrich had a dramatic story to tell his friends when he returned home, but meanwhile 252 Squadron continued its business of flying and fighting. On 12 May 1942 an experiment took place when six Beaufighters led by the commanding officer, Squadron Leader Wincott, joined up with ten Curtiss Kittyhawks of 250 Squadron led by their Australian commanding officer, Wing Commander H.C. Mayers. The single-engined Kittyhawk possessed formidable firepower: six .50 inch machine guns mounted in the wings. The purpose of this combined sortie, which took place from LG10, was to seek out German air transports flying from Crete. These had been observed landing with troops and supplies by long-range desert patrols operating behind enemy lines. Nisbet was one of the Beaufighter pilots but, after an hour of low-level flying over the sea, his port engine backfired and blew the filters out of the air intake. They stuck and restricted the flow of air into the carburettor. He had to turn back, as did one of the Kittyhawks, which also experienced engine trouble.

There was great excitement when the formation returned, for a major engagement had taken place. They had met thirteen Ju 52s and one Me 110, and had made a head-on attack. The RAF pilots thought that the enemy formation was larger, for they claimed sixteen Ju 52s and three Me 110s shot down, an exaggeration which often occurred when several fighters attacked the same aircraft. Nevertheless, the results were disastrous enough for the Germans. Nine Ju 52s were shot down, while two more crash-landed on beaches. The single Me 110 was also shot down. One Beaufighter was hit by return fire from the Ju 52s and plunged into the sea with the starboard engine on fire. Flight Sergeant Reginald A. Cripps and his navigator, Sergeant Thomas Bateman, lost their lives.

In spite of such occasional reverses, the Axis forces in North Africa were successfully supplied with war materials during the first half of 1942, by both sea and air. While Malta was suffering the protracted agony of constant air bombardment, her small force of anti-shipping aircraft was unable to strike with sufficient strength at the Axis convoys. Supplies poured across the Mediterranean, mainly to Tripoli. At the same time, the Allied forces in North Africa received huge supplies from convoys which passed round the Cape, while new aircraft continued to be delivered to Takoradi, where they were assembled and flown to Egypt. Both sides were preparing for an offensive, but it was Rommel who struck first, on 26 May 1942.

The line of the Eighth Army extended from Gazala, on the coast about thirty-five miles west of Tobruk, southwards to Bir Hakim, a strongpoint which was held by Free French troops. The thrust of the Panzerarmee Afrika outflanked this line and swept up as far as El Adem, south of Tobruk. Meanwhile the Italian forces made a frontal attack, in an attempt to penetrate the minefields. However, the Free French held out at Bir Hakim until 10 June, supported by the RAF, and seriously delayed the Axis advance. For the time being, fierce fighting stalled Rommel at El Adem and the strongpoint known as Knightsbridge, but eventually his superior generalship prevailed over the scattered units of the Eighth Army. By 15 June, the Germans had broken through and cut off Tobruk. The garrison of this port, consisting of a miscellany of units which were poorly co-ordinated and short of artillery, was unable to withstand the tremendous air and artillery bombardment to which it was subjected, and surrendered on 21 June.

The gains to the Axis forces were enormous. Tobruk contained about 1,500,000 gallons of fuel as well as 3,000,000 field rations. There was water, military clothing, tinned food, beer, whisky, and a large supply of the coveted 'desert boots' made from suede uppers with thick rubber soles. In addition to this treasure trove, the Axis armies took over 45,000 prisoners during the campaign. The road to Egypt seemed to beckon Rommel.

During the early months of 1942, the Beaufighter crews of 272 Squadron had also been operating from forward airfields such as LG10, protecting convoys and strafing roads or attacking German barges bringing supplies to the front line. But in June the squadron formed part of the RAF units ordered to protect two convoys which had set sail to relieve Malta, under the codename 'Vigorous'. One of these convoys left the Clyde via Gibraltar while the other was timed to approach Malta simultaneously from Alexandria. In response, a large Italian fleet left Taranto on a course to intercept the convoy sailing from the east. Beauforts of 39 Squadron in Egypt were ordered to make torpedo attacks on these warships, as were the Beauforts of 217 Squadron which had arrived in Malta a few days before, having flown out from Cornwall via Gibraltar.

The Operations Record book of 272 Squadron for the days of 14 and 15 June states that seven Beaufighters were lost in these attacks. It also records:

> 'In spite of the difficulties and tribulations, the spirit of the squadron remained high. One Belgian pilot at 0500 hours, just before take-off with a long trip in front of him, said: "If I have to go into the drink today, it's not because of engine failure, but because I want a bath."'

The record does not give the name of the pilot, but it does state that two Belgian pilots were among the seven shot down. It then continues:

> 'An observer, finding himself on the afternoon of the fifteenth near the Italian fleet, made a careful observation of the condition and then flashed BALLS on his Aldis lamp at the nearest cruiser, which promptly opened fire very inaccurately. They then went on and shot down a Cant Z506B.'

Once again, the name of this crew member is not given. But the book records that two more Beaufighters were lost later in the month, while strafing roads. It was a black month for 272 Squadron, as it was for the whole of the British and Commonwealth forces in the Western Desert. Moreover, the convoy from Alexandria lost a cruiser, three destroyers and two merchant vessels as a result of U-boat and air attacks, and was forced to turn back. Three of the five merchant vessels which left Gibraltar were sunk, but the remaining two limped into Grand Harbour at Valetta.

The events of May and June caused considerable dismay behind the lines at Cairo, where masses of files and papers were burnt preparatory to evacuation, for it seemed to the faint-hearted that the Axis forces would soon occupy the Egyptian capital. A similar view was taken in Rome, for the Italian dictator Benito Mussolini duly arrived in Libya ready to take his place at the head of the triumphal procession, it was rumoured in the saddle of a white horse. But the Eighth Army was still an effective fighting force and stood between Rommel and his objectives, at the little-known village of El Alamein. Moreover, the Luftwaffe failed to keep pace with the advance of the Panzerarmee, whereas the RAF's Western Desert air force, better organised and more mobile, flew back almost intact to its eastern bases. The Axis forces were strafed by day and bombed by night, with no respite. The war in North Africa became once more dominated by the problems of supplies reaching the front lines, and in this respect the British were able to overcome their difficulties while the Axis forces were once more over-extended.

In early July a renewed air assault on Malta from bases in Sicily brought sharply reduced results, following the arrival of more Spitfires and some Beaufighters. More Wellingtons also flew in, as well as a few Liberators. With the help of an improved air umbrella, five merchant vessels arrived at Grand Harbour in mid-August, although at the cost of an aircraft carrier, two cruisers, a destroyer and nine merchant vessels.

At the end of July 1942 a new pilot arrived in 252 Squadron. He was Sergeant Stanley J. Kernaghan, a twenty-year-old Canadian from Cartwright, Manitoba. He had trained at Boundary Bay in British Columbia and then went on to SFTS at Brandon in Manitoba, were he received his wings. His GR course was at Charlottetown in Prince Edward Island, and he was then sent to OTU at Catfoss in Yorkshire, where he arrived on Christmas Eve 1941. After this, he was posted to 236 Squadron at Wattisham in Suffolk, equipped with Beaufighters, but he flew on only one operation before he and his crew were posted to 252 Squadron in Egypt.

The trip out was by boat to Takoradi on the Gold Coast. Here they waited for a crated Beaufighter, a nightfighter version, to be assembled. They flew this across Africa to 108 Maintenance Unit, near Cairo, and waited with other aircrews at Almaza transit camp for further orders. The whole group, apart from Kernaghan, went down with malaria, and he was the only one to report to 252 Squadron at Idku in the evening of 31 July 1942.

Early the following morning, Kernaghan was woken up in his tent and told to report to the operations tent. His instructions were to take part in an offensive sweep of eight Beaufighters along the coast from Mersa Matruh as far as Sidi Barrani, looking for German barges bringing supplies to the Axis front line.

An experienced navigator was detailed to fly with Kernaghan. He was Sergeant Tom Armstrong, twenty-one years of age, who had volunteered as a wireless operator/air gunner at the outbreak of war. After some delay, for the RAF training scheme was unable to cope with the flood of volunteers at this stage, he completed his wireless course at Yatesbury in Wiltshire during July 1940. Then there was an opportunity to take an observer's course, and he passed through this at Weston airport, near Weston-super-Mare, which was run by the civilian Bristol Flying School. His next move was back to Yatesbury for training on Ansons, after which he qualified as a navigator/wireless operator.

The next move should have been to a course at OTU but, still with the rank of leading aircraftman, he was posted to 235 Squadron at Bircham Newton, which was equipped with Blenheim IVs. Here he was made up to sergeant and began operational flying. In June 1941 he was posted to 143 Squadron at Aldergrove in Northern Ireland, which was re-forming with the new Beaufighter IC, and crewed up with Flying Officer Michael O. Davenport. After a few weeks, the squadron was moved to Thornaby-on-Tees. From there, eight crews were selected to pick up new Beaufighters from Kemble in Gloucestershire and fly them to Malta. The aircraft were fitted with an extra internal petrol tank to make the long flight from Portreath to Gibraltar.

Arriving safely at Malta on 22 July, Davenport and Armstrong were sent out with 252 Squadron the next day to protect a convoy and attack E-boats. During the next night, their Beaufighter was blown to pieces by enemy bombing. Flying in a borrowed Beaufighter on 28 July and led by their commanding officer, Squadron Leader Gordon Yaxley, they attacked the aerodrome at Catania in Sicily. To their surprise, they found the enemy aircraft lined up wingtip to wingtip, and the Beaufighters caused a great deal of damage. However, they were attacked by three Macchi single-engined fighters and Armstrong was slightly wounded. He was taken to hospital, where he contracted fever. By the time he recovered, 252 Squadron had departed for Egypt where it was disbanded, the crews being absorbed by 272 Squadron. Armstrong was left marooned in Malta, without a unit.

At the beginning of December 1941 he managed to get off the island by flying to Egypt as a front gunner in a Wellington of 38 Squadron, which bombed Benghazi en route. He hoped to be posted to a Beaufighter squadron but instead was sent to 216 Squadron, a transport squadron with a flight of DH86Bs, four-engined biplanes which were a larger version of the Dragon Rapide but had been taken over by the RAF from a civil airline for flying urgent supplies to the front line. After some months on this work, Armstrong managed to obtain permission to transfer to the re-formed 252 Squadron at Idku. Here he crewed up with Pilot Officer I. 'Nipper' Maclean and flew on several successful operations, before being assigned to Kernaghan.

Most navigators with operational experience were reluctant to fly with novice pilots, but any hesitation which Armstrong felt was soon dispelled, for Kernaghan learned quickly and proved very skilful. During their first operation together, on 1 August 1942, the formation flew low over the sea and, after about ninety minutes, came across four German barges. The Beaufighters went into the attack.

Enemy barges might have seemed fairly easy targets to uninitiated airmen, but in fact they were very tough nuts to crack. Experts in design and construction of barges, the Germans built hundreds of these oil-driven vessels from 1942 onwards. The type employed in North Africa was the Marinfährprahm (naval ferry barge), abbreviated to 'MFP' by the Germans and 'F-boat' by the RAF. Large numbers were built in Mediterranean yards while others were constructed in Germany, Holland and Belgium. They could be dismantled and the parts were transported overland, usually by rail. There were two slightly different types, of 200 and 280 tons displacement. They could carry, at a speed of about seven knots, up to 150 three-ton trucks or large quantities of fuel or ammunition. Low in the water, with a length of 164 feet and a draught of only six feet, they were not suitable targets for torpedoes. The anti-aircraft armament was fearsome: an 88mm gun, a 37mm gun and two 20mm cannons, all mounted on steel decks. Several F-boats sailing together could put up a wall of flak. The arrival of these vessels in North Africa proved a very worrying development for the British forces.

On Kernaghan's first attack, the magazines of the cannons in each Beaufighter were loaded with a mixture of armour-piercing and incendiary shells, with the objective of breaking open the steel shells of the barges and setting fire to the cargo. The eight pilots climbed and dived down into the flak, watching their shells explode along the decks, but none of the barges caught fire and none sank. Instead, the flak caught a Beaufighter flown by Pilot Officer Alfred G.G. Machin, which crashed on the shore. Machin and his navigator, Sergeant Colin B.A. Nichols, were killed.

Three days later a similiar attack was more successful, when six Beaufighters of 252 Squadron found another convoy. One barge was seen to be sinking while two more were badly damaged; but again a Beaufighter was shot down. The Canadian pilot, Flight Sergeant Edward Babiak, and his RAF navigator, Sergeant Alfred W.T. Lancaster, survived to become PoWs.

The Bisleys of 15 (SAAF) Squadron were also brought into these attacks. On 15 August, six of these specially armoured Blenheim Vs were escorted by three Beaufighters of 252 Squadron and three more from 272 Squadron. They found a convoy of fifteen F-boats and attacked. The Bisleys claimed five hits with bombs as well as one MC200 shot down in flames, but the navigator in one of these aircraft was seriously wounded. The pilot and navigator in a Beaufighter of 272 Squadron were also injured, but all aircraft returned, claiming three F-boats sunk.

The maritime Beaufighters of 252 and 272 Squadrons were sometimes sent on detachments to Malta. On one such occasion, a flight of Beaufighters from 252 Squadron arrived at Luqa on 9 August. Moving to the fighter base of Takali two days later, they strafed the island of Pantelleria. In the afternoon of 17 August three Beaufighters, led by Flight Lieutenant A. Derek Frecker, escorted six Beauforts of 86 Squadron on an anti-shipping strike from Luqa. During the previous few weeks, Beauforts from this squadron had flown out to Malta from Cornwall, to reinforce the aircraft of 217 Squadron, which had been seriously depleted in anti-shipping attacks. Four Spitfires of 126 Squadron also accompanied the formation, as top cover.

The target was the new and fast merchant vessel *Rosolino Pilo* of 8,326 tons*, which had left Naples the day before. This Italian ship was carrying a mixed cargo of 3,429 tons, together with 112 vehicles and 101 German military personnel. She was bound for Tripoli, escorted by the destroyers *Maestrale* and *Gioberti*. The Beauforts were led by Flight Lieutenant Donald C. 'Hank' Sharman, a very experienced torpedo pilot. The formation caught up with the Italian vessels south of the island of Lampedusa, and the crews could see that four Ju 88s and two Me 109s were overhead. The Spitfires gave chase to the German aircraft, but no combats took place. Frecker led the three Beaufighters into a determined attack on the destroyers and the merchant vessel, raking the decks with cannon and machine gun fire, while the torpedo bombers made their runs. Sharman's Beaufort was hit in the nose by cannon shells, causing a fire which was put out by the navigator, Warrant Officer Roy G. Kitching, in spite of wounds to both arms and a knee. The starboard engine was also hit and poured smoke during the return journey, but all aircraft reached Malta safely.

One of the torpedoes hit *Rosolino Pilo* in the stern, immobilising her. In addition, her decks were damaged by fire from the Beaufighters. The destroyer *Gioberti* also suffered damage from cannon fire, and fires broke out. Even more serious, every officer on her bridge was either killed or wounded, including her captain, and the warship was in no condition to continue. The destroyer *Maestrale* was also damaged, although less seriously.

---

* Throughout this book, merchant ships are recorded in gross registered tonnage, while warships are in displacement.

Under the command of a junior officer, *Gioberti* headed northwards, while *Maestrale* began to take the German personnel off the stricken merchant vessel. Her captain later complained that these German troops were ill-disciplined and that there was not a single officer to control them. The merchant ship was not in danger of sinking, but she could not be repaired by her crew.

While the destroyer was still engaged in taking off the German personnel in the early evening, heavy gunfire was seen to the far north, and it seemed to the officers on the bridge that this might indicate the presence of a British cruiser. They tried to persuade the German pilots who were circling overhead to investigate the flashes, but to their exasperation could not make themselves understood over the R/T. Then they saw a series of bursts and puffs of smoke in the sky, and finally saw what they thought was the outline of a warship on the horizon. The captain decided to set course at maximum speed in that direction, hoping to divert attention away from *Rosolino Pilo*. However, whatever they had seen did not materialize, and they were ordered to make for Trapani in Sicily with the German personnel.

Meanwhile the captain of *Rosolino Pilo* also anticipated an attack and, with his ship immobilized and defenceless, ordered his crew to take to the lifeboats. This was accomplished at sunset and they pushed away from the merchant vessel. Half an hour later they heard the sound of aircraft engines and saw the first of a series of flares which 'lit up the sky like daylight', according to the subsequent report. These flares were probably dropped by Albacores from the Fleet Air Arm squadrons at Malta. They continued for several hours, until finally the Italian sailors saw an enormous sheet of flame from their abandoned ship. A hit had been scored by the submarine HMS *United*, which fired a torpedo when surfaced and at such a short range that debris from the merchant vessel caused minor damage to her own hull.

During the early morning, *Maestrale* returned to the area of the sunken vessel, together with the destroyer *Malocello*, while the rescue tug arrived fruitlessly from Pantelleria. The destroyers picked up the ship-wrecked sailors, only one of whom was lost in the entire action.

This episode is also noteworthy because it demonstrates that the collaboration between the Italians and the Germans was far from perfect. Moreover, in their report the Italians complained at the failure of their own high command to give them adequate information about the build-up of RAF strike aircraft in Malta, and stated their belief that two destroyers were insufficient to give adequate protection to such an important vessel.

The versatile Beaufighters continued to be employed in their additional role of ground attack aircraft. An aircraft failed to return from a sweep on 19 August, and Sergeants Ronald P. Williams and Frederick

J. Craven were killed. On 25 August four Beaufighters of 252 Squadron, with Kernaghan and Armstrong as one of the crews, strafed a convoy of eight trucks on the road between Bardia and Tobruk, believed to be bringing fuel to the Axis front line. Most of the trucks, some of which were towing trailers, were hit by gunfire, and several careered off the road. On 1 September two sections, each of four Beaufighters, shot up two large convoys, destroying trucks, trailers and a mobile field headquarters. Return fire brought down one Beaufighter from each section. Pilot Officer Eugene D. Vanier, an RCAF pilot from Antigua in the West Indies, was killed in one Beaufighter, together with his RAF navigator, Sergeant Harry Asquith. Pilot Officer Russell D. Jaggard and Sergeant Frank G. Dewry lost their lives in the other. Kernaghan and Armstrong returned safely from this attack, as well as from an attack against two F-boats the following day.

By then, Kernaghan's original navigator, Sergeant Bernard Andrews, had recovered from malaria and arrived at the squadron, replacing Armstrong. The crew first flew together operationally on 3 September and the sortie proved very eventful. Four Beauforts of 39 Squadron, on detachment at Mariut, near Alexandria, were ordered to attack an Axis convoy approaching Tobruk. The torpedo bombers were escorted by six Beaufighters of 252 Squadron and six more from 272 Squadron, which also flew over to Mariut. The enemy convoy consisted of the merchant vessels *Sportivo* of 1,597 tons, *Padenna* of 1,589 tons, and *Davide Bianchi* of 1,477 tons. These were carrying a cargo which consisted mainly of diesel oil and petrol, in containers. They were escorted by the torpedo boats *Lupo*, *Castore*, *Calliope* and *Polluce*. Such torpedo boats, the size of small destroyers and heavily armed with anti-aircraft guns, were the escorts most commonly employed by the Italians in the Mediterranean.

Something went wrong with the serviceability of the Beauforts. One aircraft was unable to take off on time and could not catch up with the formation. Another crashed into the sea after flying for half an hour, for no discernable reason; Pilot Officer Frank P. Winter-Taylor and his crew lost their lives. Shortly afterwards, another turned back with engine trouble, escorted by two Beaufighters.

The remaining formation reached the convoy and the pilot of the single Beaufort dropped his torpedo, which missed. He turned away for Mariut, escorted by a Beaufighter. There were three enemy aircraft near the convoy, however, and the remaining Beaufighter pilots were hungry for combat. Two of the enemy aircraft were Ju 88s, which could not be enticed away from the protective fire of the warships. But the third was not so lucky. It was an He 111, engaged on an anti-submarine patrol some distance ahead. Sergeant George A. Tuckwell of 272 Squadron was the first to attack the German aircraft, putting one engine out of action, knocking bits off the fuselage and causing one flap to drop down. Another Beaufighter of 272 Squadron also took up the attack, but the Heinkel was still flying straight and level, low over the sea, when Kernaghan closed up to it. He opened fire and, by the time he had taken his finger off the firing button, the Heinkel had hit the sea and broken up into pieces.

On this occasion, Armstrong was flying with his former pilot, Flying Officer I. Maclean. When they turned away from the convoy, the navigator pointed out that there was sufficient fuel remaining to hunt for Ju 52s flying between Crete and Derna. Maclean agreed and they headed out towards Crete. Nothing was seen for some time but, shortly before they intended to turn back, three dots appeared on the horizon, low over the water.

These turned out to be Fieseler Storch reconnaissance aircraft, single-engined monoplanes with fixed undercarriages. Closing up, Maclean blasted two of them out of the sky. They could see the wreckage of one in the sea when chasing the third. But the remaining German proved very cool and skilful, for he throttled back and put out his wing slots each time Maclean attacked, almost stopping in the sky while the Beaufighter tore past. Maclean used up all his remaining ammunition, and Armstrong took up the attack by firing his Vickers gun in the rear cupola. He fired two and a half drums, each of which contained about ninety rounds. The Storch began to break up, although it was still flying when they approached the African coast. Then the Beaufighter crew saw sand rising, signifying that enemy fighters were taking off. They turned towards Mariut and arrived after over six hours' flying, to find that they had been almost given up as lost.

Although the Italian ships were nearing their objective, they did not escape. The convoy split into two during the night in the belief that the separate parts would be more manoeuvrable, offering smaller targets to air attack. But 201 (Naval Co-operation) Group, which by then had expanded into a far more formidable force, sent out three Wellingtons and two Liberators of 221 Squadron, carrying bombs, flares, radar and homing equipment. They also despatched eight Wellingtons of 38 Squadron, some carrying bombs and others with torpedoes. These two squadrons were based at Shallufa, near the Bitter Lakes in Egypt, and operated from the advanced airfield LG226. The crews had been trained to carry out anti-shipping attacks at night.

The first vessel to be hit was *Davide Bianchi*, at a time when she was in company with *Sportivo* and escorted by the torpedo boats *Polluce* and *Calliope*. According to the Italian report, an aircraft glided towards her at night, with engines switched off, and dropped a torpedo which hit her port side. This was a Wellington of 38 Squadron flown by Sergeant

N. Jones, who is most unlikely to have switched off his engines when he released two torpedoes at low level. Jones and his crew saw a terrific explosion and then the bows and stern of a merchant vessel sticking up out of the water. The Italian report stated that *Davide Bianchi*, which was carrying 1,095 tons of petrol, sank immediately. The torpedo boat *Polluce* remained in the area until the hospital ship *Virgilio* reached the area, and then put on full speed to catch up with the other two vessels in her section.

In the other section, *Padenna* was escorted by the torpedo boats *Lupo* and *Castore*. Two hours after *Davide Bianchi* went down, two torpedoes hit the merchant ship, which was carrying 1,671 tons of combustible liquid in addition to a small mixed cargo. She sank after about half an hour, when only fifty miles from Tobruk. The torpedoes were fired by the submarine HMS *Thrasher*, brought to the target by Flying Officer Waite in a Wellington of 221 Squadron, who dropped flares and flame floats. The crew of the Wellington could see the submarine on the surface of the sea, and then saw the merchant vessel turn into a mass of flames and oily smoke. With no ship left to escort, the two Italian torpedo boats put on speed to join up with the other section of the convoy.

The miseries of this convoy were not over. By then, the torpedo boat *Polluce* had almost caught up with her section of the convoy, consisting of the one remaining merchant vessel, *Sportivo*, and her escort *Calliope*. Flares were falling some distance astern and the look-outs were watching these. Then an aircraft approached up-moon, at low level and unseen, and dropped three bombs across the stern of the torpedo boat, firing machine guns at the same time. One of these bombs hit *Polluce* between holds two and three, exploding the reserve of ammunition and starting a fire. They were dropped by a Liberator of 221 Squadron flown by Lieutenant Soukup, one of three US airmen in the ten-man crew. They dropped three 500 lb general purpose bombs and reported, quite accurately, a direct hit amidships followed by a large explosion, although they thought that their victim was a merchant vessel.

The Italian sailors did their utmost to save the warship, while *Calliope* remained nearby and the hospital ship *Virgilio* came up, but the fire proved uncontrollable and the crew were forced to abandon her. She sank about two hours after being hit. A torpedo boat of 679 tons, *Polluce* was a veteran of many convoy escorts and the Italians regarded her loss as serious. Once again, they complained that there were insufficient escorts to meet the tasks demanded of them. The only merchant ship in the convoy to reach Tobruk was *Sportivo*, which off-loaded her cargo of 1,237 tons of diesel oil.

In addition to their sorties against convoys crossing the Mediterranean, the Beaufighters of 252 and 272 Squadrons continued attacks against F-boats and road convoys, sometimes in company with the Bisleys of 15 (SAAF) Squadron. On 13 September, the crews of both Beaufighter squadrons were called upon to give maximum support to an operation being carried out by the Royal Navy. This was operation 'Agreement', a raid behind enemy lines intended to relieve the pressure on the Eighth Army in Egypt. The spearhead of the naval force consisted of the destroyers *Sikh* and *Zulu*, carrying a landing party of 350 Royal Marines, together with eighteen motor-torpedo boats and three motor launches carrying 150 troops. These were supported out to sea by the anti-aircraft cruiser *Coventry* and several other destroyers. The purpose of the enterprise was to effect a landing at night on the north side of Tobruk, shortly after a mobile column seized gun emplacements on the south side of the port. The shipping and port facilities would then be destroyed, and the landing party evacuated after about twelve hours. If successful, the operation would force Rommel's lines of communication to dependence once more on the distant ports of Benghazi and Tripoli.

There was little excitement on the first day, when twelve Beaufighters from the two squadrons were sent out in pairs to cover the warships sailing towards Tobruk. During the night, however, the operation met with disaster. The land column achieved its objectives but its 'success' signal was spotted by only two MRBs, which landed their troops. Then the destroyer *Sikh* was picked out by searchlights and disabled by gunfire. Despite an attempt by *Zulu* to tow her away, she sank; her surviving crew and marines were taken prisoner. The cruiser *Coventry* and eight destroyers turned towards Tobruk to help *Zulu* but they were attacked during the next day by swarms of Ju 87s and Ju 88s, which were able to make use of convenient cloud cover before and after their bombing runs.

On this second day, 14 September, the Beaufighters made a series of thirty sorties to help the warships under attack. One of these was flown by Flight Lieutenant Derek Frecker, with Tom Armstrong as his navigator, while Flight Lieutenant Ian Maclean flew as his 'number two'. The pair were contacted over the R/T by *Coventry* and told that there was a 'bogey' at 12,000 feet. Frecker climbed, leaving Maclean at 6,000 feet, only to find that the enemy aircraft was a shadower. Then about thirty Ju 87s dived out of the clouds below them, their main target being *Coventry*. Maclean did his best against this swarm but, by the time Frecker returned, the Stukas had done their work and disappeared into the clouds again.

Stan Kernaghan arrived over the scene a few hours later. He spotted a group of Ju 87s several miles away, but a large formation of Ju 88s appeared when he approached the Stukas. He fired a burst at the nearest Ju 87 and thought he had hit it, before tackling the Ju 88s in his solitary Beaufighter. Shells from the warships were bursting all around, while he could see Ju 88s in front of him, as well as on both sides and behind. He opened his throttles and closed on the tail of one of these, firing several bursts into the rear section and silencing the gunners. While Andrews was busy reloading the four cannons, Kernaghan saw two Ju 88s bearing down on him. He climbed and turned, flying straight towards them. His audacity paid off, for they split on either side and he flew between them to make his escape.

Meanwhile *Coventry* had been badly hit and her crew were forced to abandon her. Kernaghan watched the sad spectacle of British destroyers circling the cruiser, firing broadsides to finish her off and prevent her falling into the hands of the Germans. During the last air attack of the day, the destroyer *Zulu* was hit by a bomb, and sank that evening. Six smaller vessels were also lost in the operation, which had to be counted as an expensive failure.

As a last forlorn hope, the British raiding parties at Tobruk had been told that, if circumstances prevented their evacuation, they were to make their way to a creek about seventy miles to the east, easily distinguishable by a wrecked schooner on the north side. Here they were to hide and wait for a Beaufighter to fly over on 19 September, when they should rush out and wave their shorts. The Beaufighter would then escort waiting MTBs to their rescue. Frecker and Armstrong kept this appointment, but the beach was empty.

After operation 'Agreement', 252 Squadron was stood down for about a fortnight, for training and re-equipment. During this period, Kernaghan was sent down to a landing strip near the Suez canal to carry out a series of test flights with Beaufighter I serial X7704, which had had its four cannon stripped out and replaced with a Bofors gun. This light anti-aircraft gun fired 40mm shells at the rate of about two a second. The aircraft seemed to handle quite well, and Kernaghan made 'shadow' firing tests with a camera gun. It was intended to use the aircraft against tanks but the experiment was never carried out, for the aircraft crashed and was written off on 28 September when being flown by another pilot.

The squadron went back into action during the first week of October, in the Western Desert. On the morning of 6 October the new commanding officer, Wing Commander Peter H. Bragg, led six Beaufighters in an attack against the Italian seaplane base at Bomba, near Tmini in Libya, during which a number of Cant Z506B floatplanes were damaged. In a similar attack with four Beaufighters on the following day, several more Cant Z506Bs were damaged, as well as an F-boat. On the way back, a number of trucks were strafed near Gazala, and it was estimated that about fifty soldiers were hit.

On 9 October Bragg led four Beaufighters, including Frecker and Armstrong, together with three Bisleys of 15 (SAAF) Squadron against a train travelling on the section of the Egyptian railway which had been captured by the Axis forces. The target was huge, about twenty-six trucks, and it was considered to have been completely destroyed by bombs and cannon fire. The crews could see the smoke rising from the wreckage when they were as much as seventy miles away on their return journey.

Another of these combined attacks took place on 12 October, when Kernaghan was one of four Beaufighter pilots ordered to escort three Bisleys, once more against a train. By this time, his navigator had been posted from the squadron and replaced by Sergeant Archie Powell, whose pilot had been killed in a flying accident in Malta. As they came in from the sea, Kernaghan and another pilot spotted two large trucks on the coast road, and took one each. The trucks, which evidently were carrying petrol, exploded and gave out clouds of black smoke. The aircraft then continued and strafed the train, setting thirteen wagons on fire.

When the formation was heading back to the coast, Kernaghan saw a Ju 52 flying eastward towards the front line. His first burst put the starboard engine on fire, but the German promptly landed in the desert, with the engine still ablaze. Kernaghan circled and gave it another burst, destroying the machine and bowling over a crew member who ran along the starboard wing.

On the coast road once more, they met another line of trucks and attacked these. This was an occasion when Kernaghan almost ran out of luck, for there was a sound like a small explosion and the nose of his machine suddenly shot up into the air. Unknown to him, the elevator controls had been severed by gunfire. Of course, the Beaufighter did not respond to the control column, but Kernaghan tried the hand trim and managed to get it down from the almost vertical attitude. At this point, both engines cut out. However, they started again and, by using the hand trim, he managed to get some control and climbed to about 3,000 feet. At this stage they were about 225 miles behind enemy lines, although fortunately there were no enemy ground forces or aircraft in sight. Archie Powell declined to accept the suggestion that he should bale out, and they made their way back over the sea. Trimming the Beaufighter slightly nose down, Kernaghan put down the undercarriage and succeeded in making a good landing at Idku.

Three days later, Bragg led seven Beaufighters on an offensive sweep towards Crete. They came across two Ju 52s and shot down one, damaging the other. But one Beaufighter went down into the sea on the homeward journey, leaving only a patch of oil visible to the circling aircraft; Flight Lieutenant Kenneth J.A. Reed and Warrant Officer

Gordon D. Nash lost their lives.

The next two weeks were almost wholly occupied with strafing trucks and tented encampments, without loss of aircraft. This was the stage when final preparations were being made for the Eighth Army's offensive at El Alamein. The battle opened at dawn on 23 October and two days later Bragg led six from his squadron, including Kernaghan, against a vessel approaching Tobruk. This was the Italian *Alfredo* of 614 tons, carrying fuel, which was too small to justify torpedo attacks. She had left Taranto on 18 October and, following stops at Corfu, Patrasso and Suda, had left Crete accompanied by the torpedo boat *Perseo*. The Beaufighters caught the two vessels shortly after dawn and raked both with cannon fire. They were unable to sink the merchant vessel, but the captain was one of several who were killed on the bridge. Several sailors in *Perseo* were also killed or wounded. All the Beaufighters returned safely on this occasion.

The main task of 252 and 272 Squadron during the next few days was to escort torpedo-carrying Beauforts in the critical stage of the Battle of El Alamein, as will be seen later.

(**Above**) A Fieseler Fi 156 Storch, coded F5 + SR, a communications aircraft attached to *Fl. ber. Lfl. Kdo. 2*, over Italy in 1944. (*Archiv Rick Chapman*) (**Left**) Pilot Officer T.F. Paul Nisbet, photographed in June 1941. (*Flt Lt T.F.P. Nisbet, AFC*) (**Below**) A Messerschmitt Bf 110 fighter-destroyer at Catania in Sicily, photographed in 1941. The aircraft still bore its factory code SB + GP and was probably being ferried to a unit in North Africa when the photograph was taken. (*Archiv Rick Chapman*)

(**Above**) The Bristol Blenheim V, or Bisley, was the last of the Blenheim family. It had more powerful engines than its predecessor, the Blenheim IV, and was fitted with increased armour protection and an improved turret as well as two rearward-firing machine guns in a blister beneath the nose. The bomb load was 1,000 lb. Bisleys first arrived in 15 (SAAF) Squadron in July 1942 and continued until July 1943. This photograph is of serial DJ702, which served with 12 (P) Advanced Flying Unit at Spittlegate in Lincolnshire. (*Aviation Bookshop*)

(**Below**) 26 October 1942. The tanker *Proserpina*, almost concealed by water thrown up from the explosions of the 250 lb bombs dropped by the Bisley flown by Lieutenant Edward G. Dustow. The Bisley itself, which struck the mast of the tanker, has spun into the sea, as shown by the splashes on the left. The Beaufort flown by Pilot Officer Ralph V. Manning is the upper of the two aircraft on the left, but at this moment his torpedo is still bumping along the side of the tanker and has not yet exploded. The lower of the two aircraft is the Beaufort flown by Flying Officer Norman Hearn-Phillips, which lost its torpedo from flak. (*Roger Hayward*)

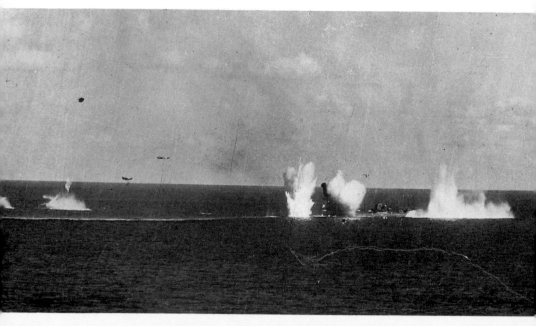

5

THE LOST SQUADRON

I n the books and articles written about the activities of the RAF during World War Two, there is rarely a mention of a squadron which was heavily involved in anti-shipping work when based at Malta from the summer of 1942 onwards. This was 227 Squadron, which was originally formed when a detachment of Beaufighters flew out from the UK in March 1942 and then moved to the Western Desert, forming part of 201 (Naval Co-operation) Group. In June, however, the aircrews were absorbed by 272 Squadron while the ground crews were posted to Palestine to serve with the Halifaxes of 10 Squadron. On 20 August 1942, 227 Squadron was re-formed at Luqa in Malta from a detachment of 235 Squadron and a few elements from 248 Squadron, under the command of Wing Commander D. Ross Shore. The Beaufighters of these two squadrons had flown out from the UK several months earlier and most of the aircrews had been in action. So little had been researched or written about 227 Squadron that survivors sometimes refer to it as 'the lost squadron'.

Many of the Beauforts of 39 Squadron were also at Luqa when 227 Squadron was re-formed, having flown there from Egypt several months previously. They had inflicted heavy damage on enemy shipping, as had the Beauforts of 86 and 217 Squadron based at the same station, but all three squadrons had suffered very serious losses.* The remaining elements of all three Beaufort squadrons were combined under the command of Wing Commander R. Patrick M. Gibbs of 39 Squadron, one of the most determined and respected leaders of the RAF's torpedo squadrons in World War Two. Each aircraft carried a single Mark XII torpedo in the bomb bay and the crews were engaged on the most dangerous work carried out by the RAF.

The combination of 227 and 39 Squadrons at Malta created the first maritime Strike Wing in the RAF, although this term was not used at the time. The first to receive the official title of Strike Wing was that formed at North Coates in Lincolnshire, consisting of three squadrons of anti-flak and torpedo-carrying Beaufighters, to tackle the German coastal trade off

---

* See *Torpedo Airmen*, by the author, for a fuller account of some of these actions.

Holland and Germany. Even then, the correct tactics of combined attacks against shipping, which had been learnt rapidly at Malta, were not employed in the UK. Following a first disastrous attack on 20 November 1942 against a German convoy, the North Coates Strike Wing did not become effective until its first major success on 18 April 1943, under the leadership of Wing Commander H. Neil G. Wheeler.*

The basic tactic of the two squadrons at Malta consisted of the protection of the torpedo-carrying Beauforts by Beaufighters armed with cannons and machine guns. The flak from the escort vessels and merchant ships was suppressed by fire from diving Beaufighters while the Beauforts made their low-level torpedo runs and, more often than not, sank some of the supply ships. Other Beaufighters acted as top cover against enemy long-distance fighters, while some carried bombs. All attacks were delivered in as short a time as possible, to confuse the enemy and spread the defensive fire. These tactics varied occasionally, depending on the size and nature of the convoy. Patrols and 'Armed Rovers' still continued, and sometimes a pair of Beaufighters armed with bombs hunted single enemy ships.

The aircrews of the anti-shipping squadrons did not realise that a remarkable form of intelligence was backing their efforts. Something was happening at the Government Code and Cipher School at Bletchley Park in Buckinghamshire which the Germans considered impossible. Indeed, Germans who were in authority had difficulty in believing the truth when it was disclosed only a few years ago. Using a captured 'Enigma' coding machine, the British were decrypting regularly the messages which the Germans were passing to their forces in North Africa. They knew the dates of sailing of almost all the Axis convoys, together with the ports of embarkation, the names of the vessels, and even the contents of the cargoes. Moreover, they knew the precise state of the Deutsches Panzerarmee and the extent of its weaknesses in war material. They did not know the exact composition of the Italian escort vessels, a deficiency which was remedied by high-level photographic aircraft operating from Malta soon after the convoys set sail. Thus, with extremely limited resources, the RAF and the Royal Navy were able to strike effectively at the vessels which contained supplies essential to the Axis forces in North Africa.

Of course, the aircrews at Malta and in North Africa realised that some form of intelligence was enabling them to find the enemy so easily, but most of them believed that the sources must be Italian dissidents. To the aircrews, there were 'men in bowler hats' somewhere in the background, assimilating such information and telling the squadrons where and when to hunt for the shipping.

---

* See *The Strike Wings*, by the author, for a history of these squadrons.

Another maritime squadron, also based at Malta, was indispensable to the activities of 227 and 39 Squadrons. This was 69 Squadron, a reconnaissance unit which was first formed in Malta in January 1941. Its original aircraft were the Martin Marylands of 431 (General Reconnaissance) Flight, but during the course of the year Hurricanes and Blenheims were also taken on strength. A year after the formation, two Beaufighters and two Mosquitos were added to the squadron. Then Spitfires were introduced, resulting in one of the most unusual squadrons in the RAF. By May 1942 this mixture had been sorted out into three flights. 'A' Flight was equipped with Martin Baltimores, partly for collaboration with the Beaufort and Beaufighter strike squadrons by photographing the convoys in advance and then during the attacks, from high level. 'B' Flight flew Spitfire IVs for other photographic work at high level and 'C' Flight continued to use the Marylands for long-distance reconnaissance work. Then a 'Special Duty' section was formed within 'C' Flight, equipped with torpedo-carrying Wellingtons for long-range attacks against shipping at night. In August 1942, the same month in which 227 Squadron was re-formed and 39 Squadron was reinforced, this composite and versatile squadron came under the command of one of its most experienced and fearless pilots, Squadron Leader Adrian Warburton; he eventually completed over 300 operational flights, earning the DSO and Bar, the DFC and two Bars, and the American DFC, before disappearing without trace during a flight on 12 April 1944.

Employing the tactics which had been developed during the previous months, the combined force of 227 and 39 Squadrons went into action on the day of their formation, 20 August 1942. A convoy consisting of the Italian tanker *Pozarica* of 7,751 tons and the German merchant ship *Dora* of 584 tons, escorted by two destroyers and two torpedo boats, had left Messina in Sicily the day before, bound for Benghazi. Ten Beaufighters led by Shore – six of which were carrying bombs – together with twelve Beauforts led by Gibbs, caught this convoy near the toe of Italy. All the torpedoes missed, but the destroyer *Camicia Nera* suffered so many casualties and so much damage to her superstructure that she was forced to leave the convoy. Two Beauforts were shot down, one flown by the Canadian pilot Flying Officer Peter K. Roper and the other by the Australian pilot R.L. Condon, but all eight men in the crews were picked up and became PoWs. A Beaufighter flown by a New Zealander, Warrant Officer Donald G. Brisco, was shot down, but he and his RAF navigator, Sergeant Douglas Paterson, also survived to become PoWs. Another Beaufighter, flown by Flying Officer John P. Eyre, came down in the sea off Kalafrana Bay in Malta. Eyre was picked up by a high-speed launch, but his navigator, Sergeant George D. Leslie, lost his life.

The following day, Gibbs led nine Beauforts to the same target, in the company of four bomb-carrying Beaufighters led by Shore. Eight Beaufighters of 248 Squadron in the fighter role escorted these aircraft. The formation found the convoy off the island of Paxos, after it had been reinforced by another torpedo boat. A Beaufort flown by a South African, Lieutenant Walter B. Wolfe, was shot down, but all four men were picked up and became PoWs. In this second attack, *Pozarica* was hit by a torpedo and was forced to beach on a bay in Corfu. She was later towed back to Italy but was so badly damaged that she took no further part in the war. In addition, many seamen in the destroyer *Aviere* were killed or wounded by the Beaufighters of 248 Squadron. One of these Beaufighters was shot down, but the two men were seen to get into a dinghy and wave to the others. They were Flying Officer Guy P. Stanton and Flying Officer Charles Bryson, who became PoWs, although Bryson died in captivity shortly before the end of the war. Five Axis aircraft were claimed as destroyed. After this attack, 248 Squadron returned to the UK, leaving 227 Squadron to continue the work of escorting the Beauforts.

The next attack took place three days later, on 24 August, but it was not successful. Eight Beauforts led by an Australian, Flight Lieutenant Wally Allsopp, were accompanied by eight Beaufighters led by Flying Officer Peter Underwood, three of which carried bombs. Their target was the tanker *Giorgia* of 4,887 tons, carrying 3,344 tons of petrol and oil, escorted by the torpedo boats *Partenope* and *Polluce*. The convoy had left Taranto at 2330 hours the previous day, headed for the Corinth Canal and then Tobruk.

One Beaufort and one Beaufighter turned back with engine trouble but Allsopp's navigator, Pilot Officer Terry A. McGarry, brought the remainder of the formation to the convoy, about thirty-five miles from the Greek coast. One Beaufort was shot down during the attack, and Pilot Officer Lawrence Dewhurst and his crew lost their lives. All the torpedoes missed, although the crews thought that they saw an explosion on the starboard bow of the tanker. Two Beaufighters bombed the tanker but the bombs on the third aircraft hung up. Three Beaufighters attacked escorting Ju 88s and claimed one destroyed, but *Giorgia* was only lightly damaged and continued to the Corinth Canal. Escorted by *Partenope* on the final part of her journey, she reached Tobruk and unloaded her cargo.

At this time a young Canadian from Alberta, Pilot Officer Dallas W. Schmidt, joined 227 Squadron. After joining the RCAF in January 1941, Schmidt trained on Tiger Moths and Avro Ansons in his home country, where he also passed through a GR course. At the end of the year he sailed in a troopship to England, where he took a course at the Advanced Flying Unit at Spitalgate in Lincolnshire. He was then posted to OTU at Catfoss in Yorkshire, where he trained on Blenheims and Beaufighters. In June 1942 he joined 236 Squadron at Wattisham in Suffolk. Then he was asked to join the Ferry Training Unit at Lyneham in Wiltshire, where he was engaged on fuel consumption tests with new Beaufighters from the Bristol factory at Filton, in preparation for their overseas flights. On his twentieth birthday 9 August 1942 Schmidt led a formation of nine Beaufighters from Portreath to Gibraltar, and then to Malta. His navigator was Sergeant Andrew B. Campbell, a Scotsman from Dunfermline. It is through Dallas Schmidt's eyes, coupled with official British and Italian records, that part of the story of 227 Squadron for the next few months can be told.

Within a few days of their arrival at Luqa, Schmidt and Campbell went into action. The merchant vessel *Dielpi* of 1,527 tons had been reported sailing from Suda in Crete, bound for Benghazi. She was accompanied by a single torpedo boat, *Cascino*. In the late afternoon of 27 August, seven Beauforts led by Flying Officer Ken R. Grant were escorted by nine Beaufighters led by Wing Commander Shore. Four Beaufighters were carrying bombs.

The whole formation kept down low, maintaining strict radio silence, with the Beaufighters weaving slightly to keep pace with the slower torpedo bombers. When they neared the enemy vessels, about sixty miles from the Libyan coast, Grant fired a yellow-yellow Very cartridge to signify that the Beauforts were ready to begin their torpedo runs. The Beaufighters streaked ahead, the bombing section releasing their 250lb bombs on the merchant vessel while spraying the deck with gunfire. Shore scored a hit on the stern and *Dielpi* began to burn, for she was carrying fuel in containers. Other Beaufighters raked *Cascino* with gunfire.

Schmidt was number five in the fighter section and thus the last Beaufighter to attack. As he climbed from sea level to begin his dive, he saw ahead a Cant Z1007, an Italian tri-motored bomber which was providing long-distance air cover for the small convoy. Schmidt made an immediate turn to starboard and got on the tail of the enemy aircraft. Then a stream of 12.7mm bullets from the twin machine guns in the ventral position of the Cant entered the Beaufighter's port engine and also put out of action the machine guns in the starboard wing. In turn, a short burst from the Beaufighter's four cannons and remaining machine guns blew the tail of the Cant to pieces. The next burst put the bomber's starboard engine on fire, and the port engine received the same treatment a few seconds later. The Italian began to go down and Schmidt followed him. Then the two Piaggio engines in the Cant's wings blew up, and Schmidt's windscreen was suddenly covered with blackened oil. From a side window, he saw the Cant crash into the sea, and turned for home.

Meanwhile two torpedoes struck the unfortunate *Dielpi*, which exploded and burned furiously. Many of her crew had already jumped into the water, and the captain of the torpedo boat *Cascino* braved the burning oil to rescue sixty of the sixty-seven men. One Beaufighter was shot down, and Flight Sergeant Eric O'Hara and Sergeant Kenneth Seddon lost their lives.

Although the port engine of Schmidt's Beaufighter had been badly holed, it continued to function until he reached Malta. It was completely dark by then, and in any event he could see ahead only by craning his neck to look out of the side windows. The aircraft ran out of fuel exactly as he touched down at Luqa, for oil and petrol had been leaking away on the return journey. He discovered after landing that the fuel selector valves had been shot away, but fortunately he had switched on to main tanks shortly before the attack.

There was another combined attack three days later. The Government Code and Cipher School had reported on 28 August that the Italian tanker *San Andrea* of 5,077 tons was loading with fuel at Taranto, and was scheduled to arrive at Tobruk on 3 September. She duly left Taranto shortly before 0600 hours on 30 August, escorted by the torpedo boat *Antares*, carrying nearly 4,000 tons of fuel, intended primarily for the Panzerarmee. Her first port of call was to be Piraeus in Greece. Just before noon on the same day, Gibbs took off with nine Beauforts, escorted by nine Beaufighters led by Shore. Five Beaufighters were carrying bombs, and Schmidt was the pilot of one of these.

Three Beaufighters turned back with engine trouble but the remainder of the formation caught up with the convoy when it was about ten miles off the heel of Italy. The crews could see three MC200 single-engined fighters and three Ju 88 bombers, all flying at medium level, as well as an Arado floatplane and a Cant Z501B floatplane on anti-submarine work.

The torpedo boat *Antares* opened fire with her heavy armament at the compact mass of RAF aircraft, but her captain ordered a cease-fire for fear of hitting the floatplanes. The Italians then began firing their 20mm cannons, but two Beaufighters swept the decks with well-directed fire, attacking from different directions. Another Beaufighter raked the deck of the tanker. Three Beaufighters dropped two 250lb bombs apiece, but these narrowly missed the tanker. Schmidt's bombs fell alongside the vessel.

The six Beaufighters then turned to defend the Beauforts, for the MC200s and the Ju 88s were diving down on them. There was a general mêlée in which three Beaufighters and one Beaufort were damaged but the RAF aircraft claimed one MC200 'destroyed', two Ju 88s as 'probables', with one Ju 88 and the Cant 'damaged'. Meanwhile, four Beauforts dropped torpedoes, one of which struck *San Andrea* and caused an immense explosion. The debris thrown up almost brought down some of the following Beauforts. All the RAF aircraft then turned for home. Later, some tugs came out of Taranto in an attempt to help the tanker, but she was doomed and went down with fifty of her fifty-five seamen. The torpedo boat went back to Taranto, with many dead and wounded among her crew.

An attack against a very heavily defended convoy took place on 6 September. Two Italian merchant ships left Taranto on that day, escorted by six destroyers and one torpedo boat. These were *Manara* of 7,120 tons, carrying 2,229 tons of ammunition and military vehicles, and *Ravello* of 6,142 tons, carrying 3,953 tons of fuel with 537 tons of varied material. These vessels were bound ultimately for Benghazi. At the same time, two more merchant ships left Brindisi, escorted by three destroyers and two torpedo boats. These were the Italian *Sestiere* of 6,400 tons, carrying 4,403 tons of ammunition and military vehicles as well as 419 tons of fuel, and the German *Ankara* of 4,788 tons, loaded with 2,127 tons of fuel and 1,304 tons of varied material. These two vessels were bound for Tobruk.

All these vessels met soon after setting sail and continued as a single formation under the command of the destroyer *Aviere*. Powerfully defended by their warship escorts and relays of German and Italian aircraft, the two sections were hoping to break through the British blockade as far as the Libyan coast, before splitting and heading for their respective destinations.

By this time, Wing Commander Patrick Gibbs had become 'tour-expired' and was posted back to the UK. Twelve Beauforts took off under the leadership of Flight Lieutenant Donald C. 'Hank' Sharman, who had led the successful attack on *Rosolino Pilo* on 17 August, as related in the previous chapter. Wing Commander Ross Shore led an escort of twelve Beaufighters, six of which carried bombs.

Four Beauforts experienced engine trouble on the way out and were forced to return, but one replacement took off and caught up with the formation. Two Beaufighters in the fighter section also turned back with engine trouble. The problems of servicing aircraft while under continual air attack, aggravated by the chronic shortage of spare parts, were responsible for these failures. The ground crews worked miracles in these conditions, but air tests in advance of operations flights were not permitted, owing to the desperate shortage of fuel.

Schmidt saw a Ju 52 before reaching the convoy and made a stall turn on to it, but turned away when he saw that it was a rescue aircraft bearing a red cross. The formation of nine Beauforts and ten Beaufighters reached their target off the coast of Corfu at about 1530 hours, to be met by a swarm of fighters and a wall of flak which seemed impenetrable.

Hank Sharman was the first to go down, crashing into the sea with an engine on fire while making a steady torpedo run. He and his crew lost their lives. The remaining Beauforts continued to fly on resolutely. Schmidt was the first to attack in the bomber section, but his bombs overshot while he peppered the bridge of a merchant vessel with cannon and machine gun fire. He was attacked by a Macchi single-engined fighter after streaking over the ship, but a short burst of cannon fire drove the Italian away. Continuous fire from the convoy surrounded his Beaufighter as he climbed to provide fighter cover, and he had no option but to fly out of range. He saw another Beaufighter crash into the sea and, unknown to him at the time, yet another was shot down. He was suffering from the intestinal complaint known as 'Malta dog', and felt most uncomfortable on the return flight.

Flying Officer Peter L. Underwood of 227 Squadron, who had bombed and gunned one of the destroyers, attacked one Macchi but in turn was attacked by three others. He saw that one of the Beauforts was in difficulties and tried to protect it, but it went down into the sea. The aircraft was flown by a South African pilot, Lieutenant Clifford Evans, and he and his crew lost their lives.

Another of the Beauforts was flown by Flight Sergeant Hubert 'Bud' Watlington from Bermuda. He was aged twenty-one and had joined the RCAF in August 1940, training on Fleet Finches and Avro Ansons in Canada. After a stint in the Atlantic Ferry Unit in the spring of 1941, he helped fly a Catalina to Scotland and was then posted to the GR School at Squires Gate. In December 1941 he passed through OTU at Chivenor and joined 217 Squadron at Thorney Island. After he had carried out nine operational sorties, in June 1942, 217 Squadron was sent overseas. He asked for a different posting, since he was a married man and did not want to be further away from his wife. He joined 86 Squadron at Skitten in Caithness, but in July the Beauforts of that squadron were sent to Malta and joined the survivors of 217 Squadron, who had been waylaid there en route to Ceylon and employed on anti-shipping operations. At the time of this attack he had completed four operations from Malta, firstly in 86 Squadron and then in 39 Squadron.

The aircrews had been briefed to expect no cloud cover and the forecast proved correct. Watlington, who was flying a Beaufort II with the more powerful Wasp engines, was attacked by Macchis on his torpedo run but his aircraft was not hit. Ahead, the barrage was like a tremendous storm, with the circling warships firing their heavy armament and raising spouts of water. Inside this circle, the water seemed as calm as a millpond.

These torpedo attacks always produced a curious physical effect on Watlington. He could think clearly and act correctly but he could not prevent a violent shivering in his legs, and he sometimes wondered if he would be able to control the rudder bars with his feet. However, he lined up carefully on a merchant vessel, using the horizontal and curved mirror sight set in front of his forehead. After estimating the ship's speed, he turned a dial which moved a light that shone on the mirror, giving the 'aim-off' angle for the correct dropping distance of 1,000 yards at an altitude of 80 feet and a speed of 140 knots. A cool head and a steady nerve was required to perform such a task under fire.

Watlington released his torpedo, put the engines in fine pitch and full throttle, and then streaked over the bow of the merchant vessel. The warships opened up on the Beaufort again, but it got through the curtain of fire. Then a stream of tracer came from a fighter aircraft and Watlington could tell that his aircraft had been hit. He applied hard left rudder and right aileron, to spoil the aim of his attackers, and began jinking up and down. There were seven attacks in succession from fighters, but the Beaufort survived all of them. Watlington even managed to get off a burst with the two forward-firing Browning guns against a Cant Z506B, but had no time to look for the results.

The two men at the back of the Beaufort, who had been fighting off the Macchis, were wounded. The wireless operator, Sergeant Hugh McIllaney, who had left his seat to man the Vickers guns in the starboard and port beam positions, had been hit in a thigh by shrapnel. In the turret, Sergeant Leslie H. Tester had been wounded in an arm by shrapnel, while his right knee had been hit on the left by a bullet as well as deeply scored on the right by a 20mm cannon shell. From the navigator's position, Sergeant Charles M. Grant, a twenty-two-year-old Scotsman from Edinburgh, went back to help. He dragged Tester from the turret and applied a rough tourniquet to staunch the blood which was pouring from his leg. Then he slapped another ammunition pan on the Vickers gun in the port entrance hatch and opened fire on a fighter, but the gun soon jammed.

By some miracle, Watlington managed to fly clear and eventually found that they were over water without another aircraft in sight. They had been flying in a generally southern direction, and it was necessary to get back to Malta as soon as possible so that the wounded could receive medical attention. He asked Grant for a course, and the navigator went back to his chart table in the nose.

'How long do you think we've been flying south?' asked Grant.

'About fifteen minutes,' replied Watlington.

Grant had to make a number of calculations. They had flown in formation for three hours, following Sharman's Beaufort and without radio aids. The sea was like a sheet of glass and he had been unable to take drifts with the course-setting bombsight. While he was plotting a 'dead-reckoning' position, Watlington asked twice for the course, being told on each occasion, 'I'm working on it.'

Eventually Watlington lost his patience and snapped, 'I know why you haven't given me a course! You're goddamned lost!' Back came the dignified reply: 'A navigator may be temporarily unsure of his position, but he is *never* lost!' Watlington was so astonished that he said no more until Grant handed him the course. The navigator then went back once more to see if he could help the wounded. In spite of the pain from his wounds, Tester took up a position with the wireless set and managed to get a bearing on the medium-frequency beacon sited on Malta. When they approached the island, he also obtained a QDM (a course to steer with zero wind) from Luqa. An alteration of course brought them within sight, when they fell seriously short of fuel. The Beaufort had been hit in the hydraulics, flaps, tail assembly and turret, but Watlington made a safe landing.

Most of the remaining Beauforts had also been hit, but a WOp/AG in Sergeant G. Sanderson's crew, Flight Sergeant James D. Cunningham, was killed. The four men in the two Beaufighters shot down were also killed. One was flown by an Australian, Pilot Officer Dennis de M. Partridge, with an RAF navigator, Sergeant Anthony W. Vivian. The pilot was a South African, Lieutenant Frederick O. Noome, with another RAF navigator, Sergeant Albert J. Cusworth.

However, the convoy did not emerge unscathed. A torpedo struck *Manara*, which remained afloat but could not steer. The destroyer *Freccia* took her in tow and beached her on a bay in Corfu, while the remaining vessels continued their journey. They were bombed during the night of 7/8 September by three Wellingtons of 69 Squadron but no damage was caused and they reached their destinations.

Watlington and Tester were awarded DFMs after this sortie. When Watlington visited his two wounded crew members in hospital, Tester was picking at a scab under his left eye. A doctor had removed a rivet from this wound, which was one of those holding the turret perspex.

On 15 September a signal decrypted at Bletchley Park revealed that the merchant vessel *Carbonia* of 1,237 tons had left Naples three days before. At this stage her destination was not known but the following day a further decryption indicated that she had arrived in Tunis and was scheduled to leave that port the same evening, headed for Tripoli. She was not escorted, for the Italians sometimes hoped that smaller ships could slip through the blockade unobserved, and indeed so far she had been successful.

At 1615 hours on 17 September, Squadron Leader William C. Wigmore of 227 Squadron took off at the head of six Beaufighters, each carrying two 250lb bombs. The target was considered too small for the torpedoes of 39 Squadron. One Spitfire of 69 Squadron accompanied them for observation and high-level photography, flown by Adrian Warburton, who by then had been promoted to wing commander.

The formation hunted along the coast until, two hours later, the aircrews spotted *Carbonia* in the Gulf of Hammamet. Each Beaufighter attacked the vessel several times with bombs and gunfire, while yellow tracer curved up to meet them. Wigmore's cannons refused to work and his bombs hung up. All the remaining bombs overshot, save one dropped by Dallas Schmidt. He was the second to attack, following Peter Underwood, and came down to forty feet for the bombing run, giving the bridge a squirt of gunfire at the same time. His first bomb missed by about thirty feet but the second hit the merchant ship squarely on the funnel. There was an explosion and *Carbonia* immediately began to list. Schmidt went in five more times at deck level, firing cannons and machine guns.

By the time the Beaufighters and the Spitfire left, *Carbonia* was listing steeply and white smoke was pouring from her. Most of her seamen took to the lifeboats, and she sank quickly. Italian motor boats came out from Pantelleria, about sixty miles away, and rescued thirty-two men. The success of the operation was marred for 227 Squadron by a Beaufighter which crashed into the sea during the return journey. It was flown by Pilot Officer John D. Moffatt, who was on his first operational flight; he and his navigator, Pilot Officer John S. Dicker, lost their lives.

Two days later, Underwood led four Beaufighters, one flown by Schmidt, on a sweep eastwards along the coast from Tripoli, where they found three schooners under sail. It was known that the Axis forces were using these small auxiliary vessels to bring supplies to their front line, possibly in the belief that they would be considered too unimportant to attack. On this occasion, each Beaufighter carried two 500lb bombs. The pilots usually made their attacks at sea level, partly because maximum surprise was more likely to be achieved at this height and partly because the enemy gunners had difficulty in traversing their guns almost horizontally against fast-moving aircraft. The bombs were thus more likely to hit the sides of the ships than their decks, but they often passed overhead. While making these attacks, the pilots always continued to fire at the enemy decks. Then they pulled up slightly to clear the masts and dropped down to sea level on the other side, skidding and jinking to put the gunners off their aim. All the bombs overshot on this occasion, but the pilots raked the decks with gunfire. They left the schooners smoking, but none was seen to sink. Schmidt brought back one of his bombs.

On 22 September a combined attack took place against a target which was destined to play a key role in the Battle of El Alamein, just over a month later. This was the tanker *Proserpina* of 4,869 tons, formerly the French *Beauce*, which had been captured by the Italians at Marseille in July 1940. The tanker had left Taranto during the previous night, escorted by the destroyers *Lampo* and *Euro*, together with the torpedo boat *Partenope*. The convoy was bound for Suda in Crete, following a stopover in Piraeus.

The attackers headed for the island of Antipaxos, to catch the ships before they entered the Gulf of Corinth. Nine Beauforts were led by Wing Commander M. 'Larry' Gaine, who had taken over command of 39 Squadron early in the month. He was thirty-one years of age and was well known as a skilful torpedo pilot. His initial training had been in 1931, on the Avro 504N and the Armstrong Whitworth Atlas. He then joined 100 (Torpedo Bomber) Squadron at Donibristle in Fifeshire, which was equipped with Hawker Horsleys, following which he served for over four years in 36 (Torpedo Bomber) Squadron at Singapore, first flying Horsleys and then Vickers Vildebeests. On his return to the UK in 1937, he joined 148 Squadron at Finningley in Lincolnshire, one of the first squadrons to be equipped with the new Vickers Wellesley long-distance bomber. In July 1938 he took part in a flight of four Wellesleys to the Persian Gulf and Egypt, and then in a record-breaking flight of three Wellesleys from Ismailia to Darwin. Much valuable information was gained from these flights and Gaine was awarded an AFC. He then became a torpedo instructor, first at Gosport and secondly at Abbotsinch. His next position was as commanding officer of 431 (General Reconnaissance) Flight, which was based at Bircham Newton in Norfolk and then Kemble in Gloucestershire. This flight was equipped with Martin Marylands of the former Armée de l'Air, several of which were later sent to Malta and eventually acquired by 69 Squadron. Gaine also tested Wellingtons, Bothas, Hampdens and Albemarles for conversion to torpedo bombers. He was known to his crews in 39 Squadron as a careful and precise pilot who 'did everything by the book'.

Gaine's navigator was Pilot Officer Terry A. McGarry, aged twenty-nine, who was very experienced operationally. He had joined the RAFVR in May 1940 and trained at Prestwick in Ayrshire and Penrhos in Caernarvonshire before qualifying as an air observer. At OTU in Chivenor he crewed up with Pilot Officer Jack Urquhart, with Charles Walker as wireless operator and Sergeant Peter Exton as air gunner. The crew was posted to Egypt and picked up a new Beaufort from the Bristol factory at Filton, but their attempt to reach Gibraltar from Portreath ended in disaster. Both engines cut out when making their final approach to the airfield at Gibraltar. The wheels were down and McGarry was in the nose, flashing the letters of the day with his Aldis lamp. His thoughts were 'This can't be happening to me!' when the Beaufort hit the water and dived in, tearing off both wings. He was knocked unconscious but came to in the cold water and inflated his lifejacket, to find that the fuselage was still floating, with Walker sitting on top of it. They tore the cupola off the turret, where Exton was still trapped, and pulled out the gunner. All four crew members were rescued by the cruiser HMS *Hermioine* and sent back to the UK.

In May 1942, McGarry joined 86 Squadron at Skitten and flew on a dozen operations with Squadron Leader Barnard J. Sandeman. At the end of July many of the crews were posted out to the Middle East. McGarry flew out once more in a Beaufort, with Warrant Officer R.E. Brown as pilot. At Malta, McGarry crewed up with an Australian flight commander, Flight Lieutenant Wally Allsopp, with Sergeant J.G. 'Maxie' Miller and Sergeant Jack Featherstone as wireless operator/air gunners. The crew carried out four operations, including the attack on *Rosolino Pilo* described in the previous chapter, and then Allsopp was posted from the squadron. Wing Commander Gaine took over this crew when he joined the squadron and McGarry was appointed as squadron navigation officer. (The entire crew received awards eventually. Larry Gaine was awarded a DSO and McGarry a DFC. Jim Miller and Jack Featherstone were awarded DFMs and commissioned. Flight Lieutenant Jack Featherstone lost his life in 1945, flying in a Halifax of 502 Squadron.)

On the attack against the tanker *Proserpina* and her escorts, the nine Beauforts of 39 Squadron were escorted by six Beaufighters of 227 Squadron led by Wing Commander Shore. Three Beaufighters were allocated the task of suppressing flak while the other three were to act as top cover. The aircraft kept down low, with the Beaufighters weaving slightly at the rear. By then, the Beaufort pilots had been instructed to operate in 'fluid pairs' so far as possible, these being more manoeuvrable than the older formations of vics of three. Since resources at Malta were so limited, they had also been told that their targets should be ships of at least 5,000 tons, unless smaller vessels were known to be carrying cargoes of particular importance. Their method was to attack simultaneously from all points of the compass, to spread the defensive fire more thinly.

A calamity occurred before they reached the target. Flying as number two to Shore in the anti-flak section, Schmidt saw their number three, flown by Sergeant A.J. Phillips of the RAAF, collide with a Beaufort flown by a Canadian, Pilot Officer Aubrey F. 'Izzy' Izzard. The tail of the Beaufort was damaged and it dived into the sea, killing all the crew members, but Phillips managed to regain control of his Beaufighter and returned safely to Luqa. The remaining thirteen aircraft continued their outward journey.

McGarry's navigation brought the formation directly to the convoy. The three warships began sailing in a circle around *Proserpina*, putting on speed and making smoke. Several Ju 88s and two MC200s were overhead. McGarry fired a yellow-yellow Very cartridge from the side window, and the formation attacked. Shore made two cannon and machine gun sweeps over a warship and then raked the tanker. His Beaufighter was hit but he eased it back to Malta and crash-landed near Luqa, both he and his navigator unhurt.

Schmidt strafed a destroyer and seemed to score a hit on some ammunition, for there was a small explosion forward of the bridge. He was attacked by a Ju 88 but outflew the German pilot. To his surprise, he saw the warships open fire on another Ju 88 after it had fired a recognition signal. The remaining Beaufighters attacked several Ju 88s, but without visible results. From the turret of Gaine's Beaufort, Miller hit a Ju 88, which was listed as a 'probable'. In spite of repeated attacks on them, all eight Beauforts dropped their torpedoes at the tanker, which was partly screened by the smoke, but she was able to avoid them. With damage to their upper decks and nursing their wounded, the four Italian vessels continued via the Corinth Canal to Piraeus, arriving at 2300 hours the following day.

In the late evening of 27 September, three Beauforts of 39 Squadron took off to intercept at night a convoy which was known to be sailing down the coast of Greece en route for Benghazi. This consisted of the the merchant ship *Barbaro* of 6,343 tons and the tanker *Unione* of 6,017 tons, escorted by two destroyers and four torpedo boats, headed for Benghazi. This convoy had been attacked in the late afternoon by the submarine HMS *Umbra*. She had torpedoed *Barbaro*, which was carrying 135 soldiers as well as about 4,500 tons of ammunition and other supplies. The merchant ship began to sink, while the warships attempted to tow her to safety. The weather was dark and overcast, but two Beauforts found the convoy. One was flown by Lieutenant Don P. Tilley, a South African who had been seconded to the RAF at the end of 1941 and had joined 39 Squadron in July 1942; he was to establish himself as one of the premier torpedo pilots of the war. Tilley torpedoed the tanker *Unione* soon after midnight, but she did not sink and was also taken into tow. She was loaded with over 4,000 tons of fuel and other supplies. The merchant ship *Barbaro* went down about four hours later, but the warships rescued 248 of the 278 men who had embarked with her. The tanker was towed to the port of Pylos (known as Navarino by the Italians) in south-west Greece, and arrived in the morning of 29 September.

After this attack, for which Don Tilley was awarded a DFC, 39 Squadron was sent back to Shallufa in Egypt. The crews flew there in their Beauforts during the first two days of October and were granted a short leave while their aircraft were serviced. It was originally intended that they would fly back to Malta on 12 October but this order was cancelled. Instead, a large detachment was sent to the forward airfield of Gianaclis, about seventy miles west of Alexandria. The crews were not aware that the Battle of El Alamein would begin on 23 October and that their role would be to assist in attacking Axis supply ships approaching the port of Tobruk.

Meanwhile, 227 Squadron continued anti-shipping attacks from Malta, but a series of events sapped the strength of the squadron during the next few weeks. On 4 October, three Beaufighters carrying 500lb bombs were sent out against a target, but they did not reach their objective. After about thirty minutes a Beaufighter flown by a Canadian, Flight Sergeant George P. 'Red' Fargher, lost power and dived into the sea. Flying as number two in the formation, Dallas Schmidt saw the navigator, Pilot Officer K.C. Briffett, floating in the water. He was wearing his Mae West but had no dinghy. Schmidt's navigator, Sergeant Andrew Campbell, threw his dinghy out to Briffett, but it failed to open. Campbell then went forward and threw out Schmidt's 'K-type' pilot's dinghy. This time, Briffett managed to open it and get inside.

Schmidt and the other pilot flew back to Malta and alerted the rescue services and then went out again on a search for the dinghy. But night fell and the search had to be abandoned for the day. Schmidt took off again early the following morning, in company with a Beaufighter flown by Squadron Leader William Wigmore. They came across Briffett floating in his dinghy, but then Wigmore's engines failed and he also ditched in the sea. Fortunately he and his navigator, Pilot Officer A.M. 'Jimmy' Crow, managed to get into their dinghies. A high speed launch came out from Malta and picked up the three men, but Red Fargher had been drowned and two Beaufighters were lost.

When he landed back at Luqa, Schmidt learned that he had been awarded a DFC, which was gazetted twelve days later. On 12 October Wing Commander D. Ross Shore, who had also been awarded a DFC, was posted from the squadron. His replacement was Wing Commander Cedric A. Masterman OBE, who assumed command when the fortunes of the squadron were reaching a low ebb. They were to fall even further.

On 14 October, three Beaufighters were sent out to attack a convoy consisting of the German merchant vessel *Trapani* of 1,855 tons escorted by the torpedo boat *Medici*. These two vessels had left Tripoli in the early morning and were headed along the coast of North Africa to Benghazi. Two Macchi fighters circled overhead.

The three Beaufighters reached the enemy convoy at 1230 hours and attacked. The results were described in a report written by the commander of the torpedo boat, Tenente di Vascello Antonio Furlan:

'At 1237 hours the convoy was attacked at very low level by three bombers. The first bomber attempted to fly across the merchant ship from port to starboard but was too low. Probably hit by machine gun fire, it hit the mast at the stem, crashed into the sea on the starboard side, and exploded. The second aircraft tried a similar manoeuvre from the opposite direction but, noticing that it was too low, tried to turn away and dropped two bombs on the starboard side, neither of which exploded. At the same time, it was firing its machine guns. Caught between fire from *Trapani* and *Medici* (which was well within range, being only 300 metres away), the aircraft was hit in the engines. It lost height as it flew off and was seen to crash into the sea. The third bomber did not carry out an attack but was chased and overtaken by the escorting fighters, which shot it down. I steered towards the position where the second aircraft had crashed into the sea, this position having been indicated to me by an escorting fighter. I spotted a rubber dinghy and rescued the crew, which consisted of an officer and a sergeant ...'

This vivid account was somewhat inaccurate in parts, as was often the case when fast-moving events were witnessed. The first Beaufighter was flown by Squadron Leader Peter L. Underwood, who was by then a flight commander and nearing the end of his operational tour. He was notable for the determination of his attacks, as well as for his frequent support of Beauforts in difficulties. Both he and his navigator, Flight Sergeant Ivor R. Miller, lost their lives. The second Beaufighter was flown by Pilot Officer J.M. Bryce and navigated by Flight Sergeant S.W. Cole. Fortunately they were picked up by *Medici*, and became PoWs. The third Beaufighter was not shot down and in fact made two attacks on *Trapani*. The bombs hung up on the first occasion and they overshot on the second. The Beaufighter, flown by Pilot Officer Tom St B. Freer, was badly hit and the hydraulics were shot away, but the pilot nursed it back to a crash-landing at Luqa. The fighter aircraft which guided *Medici* to the downed airmen was not an Italian but a Spitfire of 69 Squadron flown by Wing Commander Adrian Warburton. He had seen the dinghy from above and dived down to help, shaking off attacks by Macchis while on his errand of mercy.

By this time the strength of 227 Squadron was reduced to six Beaufighters, of which only three were serviceable. This was the period known as the 'mini-blitz', when Malta came under renewed attack from Sicily. One of these machines was burnt out in a blast pen on 17 October, following an air raid. A single replacement Beaufighter arrived five days later, but was not fitted up for operational work. By 24 October the squadron could muster only one serviceable aircraft, with two more capable of readiness within twelve hours, two more within a day, and the new aircraft still being fitted up. Then yet another Beaufighter was damaged during the air raids.

On 30 October, Masterman and seven crews were detached to Idku, flying there in the four Beaufighters which were capable of taking to the air. Dallas Schmidt had been promoted to flight lieutenant and appointed as a flight commander, while Squadron Leader William Wigmore continued as the other flight commander. The squadron needed to re-equip and take a short rest before making itself available for the next phase of its operational work from Malta.

(**Above**) *Left to right*: Flight Sergeant Barnes (who replaced C. Nimerovsky), Pilot Officer C. Bladen, Flying Officer N.G. Spark, Squadron Leader R.V. Manning. Bladen, Spark and Manning were part of the crew which sank the tanker *Proserpina* on 26 October 1942 outside Tobruk. The photograph was taken at Vavuniya in Celyon in April 1944. (*Flight Lieutenant N.G. Spark*) (**Right**) Dallas W. Schmidt (*Flt Lt D.W. Schmidt*) (**Below**) A Beaufighter IC taking off from Luqa. (*Aeroplane Monthly*)

Two pilots who flew with 227 Squadron in Malta. *Left to right:* Sergeant A.J. 'Jack' Phillips (RAAF) and Sergeant C.M. 'Cas' de Bounevialle (RAF). (*Flt Lt C.M. de Bounevialle, DFC*)

A photograph taken at Takali in Malta on Christmas day 1942. *Left to right:* Wing Commander C.A. Masterman, who commanded 227 Squadron; Wing Commander John K. Buchanan, who commanded 272 Squadron and then 227 Squadron; Squadron Leader Anthony Watson (recently returned after having been shot down over Tunis), who commanded 272 Squadron and then 227 Squadron; Flight Lieutenant P.C. Cobley of 272 Squadron. (*Group Captain C.A. Masterman*)

6

Fuel for the Panzerarmee

The Achilles' heel of the Axis powers was oil. With the Romanian oilfields as the only major source of crude oil in Europe, Germany had applied her technical expertise to the manufacture of synthetic oil, primarily from coal. But the gap between consumption and production during the war was never satisfactorily closed, especially when oil was being consumed at a high rate in major military actions.

Italy was in an even worse situation than her ally since she had only tiny sources of crude oil, while a synthetic industry was restricted by her lack of indigenous coal supplies. The conquest of Albania had yielded a small supply of crude oil, but otherwise Italy was almost wholly dependant on imports from Romania. This was transported over a mountainous route through the Balkans and the supply was controlled by the Germans, who allocated only sufficient quantities to keep certain fighting units in battle readiness.

In the early part of the war, the fuel requirements of the Italian Army and Air Force were partly satisfied by restrictions on civilian allocations, the curtailment of military training and the admixture of up to thirty per cent of alcohol. But, as soon as pre-war stocks of fuel oil were exhausted, the deficiency became particularly serious in the Italian Navy. Towards the end of 1941 consumption was running at about 75,000 tons per month, but existing supplies were available for only about half that amount. Early in 1942 the Germans pressed the Italians to reduce their activities in the Mediterranean Sea, while the Kriegsmarine was forced to limit its commitments in the North Sea. It seems that the Germans did not believe that the supply of naval fuel to Italian capital ships was a good investment, since these had avoided action with weaker British warships at a time when stocks had been available.

The Axis forces in North Africa consumed an average of 13,000 tons of liquid fuel per month. The Germans used far more than the Italians, since their units were composed mainly of Panzers and other mechanised vehicles. The only adequate method of supply was by sea, choosing routes which were furthest from RAF bases. But the tankers required escorts from destroyers, torpedo boats and other vessels, and these required fuel. After an abortive foray in June 1942 to attack a Malta-bound convoy, the large Italian warships received no more supplies of fuel and were immobilised until the surrender of Italy in September 1943. Most of the available fuel was allocated to the supply ships and their escorts.

On the evening of 23 October 1942 an artillery barrage of enormous weight and violence opened on the Axis forces from the Allied lines in the Western Desert. When this prelude to the Battle of El Alamein began, Generalfeldmarschall Erwin Rommel was resting at Semmering in the Austrian Alps, where he was undergoing a cure for intestinal and liver disorders caused by a poor diet and the strain of his duties. His replacement in North Africa, General Georg Stumme, was reported missing on the morning of 24 October. He was found dead in his staff car the next day, apparently having died of a heart attack while being strafed by the RAF. During the same morning, Rommel reached Rome en route for Africa, having agreed to resume his old command. Here he learned that his mechanised units were so short of fuel and spare parts that the Panzerarmee could continue fighting for only four days. No amount of courage or generalship could replace this urgent need. The whole future of the campaign in North Africa was at stake.

Rommel did not hold his Italian allies in high regard. The Italian Navy was responsible for the safe transport of supplies to North Africa, but only half the vessels had arrived in the previous few weeks. The ships were being sunk with uncanny regularity by Allied aircraft and submarines. Rommel decided that the Allies must be aware of the movements of these convoys, and he asserted that Italian traitors were betraying sailing times, contents of cargoes and destinations to the enemy.

In Rome, the Luftwaffe officer Feldmarschall Albert Kesselring had been appointed C-in-C of the German forces in southern Europe. He also acted as liaison officer between the German forces in North Africa and the Italian Supreme Command. Rommel demanded the immediate despatch of tankers and ammunition ships to Tobruk, the nearest port to the front line. The safer port of entry was Benghazi, further west, for this was outside the range of medium bombers operating from either Malta or Egypt, but from this port the supplies had to be transported about 1,000 miles to the front line. Even supplies landed at Tobruk took two days by truck to reach the Panzerarmee.

By the time Rommel had flown to his headquarters in North Africa, on the evening of 25 October, Kesselring was able to send a highly secret and urgent radio message: Mussolini had given firm assurances that a convoy carrying these vital supplies would arrive in Tobruk the following evening. It was code named convoy 'TT', from Taranto to Tobruk.

Rommel was quite correct in his belief that the Allies knew the secrets of the Axis convoys in the Mediterranean, but the fault did not lie with the Italians. As we have seen in the previous chapter, the answer lay in the Government Code and Cipher School at Bletchley Park. Although the troops of the Eighth Army came to believe that their new commander, General Bernard Montgomery, possessed extraordinary powers of perception regarding the disposition of the Axis forces and their supplies, much of the intelligence information care from this decrypting service.

In its final form, convoy 'TT' consisted of seven vessels. The most important was the tanker *Proserpina* of 4,869 tons, the vessel which the strike force of 39 and 227 Squadrons had attacked unsuccessfully on 22 September. This tanker had left Taranto at 0428 hours on 22 October and, escorted by two torpedo boats, had passed through the Corinth Canal and reached Piraeus. She was carrying 4,553 tons of fuel, 888 tons of which were destined for the Luftwaffe, 2,500 tons for the Panzerarmee, and 1,165 tons for the Italian forces. These facts were known by British Intelligence.

A small freighter had arrived in Piraeus on 21 October, from Salonika. This was the German *Dora* of 584 tons, which had survived the attack of 39 and 227 Squadrons on 20 August. There are no records of her cargo, but she probably carried about 400 tons of military equipment.

Proserpina and *Dora* set sail from Piraeus at 0634 hours on 24 October, a few hours after the opening of the artillery barrage at El Alamein, accompanied by three torpedo boats. There was an alarm five hours later when a submarine was located by sonar and bubbles were seen on the surface. Two salvoes of depth charges were fired but no results were seen and the convoy continued south.

Meanwhile another merchant vessel sailed to join the convoy, leaving Suda in Crete at 0934 hours on 24 October, escorted by two more torpedo boats. She was the Italian *Tergestea* of 5,890 tons, carrying the dangerously explosive mixture of about 1,000 tons of fuel and 1,000 tons of ammunition.

The two sections of the convoy made their rendezvous during the morning of 25 October. They set course for Tobruk across that stretch of the Mediterranean Sea which British seamen had dubbed 'Bomb Alley' when they were attacked by Stukas during their attempts to relieve Malta from the east. The course of the convoy was slightly circuitous, curving westwards to keep equidistant from the RAF's bases in Malta and Egypt. There were about thirty-two hours of sailing time ahead of convoy 'TT' at its speed of nine knots. Only in the last few hours of their journey would the vessels come within the range of Beauforts based in Egypt.

One of the torpedo boats turned away on another mission. The three merchant ships formed up in line astern, with *Dora* in the lead, followed by *Proserpina* and with *Tergestea* in the rear. Each vessel carried flak armament. On their flanks zigzagged the four Italian torpedo boats *Partenope*, *Lira*, *Ciclone* and *Calatafimi*. Relays of three to five aircraft circled overhead during daylight hours, expected to be doubled in strength when the convoy neared Tobruk. The commander of the convoy was Capitano di Corvetto Gustavo Lovatelli in *Partenope*, who bore the heavy responsibility of bringing these vital supplies to the Axis forces during the battle.

The daylight hours of 25 October were fairly uneventful, although the air escorts warned the commander that the convoy was being shadowed by RAF reconnaissance aircraft. Of course, the strike aircraft of 201 (Naval Co-operation) Group were ready and waiting. During the night, long-range Wellingtons attacked from Egypt. These were nine torpedo bombers of 38 Squadron, based at LG226 at Gianaclis, together with one ASV aircraft of 221 Squadron and one of 458 (RAAF) Squadron, both based at Shallufa.

The Wellington ICs of these squadrons had been converted to carry two Mark XII torpedoes, the nose turrets having been removed to save weight. The crews had been trained to operate in concert with each other in night attacks on shipping. Some were termed 'Snoopingtons' or 'Goofingtons' and used their ASV to locate targets and then switched on their 'Rooster' radios so that the strike aircraft could home on them. Those carrying torpedoes were termed 'Fishingtons' while those with bombs were 'Bombingtons'. The ASV Wellingtons dropped flares which lit up the targets or silhouetted them against the horizon.

These techniques had worked well on previous occasions but they proved unsuccessful on this night. Two torpedoes were aimed at *Proserpina* at different times, but the Italians were vigilant and the tanker manoeuvred out of the way. Then the seamen on *Calatafimi* spotted two tracks running towards them, and the torpedo boat also took avoiding action. A stick of bombs straddled the bows of *Lira*, narrowly missing the warship. The last Wellington turned for home at 0400 hours and the first escorting Axis aircraft arrived half an hour later. Convoy 'TT' had come through the night unscathed and was only fourteen hours away from Tobruk.

During the early hours of the following morning, 26 October, RAF reconnaissance aircraft relocated the convoy and transmitted the disappointing news that all the vessels seemed undamaged. Between 1210 and 1230 hours, when the convoy was only about fifty miles from Tobruk, three waves of B-24 Liberators appeared at 20,000 feet. These were eighteen aircraft of the 98th Bombardment Group, an American unit based at Fayid in Egypt and temporarily under the control of the RAF. The Liberators flew in three boxes of six and all dropped salvoes of bombs which fell very close to the merchant vessels. Several bombs narrowly missed *Proserpina*, but there was no damage, although some US airmen reported hits. It was extremely difficult to hit a moving target from that altitude, even when aiming carefully through the advanced Norden or Sperry bombsights.

So far, convoy 'TT' had borne a charmed life. But the first stroke of misfortune fell at 1430 hours, when the vessels were only thirty miles from Tobruk and steaming eastwards along the coast. *Proserpina* suddenly developed a fault in her engine room and fell back, protected by the torpedo boat *Calatafimi*. However, repairs were effected rapidly and after only half an hour the tanker and her escort began to close the gap with the other vessels. Then the sailors saw about fifteen twin-engined aircraft approaching from the east, skimming just above the surface of the sea.

In early October 1942 the crews of 47 Squadron, based at Shandur in Egypt, were busy converting on to Bristol Beaufort Is as replacements for their outdated Vickers Wellesley Is. They had been joined during the previous month by a detachment of aircrews from 42 Squadron, which had been operating with Beauforts in the UK since April 1940. But the Beaufort I, which was in any event underpowered, did not have the range to reach Tobruk when carrying a Mark XII torpedo of 1,610lb. One problem was that these aircraft had been 'tropicalised'. Two ungainly air filters, something like ships' ventilators in appearance, stuck up above the engine cowlings. ASV aerials called 'Yagi' aerials – protruded from underneath the leading edges of the wings and caused further drag. The aircraft were fitted with rhodoid instead of perspex windows, and the heat and humidity had caused these to buckle inwards, affecting the streamlining. The tropicalised Beaufort in Egypt lumbered along in a tail-down attitude, sometimes below the critical speed for single-engined flying.

One of the new arrivals at Shandur was Flying Officer Norman Hearning Phillips DFM, a twenty-seven-year-old pilot with considerable experience of Beauforts, both operationally and as an instructor. Known as 'H-P' in the small world of Beaufort aircrews, he was a person with a detailed technical knowledge of the aircraft as well as a flair for improvisation.* The commanding officer of 47 Squadron, Squadron Leader Robert L.B. Carr, seized on the opportunity of discussing the problems of his new Beauforts with H-P. Together with the squadron engineer officer, they set about experimenting with modifications to one of the Beauforts.

Firstly, they reduced the height of the Vokes air filters and fitted aluminium fairings around the square fronts. Then H-P suggested that

---

* See *Torpedo Airmen*, by the author, for a fuller description of this pilot.

the ASV aerials might work satisfactorily if they were fitted straight out of the leading edges of the wings instead of slung beneath them. This proved to be correct, for it was found that the wings acted as reflectors and that there was no difference in reception, but drag was further reduced. Lastly, they realised that the new mid-upper turret, which had been equipped with two guns instead of one, was too high. They took off the cupola and replaced it with low fairings. The gunner was partly exposed to the elements, but this was not a disadvantage when flying at low level in the baking heat of the desert. These improvements almost restored the normal airspeed of the Beaufort, and gave it an extra range of about 100 miles. With official approval, the engineers on the squadron began to modify all the Beauforts.

On 24 October some of the modified Beauforts of 47 Squadron were flown westwards to the forward airfield of Gianaclis. From there they could now reach Tobruk while carrying a torpedo and with a reasonable safety margin. It was a round trip of about 720 miles, or about five and a half hours' flying. There were eight Beauforts in the detachment, including one flown by the new commanding officer, Wing Commander Richard A. Sprague.

At 1230 hours on 26 October the eight Beauforts took off to attack the approaching convoy 'TT'. Although Sprague was one of the pilots, he had had little experience of torpedo attacks and instructed another newcomer to lead the formation. This was Flight Lieutenant Ronald Gee, a very experienced Beaufort pilot and instructor, who was nicknamed 'Auntie' as a result of his careful and exact approach to life and the problems of flying.

Accompanying the Beauforts were six Bisleys of 15 (SAAF) Squadron, ordered forward to Gianaclis from their base at Mariut. Each carried a load of four 250lb general purpose bombs, and their dangerous task was to make low-level attacks on the merchant vessels at the same time as the Beauforts released their torpedoes. A fighter escort was provided by four Beaufighters of 252 Squadron and five more from 272 Squadron, which had also moved forward to Gianaclis from their base at Idku. Their job was to suppress flak as well as to tackle enemy fighters.

The Beauforts kept down low, at about 100 feet over the surface of the sea. The Beaufighters were stacked up at various heights above them, weaving slightly to keep pace with the slower speed of their charges. One of the Bisleys was late in take-off, owing to a delay in refuelling, and returned to base after a fruitless attempt to catch up with the formation. The remaining twenty-two aircraft flew in a westerly direction, keeping out to sea about fifty miles from the enemy coastline.

H-P flew to the right of the formation. On the far right was Pilot

Officer Ralph V. Manning, a twenty-six-year-old Canadian. His navigator was a twenty-three-year-old Londoner, Sergeant Norman G. Spark, and Sergeant Charles Bladen manned the wireless set. Sergeant Cyril Nimerovsky, from a Jewish family in Manchester, occupied the turret. Manning's crew was under a cloud, although they were experienced in Beauforts and had already flown on fourteen operations. They had been part of four Beauforts, four Bisleys and six Beaufighters which had been sent out the day before, looking for merchant vessels. They found some F-boats and, although Sprague and two Beaufort pilots had dropped their torpedoes against these, Manning had brought his back in the belief that the draught of the barges was too shallow for the torpedo settings. Although he was proved correct, there remained the suspicion that he had avoided combat for a different reason.

At 1440 hours, according to Spark's navigation chart (which still exists, with pencilled times and positions), they approached Tobruk and came under fire from heavy flak batteries. Turning north-west to hunt along the coast, they next came across a large concentration of F-boats, which also opened fire. No mistake was made on this occasion and Gee led the formation away from these unprofitable targets. The aircrews were under strict orders to find the correct convoy and concentrate their attacks against the tanker.

The Beaufighters waggled their wings at 1525 hours. From their higher altitude, they had spotted the first section of convoy 'TT', with the little ship *Dora* in the lead, followed by the ammunition ship *Tergestea*. Two torpedo boats, *Partenope* and *Ciclone*, guarded the seaward flak, while *Lira* was at the rear. Above them circled two Ju 88s, an Me 109 and two MC202s. The Beaufighters made for these air escorts while the majority of the Beauforts and Bisleys altered course to attack the merchant vessels. The sunlight was so bright that the aircrews could barely see the lines of tracer curving up to meet them, but the jagged black puffs of exploding shells were clearly visible in the bright blue sky.

The crews of these squadrons had not developed the precisely co-ordinated attacks against shipping learned by 39 and 227 Squadrons in Malta. There was a general plan of attack, but each pilot chose his own target. Looking at the convoy, most pilots assumed that *Dora* in the lead must be the important tanker they had been ordered to sink. A yellow-yellow Very light soared up from Gee's Beaufort.

Three of the South African Bisleys went in first, at low level. Lieutenant James Lithgow led this trio, but his bombs missed narrowly and his aircraft was damaged by flak as he pulled away. Close behind, Lieutenant Algie B. Groch released his bombs but his aircraft was hit by cannon fire. The port wing clipped the mast of *Dora* and the aircraft spun into the sea, killing the navigator, Lieutenant A. McL. Johnson. Groch and his gunner, Air Sergeant R.E. Twigg, managed to get into their dinghy and became PoWs. The bombs dropped by Lieutenant Sven E. Leisegang in the third Bisley also missed. The aircraft appeared to have been hit, but it continued flying.

During this attack, five Beauforts aimed their torpedoes at *Dora*, while one chose *Tergestea*. All six torpedoes missed. Sprague's aircraft was hit but he regained control, with half the rudder shot away. Another Beaufort pilot was Flying Officer Haraldur J. Davidson, a Canadian on his first operational flight. He had exchanged good wishes with Manning shortly before take-off. The flak caught his aircraft immediately after he dropped his torpedo. It turned on its back and crashed, killing all the crew save the navigator, Pilot Officer Trevor H. Jones, who survived to become a PoW.

Two Beauforts did not attack, nor did two Bisleys. One of the Beauforts was flown by Ralph Manning, who looked at the two merchant ships coolly and carefully. Neither had the outline of a tanker.

'I don't think the tanker's there, Norm,' he said to his navigator, Sergeant Norman Spark. 'It must be further down the coast.'*

This was a remarkable decision for a junior officer to take, especially when both his commanding officer and his formation leader had attacked other vessels, while he was already under suspicion of avoiding combat. But Manning turned and flew along the coast. His decision must be classed as one of the most important of those which affected the Battle of El Alamein.

Another pilot who realised that the wrong targets were being attacked was Norman Hearn-Phillips, one of the steadiest and most careful of all the Beaufort pilots. He had not participated in the fruitless attack against the F-boats the day before but he had heard about it and had no intention of making a mistake on this day. He followed Manning.

Looking around, the two Beaufort pilots were relieved to see that two Bisleys were with them. Major Douglas W. 'Pip' Pidsley, the commanding officer of 15 (SAAF) Squadron, also doubted whether the little *Dora* was a tanker. Lieutenant E. Gerald Dustow in the other Bisley continued to format on him. They did not communicate with the Beauforts by R/T but guessed what the pilots were doing.

These four pilots were proved correct after a few minutes. A plume of smoke on the horizon resolved itself into the tanker *Proserpina*, with the torpedo boat *Calatafimi* guarding the seaward flank. But meanwhile H-P's Beaufort was hit, probably by one of the shells fired by *Lira* at the

---

* The remarks made on this day are remembered vividly by surviving aircrews.

tail of the first section of convoy 'TT'. A chunk of flak passed through the wireless operator's position from port to starboard, smashing the electrical panel in the fuselage. Fortunately the wireless operator, Flight Sergeant P.G. 'Ginger' Coulson, was further forward at the time, in readiness to take photographs with H-P's 35mm camera. But the damage to the electrical circuit caused the torpedo to drop from the bomb bay. All that H-P could do was to draw enemy fire and watch while Manning made an attack with the last torpedo.

When Manning looked at *Proserpina*, he realised that he had found the right target. But the Italian master of the tanker knew what to expect and turned to port, towards the torpedo bomber, spoiling Manning's aim. The Canadian pilot circled over the shore while under continuous fire, to find a better angle. The master of *Proserpina* watched him and began to reverse his turn, to point the bows once more at his attacker. For a few moments, *Proserpina* was almost montionless in the water and Manning saw his chance. He flew straight at the tanker at 80 feet and 140 knots, the correct altitude and speed for dropping a torpedo. The distance for release was 1,000 yards, but he flew closer before pressing the release button, in his determination to score a hit. As he did so, the two Bisleys streaked ahead on their bombing run while a Beaufighter dived out of the sky at *Calatafimi*.

The two Bisleys attacked almost simultaneously, under intense fire. Pidsley released his bombs and cleared the tanker, although his aircraft was peppered with holes. Dustow's aircraft was more seriously hit and did not recover. It struck one of the masts of *Proserpina* and cartwheeled into the sea. There were no survivors.

Manning watched the scene ahead in shock and fascination. Out of the corner of one eye, he saw the bridge of *Calatafimi* disappear under a cloud of smoke from the exploding shells of the Beaufighter. His attention was so distracted that he almost failed to climb over the masts of the tanker before coming down on the other side and skidding just above the surface of the sea. The delay-action bombs from the Bisleys exploded almost underneath his Beaufort and there was an enormous jolt. It was discovered later that a piece of the ship's superstructure had passed through the whizzing propeller on the starboard side and dented the wing between the engine and the fuselage.

At this point, the Beauforts and Bisleys which had survived the attack against the first section of the convoy caught up with Manning and Hearn-Phillips. Pilot Officer D.H. Francis, the navigator in Gee's Beaufort, could see Manning's torpedo running through the clear sea towards the tanker. But *Proserpina* continued to turn to starboard and the torpedo bumped along her starboard side.

The Mark XII torpedoes were of two types, 'contact' and 'duplex'.

Both exploded on contact with the pistol in the nose, but the duplex was also activated by the magnetic field of the ship. The records do not state which type of torpedo was carried on this day, nor can the surviving aircrews remember. However, it seems likely that the torpedo dropped by Manning was of the simple contact type, since the duplex had proved somewhat unreliable and was used less often. What probably happened is that Manning dropped his torpedo less than 600 yards from the target, this being the distance in which the torpedo flew through the air and then travelled in the sea before becoming armed. While the torpedo was bumping along the side of the tanker, it was probably still arming itself. But when it reached the stern, it exploded.

'We've hit her!' shouted Cyril Nimerovsky, from the turret of Manning's aircraft.

'Hurrah! He's hit her!' shouted Ginger Coulson, from the seat beside Hearn-Phillips.

'Take a picture!' H-P shouted to Coulson.

Sheets of flame came from the tanker, followed by a billowing mass of smoke. The crew of *Proserpina* thought that they had been hit by two torpedoes, but the first explosion must have come from one of the bombs dropped by the Bisleys. The vessel sank almost immediately. *Calatafimi* and *Lira* picked up sixty-two survivors from the sea, but fifteen of the crew lost their lives.

The Beauforts and Bisleys grouped together in a loose formation, ten aircraft in all, to begin their journey back to Gianaclis. But the action was not yet finished. While the anti-shipping attacks had been in progress, Beaufighters had been in combat with enemy aircraft. One Beaufighter of 252 Squadron got in a long burst at a Ju 88; bits flew off the fuselage of the German aircraft, which then made for shore. Another Beaufighter of 252 Squadron was shot down into the sea, but both Pilot Officer J.S. Adams and Sergeant C.L. Barringer got into their dinghy and were picked up by the Italians. Sergeant W. Russell of 272 Squadron was pursued for about sixty miles by an Me 109E which badly holed his Beaufighter, but he brought the aircraft back to Gianaclis. A few MC202s were still circling around the Beauforts and Bisleys, and H-P had his first indication of these when Flight Sergeant A.T. Johnson called from the turret: 'Macchi coming in on our starboard quarter!' 'O.K.,' replied H-P. 'Tell me what to do.'

The Macchis dived again and again on the Beauforts and Bisleys, being met by return fire from the gunners in their turrets. But Johnson could not operate his turret, since the electrical circuit had been severed. All he could do was to give instructions to H-P, who obeyed them coolly and precisely. Manning was also attacked, and he found later that one of the Macchis had caused mainspar damage to his Beaufort. No aircraft were lost in these attacks and eventually the

Italians turned away, probably having exhausted their ammunition. More enemy fighters were seen but the Beauforts and Bisleys kept down low and were not attacked again.

However, the damage sustained by the returning aircraft still had to take its toll. H-P saw one of the Bisleys, flown by Lieutenant Leisegang, begin to weave. It will never be known what was wrong with the aircraft but it must be assumed that either the machine or the pilot had been hit during the attack on *Dora* or by one of the Macchis. The Bisley slid sideways under a Beaufort and then climbed. H-P watched in dismay but was unable to give a warning since his R/T – never an efficient instrument at the best of times – had been put out of action. He remained helpless while the Bisley collided with a Beaufort flown by an Australian, Pilot Officer Walter Garriock. Locked together like a biplane, the two aircraft crashed into the sea, killing all crew members. Only sixteen aircraft returned from the twenty-two which had set out for convoy 'TT'.

It was believed at 201 (Naval Co-operation) Group that the tanker must have sunk, but there was doubt about the other two vessels. A second strike force, consisting of five Beauforts of 39 Squadron, led by Squadron Leader Les Wordsell, and nine Beaufighters of 252 and 272 Squadrons, were sent out from Gianaclis. The formation met five He 111s off the enemy coast and the Beaufighters attacked, while the Beauforts continued to hunt for the convoy. Pilot Officer A.I. Smith of 272 Squadron destroyed one Heinkel, while Pilot Officer G.G. Pattearson from the same squadron set another on fire and saw it limping back to the coast on one engine. Sergeant Stan Kernaghan of 252 Squadron followed Flight Lieutenant Derek Frecker into a head-on attack. For Kernaghan, the attack was like sitting in a car during a hailstorm while nearly forty bullets riddled his Beaufighter, many passing through his cockpit. But he positioned himself above and behind the Heinkels, until he spotted one on the left flying slightly apart from the others. He dived, and shot the German down into the sea. The Heinkel exploded, part of the debris damaging the starboard wing of the Beaufighter.

A Beaufighter of 252 Squadron was shot down. It was flown by another Canadian, Pilot Officer E.R. 'Buzz' Derick, who managed to get into his dinghy, together with his wounded navigator, Pilot Officer M.J. McCann. They floated for eight days before reaching the coast. McCann went off to try to find water and was taken prisoner, but Derick was helped by friendly Arabs and returned to his squadron on 9 November.

After this air combat, the other eight Beaufighters chased after the five Beauforts and met them coming back. They had not found the convoy but three had dropped their torpedoes against a convoy of F-boats and an escort vessel, without result. Wordsell and one other pilot brought back their torpedoes.

There was now anxiety at 201 Group about the Axis convoy, for it was realised that the vessels would be able to unload their cargoes after nightfall. Three torpedo-carrying Wellingtons of 38 Squadron from Gambut took off in the late afternoon, in a last attempt to sink the two merchant vessels.

In the early evening, when the remaining ships of convoy 'TT' were picking their way around the sunken wrecks which littered the passage towards Tobruk, the sailors saw the three Wellingtons flying towards them from the sea. Every gun on the ships and on the shore was brought to bear. But the three Wellingtons, led by an Australian pilot, Flight Lieutenant Albert L. Wiggins, continued steadily on their run and dropped their torpedoes. One aircraft, flown by Sergeant George Viles, was hit and crashed in a fuel dump near the port, but all the crew members survived. Three were taken prisoner, but Sergeant Herbert E.G. Hale and Sergeant James McPherson managed to evade capture and reached British lines on 11 November.

Wiggins and the other pilot, Pilot Officer R.H. Bertram, were able to turn for home, in spite of damage to both Wellingtons. At least one torpedo hit the stern of *Tergestea*. The merchant ship, loaded with fuel and ammunition, disintegrated. A pall of oily black smoke rose to 3,000 feet above the wreckage. There was not a single survivor from her crew of eighty seamen.

Only the little *Dora* was able to enter Tobruk and unload her cargo of about 400 tons. The Germans along the shore had watched with dismay the destruction of the other two vessels, for they knew that with them went their best hopes of retrieving the situation at El Alamein.

Well-merited awards for the Allied airmen who had shared in the successful attacks arrived several days later. Wiggins, who had led the Wellingtons, was awarded a DSO. Gee, who had led the Beauforts, received a DFC. Pidsley, who had led the Bisleys, also received a DFC. But Manning did not receive an award, although Wing Commander Sprague put in a strong recommendation for his DFC. It was not until later in the war, on a quite different occasion, that he was awarded a DFC.

Even after the loss of his supplies in *Proserpina* and *Tergestea*, Rommel refused to admit defeat. British Intelligence knew that many of his armoured vehicles were unserviceable and that fuel was almost exhausted. There was a severe shortage of artillery shells, while his troops were being strafed continually by the RAF. But so far the Eighth Army had been unable to make an effective penetration of the Axis minefields. The fighting quality of the Deutsches Panzerarmee remained high. If only adequate supplies could be brought to the front line, Rommel hoped to win the battle.

Another convoy was scheduled to arrive at Tobruk shortly after convoy 'TT'. This was convoy 'J', consisting of the tanker *Luisiano* of 2,552 tons, loaded with 1,460 tons of army fuel, and the merchant ship *Etiopia* of 2,143 tons, carrying an unrecorded quantity of aviation fuel in containers. Escorted by a destroyer and two torpedo boats, the convoy left Taranto during the evening of 25 October. Of course, its movements were monitored by Bletchley Park. The vessels soon found that they were being shadowed by RAF reconnaissance aircraft, which came from Malta. Correctly anticipating an attack, they put into Navarino in Greece during the early hours of 28 October, at a time when the Battle of El Alamein was at its peak.

In Navarino, it was decided that the chances of success would be improved if the convoy were split into two parts. At dusk on the same day, *Luisiano* left the port, accompanied by two torpedo boats, her destination having been changed to the more distant but safer port of Benghazi.

The merchant ship *Etiopia* left a few minutes later, accompanied by a torpedo boat, for her original destination of Tobruk. As she was manoeuvring out of the anchorage, she was struck by a torpedo. This was dropped by a Wellington of 69 Squadron, flown by a Canadian, Pilot Officer Harry W. Donkersley. She was not seriously damaged, although she was forced to put back into Navarino for repairs.

Meanwhile, the tanker *Luisiano* continued her journey to Benghazi. Three hours after leaving port, RAF aircraft began to hunt for her with ASV and flares. In the late evening she was hit by a torpedo dropped by another Wellington of 69 Squadron flown by Pilot Officer W.H. Matthews. The unlucky tanker exploded and sank within minutes. Only eight of her crew survived, being picked up by one of the torpedo boats.

It is said that this was the point at which Rommel realised that the Battle of El Alamein was lost. At midnight on 28 October, Bletchley Park picked up a signal sent by him to Kesselring, demanding the immediate despatch of reinforcements for his air units and fuel for his forces. Kesselring ordered the air transports in Crete to carry supplies to North Africa 'by day and night down to the last crew and the last aircraft'. The crews obeyed and many Ju 52s were shot down by the waiting Allied fighters. Nevertheless, the transports did succeed in bringing small quantities of fuel and personnel to the Axis forces.

By 29 October, Bletchley Park learned that fuel stocks for the Panzerarmee were down to less than two days' supply and that serviceable tanks were reduced to 197 Italian and 81 German, about half the number available when the Eighth Army began its offensive.

At this time, Rommel ordered fuel and other supplies to be brought forward by ships and trucks from Benghazi, where stocks had been augmented by the small tanker *Morandi*, which had succeeded in off-loading 300 tons at that distant port. Bletchley Park decrypted signals giving details of a convoy scheduled to leave Benghazi in the afternoon of 30 October, heading along the coast for Tobruk. This consisted of the Italian merchant ship *Tripolino* of 1,464 tons, carrying 440 tons of rations and 318 tons of ammunition, and the German *Ostia* of 359 tons, carrying 57 tons of rations and 52 tons of ammunition. They were escorted by the torpedo boat *Circe*.

The night passed without incident and the Axis convoy came under the umbrella of a strong air escort during the following day. But the aircraft left at dusk and shortly afterwards a series of flares began to light up the convoy. The vessels were being hunted by the ASV Wellingtons of 221 Squadron, the Wellington bombers of 458 (RAAF) Squadron, and the torpedo Wellingtons of 38 Squadron.

The flares became more frequent around midnight and the sailors knew what was in store for them. *Circe* put on speed and began to circle the two supply ships, making smoke. These tactics kept the Wellingtons at bay for about four hours, but then the smoke drifted away from *Tripolino* for a few minutes. Sergeant McNall of 38 Squadron spotted the vessel and approached up-moon, dropping his two torpedoes. There was a colossal explosion and the vessel began to sink. Capitano di Corvetto Stephano Palmas in *Circe* had to make a difficult decision, for his orders were to bring the supplies to Tobruk at all cost. He deliberately steered away from the sinking vessel, changing direction to the north while continuing to make smoke around *Ostia*. He hoped to confuse his attackers, but the relentless Wellingtons followed the vessels and made further attacks, although their torpedoes missed.

The two vessels returned to the position of the sunken *Tripolino* at dawn, but found only one seaman, who was badly wounded. Meanwhile three Beauforts of 47 Squadron had been sent out from Gianaclis to hunt for the remaining supply ship in the early light. One Beaufort, flown by Pilot Officer Frederick J. Pile, spotted the enemy vessels west of Tobruk and made a torpedo run. The two ships opened an intense fire and bracketed the Beaufort, which was hit in the turret and wireless equipment. Pile turned away but then made another attack and released his torpedo at 800 yards. It ran true to the small target and hit *Ostia* in the bows. There was an explosion, followed by an even larger one when the ammunition blew up. She sank immediately, but *Circe* picked up a few survivors and landed them at Tobruk, about thirty-five miles away.

The Axis forces were now in a truly desperate situation. On learning of the destruction of the various supply ships, Rommel considered a general withdrawal, but shortage of fuel hampered this. Then Bletchley Park decrypted signals giving details of another convoy, which had left Brindisi on 30 October. This consisted of two auxiliary naval vessels: *Zara* of 1,976 tons, carrying an unrecorded amount of fuel in containers, together with *Brioni* of 1,987 tons, carrying a cargo which included 255 tons of ammunition. These supplies were intended for the Panzeramee. The two vessels were joined by the torpedo boat *San Martino* near Crete, and set course for Tobruk in the afternoon of 1 November.

Wellingtons made several attacks during the night, but without success. At 1000 hours the following morning, the Italian sailors saw a compact formation of aircraft approaching them at low level, when they were only fifty miles from Tobruk. These were six Beauforts of 39 Squadron, led by Wing Commander Larry Gaine, escorted by seven Beaufighters of 272 Squadron. By this time there was air cover over the convoy: two Me 110s, two Ju 88s and two MC202s. The Beaufighters attacked the enemy aircraft, shooting down a Ju 88 for the loss of one of their number. The crew of the Beaufighter – Pilot Officer A.J. Proctor and Pilot Officer E.A.C. Young – floated in their dinghy for eight days before they were picked up by the British, in an extremely weakened condition.

The Beauforts aimed their torpedoes at the two auxiliary vessels, but two aircraft were shot down. One was flown by Squadron Leader Ken R. Grant, and he and his crew were picked up by the Italians. The four men in the other, flown by Flying Officer Oscar M. Hedley, lost their lives. Three torpedoes were aimed at *Brioni*, but she was so fast and manoeuvrable that she managed to avoid them. *Zara* was not so lucky. She was hit amidships and stopped, giving out a great column of smoke. However, she did not sink immediately and the torpedo boat *San Martino* put a line on board and began to tow her to Tobruk. The auxiliary vessel remained afloat for thirteen hours, slowly nearing her destination, but she gradually settled lower and went down at 2300 hours.

Meanwhile, *Brioni* put on full speed and arrived unescorted at Tobruk at 1430 hours. Her precious cargo was being unloaded when, at 1700 hours, B-24 Liberators of the USAAF appeared unexpectedly over the port. What happened is contained in the Italian report:

> '*Brioni* received direct hits from a bomb and a canister of incendiaries. Soon the ship was like a furnace, inside which the ammunition on board was exploding, as well as the small quantity which had been off-loaded on the quayside. Only a few of the crew were wounded, for they had been able to take refuge in a nearby air-raid shelter.'

With the destruction of *Zara* and *Brioni* went the last faint hopes that the Axis forces had of resisting the onslaught of the Eighth Army. On the evening of that day, 2 November, Rommel sent a message to his headquarters in Berlin:

'The Army will no longer be in a position to prevent a further attempt by strong enemy forces to break through, which may be expected today or tomorrow ... The stocks of ammunition still available are in the front area, while there are no stocks worth mentioning in the rear area. The tiny stocks of fuel do not permit a movement to the rear over great distances. On the single road available, the Army will certainly be attacked day and night by the RAF. In this situation, in spite of heroic resistance and the excellent spirit of the troops, the gradual annihilation of the Army must be faced.'

Hitler's response was to send a directive ordering Rommel not to yield a step and to use every man and weapon available. He exhorted Rommel to 'show no other road to your troops other than the road leading to death or victory'. Rommel, who hitherto had been devoted to his Führer, did his best to obey these instructions for the next day but was then heard to express the opinion that they were crazy. On 4 November he asked Hitler's permission to retreat and began to do so before a reply was received. It is believed that this action marked the beginning of Rommel's fall from grace, leading to his enforced suicide almost two years later.

Most military analysts now seem to agree that it would have been possible for the Eighth Army to encircle and destroy the remaining elements of the Axis forces. But Montgomery acted only on certainties and he feared that his resourceful enemy might still spring a trap. In any event, he knew that Anglo-American forces would begin landing in Algeria four days later and that eventually his enemy would be crushed.

Rommel's retreat was facilitated by the arrival in Tobruk on 3 November of *Etiopia*, carrying aviation fuel. The tanker had been repaired in Navarino and had slipped through the blockade. A few other vessels also arrived at Tobruk, Benghazi and Tripoli within the next few days. The withdrawal became orderly, but the legend of Rommel's invincibility was smashed. The maritime RAF and British Intelligence made a major contribution to the Allied victory. In November 1945, Generalmajor Johann Cramer of the Deutsches Panzerarmee gave his verdict: 'Alamein was lost before it was fought. We did not have the fuel. Vast stocks of fuel and material were lying around in Italy and the Italians were supposed to bring them over, but they could not do it.'

A Messerschmitt Bf 110 of *Zerstoergeschwader 26* in December 1941, probably taken in Sicily. The officer standing in front is *Hauptmann* Hornung, who commanded *4./Kampfgruppe-zbV 400*. (*Archiv Karl Kössler*)

The Norwegian tanker *Thorsheimer* of 9,955 tons, which was taken over by the Germans. After damage from US and FAA aircraft, she was torpedoed and sunk by Beauforts of 39 Squadron from Malta in the evening of 20 February 1943. (*Roger Hayward*)

Leutnant Rolf Schlegel of *Jagdgeschwader 53,* easing himself out of the cockpit of his Messerschmitt Bf 109G-6/Trop 'White 6', at Tunis in 1943. (*Archiv Rick Chapman*)

A Beaufort Mark II in a blast pen at Luqa in Malta, fitted with Vokes air filters above the Wasp engines, twin Vickers .303-in machine guns in the nose and a Yagi aerial under the nose for the Air to Surface Vessel radar. (*Roger Hayward*)

7

FIGHTERS FROM MALTA

The retreat of the Axis forces in Egypt and Libya, coupled with the landing of Anglo–American forces in Algeria under the code name of operation 'Torch', transformed the military situation in North Africa. However, the Axis responded immediately by gaining acceptance from the Vichy French for the use of bases in Tunisia. Supplies began to pour into El Aouina, the main aerodrome for the port of Tunis. New fighters and bombers were flown across the 100 miles which separate Tunisia from Sicily. German troops began to arrive by air at the rate of about 750 a day, for Fliegerkorps II had been able to increase its transport aircraft from about 250 to 750 during the previous few weeks. In addition, supplies were sent by sea to the Tunisian ports of Bizerta, Tunis, Sfax and Sousse, as well as to the Libyan port of Tripoli.

The sustained pursuit of the Axis forces by the Eighth Army resulted in the capture of Tobruk on 13 November 1942, but the port had been almost demolished and could not be used. It was not until 23 January 1943 that Tripoli was entered and the Axis forces were bottled up in Tunisia. Meanwhile the threat to Malta diminished and the air assault petered out, although living conditions remained harsh. Four merchant ships docked at Malta on 20 November 1942, heavily escorted by the Royal Navy and bringing welcome supplies of aviation fuel and ammunition. Food rations continued at little more than starvation level, however, and did not improve until the following January. The 'siege rations' for 227 Squadron at Takali, the fighter base to which the squadron moved on 25 November, were recently described by a former fitter/armourer, Sergeant Fred A. Brinton:

'A typical day would begin with breakfast in the sergeants' mess in a requisitioned hotel on the side of a small and open square on the edge of Rabat. As each senior NCO collected his meal from the serving hatch, his name was deleted from the ration list for that meal. I recall that breakfast consisted of one and a half slices of bread, together with half a sausage cut horizontally, and one cup of tea. Many times we cast quick and surreptitious glances at those sitting with us, wondering if they had a slightly thicker slice of bread or a larger half-sausage than ourselves.

For those prepared to question the weight, a pair of scales was available. I remember them being used – but only once!

'After breakfast we usually walked down to Takali aerodrome and about midday the soup wagon arrived to serve what was laughingly called "cabbage soup" – one small cabbage to about two gallons of water, we calculated! At some time during the day we ate one small square of chocolate issued previously, together with part of a hard "issue" biscuit. But such additions to our daily diet were always eaten in some quiet corner. No one ate such extra delights in front of his fellow airmen!

'On return to the sergeants' mess after work, we ate the last meal of the day. This would consist of another one and a half slices of bread, with perhaps two small sardines, and one cup of tea. To counteract the lack of fresh fruit we were issued with ascorbic acid tablets, containing vitamin C.

'Surprisingly, we remained quite fit on such rations and were always able to service our aircraft. However, we were always hungry and often used to describe the wonderful meals we would eat when the war was over. As well as guarding our own screwdriver, pliers and a spanner or two, we always took our own tin mugs wherever we went, as well as our knives and forks. Quite often, we used a knife and fork to help remove and replace split pins when servicing our aircraft. In spite of this, morale was high and there was always someone on hand to make the required effort and ensure that the work was completed.

'With darkness at the end of the day, we went to bed. There was no lighting, so bed was the obvious place. However, we contrived to make our own wick-type lamps, based on a round cigarette tin. These gave some light, even though there was a lot of smoke, and were better than nothing.

'On a day off we would walk to Valetta, perhaps getting a lift on the way. Once there, we could obtain a small plate of diced beetroot for fourpence at the Royal Navy Club. Big eats indeed! However, we did have unlimited supplies of cold and clear water at the turn of a tap. After all our days in the desert and our way of life in the previous few months, this was our idea of heaven!'

Fred Brinton, who was a twenty-two-year-old sergeant at the time, had volunteered for service in the Middle East when an armament instructor in the relatively comfortable circumstances of the Empire Air Training Scheme in Southern Rhodesia, but he never regretted his decision. It would have been unlike the RAF if the ground crews had not grumbled, frequently and in very colourful terms, but most were intensely proud of the work they were doing. Their resolution never faltered. To them, the Beaufighters were 'our aircraft', not 'the aircraft'.

Wing Commander Cedric A. Masterman had taken over command of 227 Squadron on 12 October 1942, but the destruction of so many

Beaufighters in combat or in the 'mini-blitz' of that month had almost eliminated operational flying for a short while. But new crews and new aircraft soon arrived in Egypt and these were flown out to Malta on 7 November. None of these new crews had had any operational experience, but a few crews from the old 227 Squadron were able to give them some advice. In the same month, Beaufighters of 272 Squadron also arrived in strength at Takali.

Both squadrons had been equipped with the new Beaufighter Mark VIC. This was fitted with a dihedral tailplane instead of the straight tailplane of the Mark IC and was thus more stable in flight although somewhat less manoeuvrable. The engines were more powerful, 1,670hp Hercules VIs or XVIs replacing the 1,425hp Hercules IIIs, while a rearward-firing .303 inch machine gun was provided in the navigator's cupola.

The main task of these two Beaufighter squadrons in Malta was to intercept the Axis transports flying between Sicily and Tunisia. In addition, the Beauforts of 39 Squadron had been brought up to full strength and had flown back to Malta, being based once again at Luqa. Their main task was to hold themselves in readiness to attack the Italian Fleet, if the capital ships left their ports to intercept the relief convoys approaching Malta.

Before taking up command of 227 Squadron, at the age of twenty-eight, Wing Commander Cedric Masterman had had an unusual and varied career in the RAF. He had qualified as a pilot with a short-service commission in March 1935 at Digby in Lincolnshire, where he trained in Avro Tutors and Hawker Harts. Then he volunteered for an army co-operation course at Old Sarum, followed by service in India. He was posted to Ambala in September 1935, from where he flew Hawker Audaxes over the North-West Frontier. However, he then decided to take an engineering course, at Henlow in Bedfordshire, which gained for him a permanent commission.

By October 1939, Masterman was flying Westland Lysanders with 225 Squadron at Odiham in Hampshire. Soon afterwards, he went up to Dyce, near Aberdeen, from where it was intended that he would fly a Lysander to Finland and then take part in the war against the invading Russians. But Sweden refused to allow the aircraft to fly over their territory and Masterman returned to his squadron. When Norway was invaded by Germany, he went over with the British forces to help build airfields, and was eventually brought back to Britain by the Royal Navy. He was awarded an OBE in the New Year's Honours List.

Back in 225 Squadron, which by then was based at Tilshead in Wiltshire, he was promoted to squadron leader and engaged on reconnoitring the build-up of German invasion barges in the Channel ports. Then followed a stint with 13 Squadron at Hooton Park in

Cheshire, helping to rebuild the squadron after its Lysanders had been severely mauled in France. By the spring of 1941 he was up at Loch Fyne in Argyllshire, preparing with the RAF Commandos of 110 Force to invade the Azores, in order to provide a refuelling base for ferrying aircraft across the Atlantic. But this matter was settled by negotiation with Portugal, and the enterprise was cancelled.

He then converted to Spitfires and was posted to 72 Squadron at Gravesend, eventually taking over command of the squadron. On completion of his operational tour, he was appointed as a wing commander to lead a squadron of Spitfires flown to Malta on 20 April 1942 from the US carrier *Wasp*. He flew out in a Catalina via Lisbon, only to find that his new command did not exist, since most of the Spitfires had been destroyed. Instead, he was appointed as air adviser to the governor of Malta, Lord Gort, and remained in that capacity until the command of 227 Squadron became available. He then converted rapidly on to Beaufighters, and Pilot Officer Gordon Burnside became his navigator in 227 Squadron.

The first major attack by the new Beaufighters from Malta occurred on 12 November when Squadron Leader Anthony Watson, the commanding officer of 272 Squadron, led six aircraft to the area of Pantelleria. Here they encountered six SM75 tri-motored transports and destroyed all of them, four going down in flames.

A much larger enemy formation was intercepted the following day, when Masterman led a section of four Beaufighters of 227 Squadron, with Dallas Schmidt leading four more. The eight aircraft ran into mist near the Tunisian coast and became somewhat dispersed. When the weather cleared, Schmidt found himself near the Tunisian coast and alongside a South African pilot from Masterman's section, Lieutenant J. Clements. They spotted a Do 24 flying boat and promptly shot it down, watching it crash into the sea. As Schmidt turned away, he saw about sixteen Ju 52s in three vics, and attacked immediately. His first burst damaged one of the transports and a few seconds later he destroyed another. Continuing his attacks, he shot down another and damaged yet one more. But three more vics of enemy transports appeared, consisting of about thirty tri-motored SM 81s. Masterman shot down one of these Italian aircraft, while Clements and a New Zealander, Sergeant Ford J. Franklin, disposed of two more. Finally, Masterman and Sergeant B. Megone shared in the destruction of another SM 81, making the total score six transports shot down, apart from those which were damaged.

The German and Italian transports were not without defences. In addition to their normal gun positions, troops lined the windows of the fuselages, firing automatic weapons. Pilot Officer R. Wills was hit in the ankle but his navigator, Pilot Officer N. Lewis, took over the controls and brought the aircraft back to Luqa, where Wills managed to land it safely. Another Beaufighter went down into the sea on the return journey. It was flown by a Canadian pilot, Sergeant John M. Stephen, and he and his RAF navigator, Sergeant Samuel H. Whear, lost their lives.

Schmidt's Beaufighter was badly hit. The port engine burst into flames but he managed to climb gradually to about 400 feet, skidding to starboard to prevent the flames spreading, while putting the fire precautions into effect. He switched off the port engine and the fire burned out in about ten minutes. But the Beaufighter was still in great danger. Two Me 109s flew near, as did three Ju 88s, but fortunately none attacked. Schmidt cleared the Tunisian coast and headed his machine towards the islands of Pantelleria and Linosa. It was nearly dusk when he arrived at Malta but he managed to make a forced landing at Luqa without injury to himself or his navigator, Sergeant Andrew Campbell. They counted about thirty bullet holes in the machine during the following day and strung threads through those in the pilot's cockpit. They could not understand how they had all missed Schmidt's body.

On the same day as this air combat, Watson led seven Beaufighters of 272 Squadron on a strafing attack against El Aouina in Tunisia. They met an unlucky He 115 floatplane on the way out, and Flying Officer R. Rankin shot it down into the sea, where it burst into flames. When they reached the aerodrome they were met by a signal rocket followed by an intense barrage of flak. Watson led the first section of four Beaufighters, which destroyed several Ju 52s on the ground; his aircraft was hit by flak and he force-landed on a beach several miles away, while Sergeant N. Russell silenced the gun post which had caused the damage. In the second section, Flight Lieutenant Aubrey N. Bale went in twice but was then seen being chased by three fighters; he and his navigator, Flight Sergeant Robert H. Soutter, lost their lives. But Watson and his navigator, Sergeant Cyril N. Cutting, managed to evade capture and reach Allied lines. They returned to their squadron on 30 November.

An attack by eight Beaufighters of 227 Squadron on 14 November was not successful. Masterman led the formation against the enemy aerodrome and seaplane base at Bizerta, where they flew over four warships and were met by a swarm of single-engined fighters. The Beaufighters tried to make for cloud cover but one was shot down; Sergeant John E. Hughes and Sergeant Cecil G. Candler were killed. Then another Beaufighter went down and the Canadian pilot, Flight Lieutenant David M. Witherspoon, was killed, together with his RAF navigator, Pilot Officer Robert B. Pearson. An American pilot in the RCAF, Pilot Officer Carl L. Johnson, shot down an Me 109, which was no mean achievement in a Beaufighter. He followed this by disposing of a Ju 88. On the way back, Masterman and Clements shot down an SM 82. Masterman saw a man in the water after this attack and dropped a dinghy near him; like many RAF airmen who frequently risked their own lives, he believed that the war should be fought with as much chivalry as possible.

On 20 November, 227 Squadron went out in strength, with three sections of four Beaufighters apiece. The first section, led by Masterman, took off at 0245 hours and met two enemy aircraft at dawn, shooting down both. Masterman and Clements, who each destroyed an aircraft, thought they were Ju 88s, but a post-war examination revealed that they were twin-engined Ca 314s.

The second section took off for a patrol along the Tunisian coast. It was led by Carl Johnson, who by then had been promoted to flight lieutenant. All the Beaufighters in the squadron had been fitted up with bomb racks and one aircraft, flown by Pilot Officer Tom St B. Freer, was carrying two 250 lb bombs. They found a small merchant vessel after less than an hour, near Pantelleria, and attacked. Freer claimed a hit with one bomb and the vessel, which was hit repeatedly by cannon shells and machine gun fire, was left on fire and listing.

At 1455 hours, Wing Commander Larry Gaine led three Beauforts of 39 Squadron to finish off the vessel, escorted by three Beaufighters of 272 Squadron. They came across the ship, which by then was well down by the stern. The Beaufighters did not attack, since there was no sign of flak, but the Beauforts dropped their torpedoes. A plume of black smoke was seen to rise from the vessel.

The RAF records, though accurate, do not convey the full horror of the strike on this vessel, although more graphic details can be found in the Italian naval history. She was an auxiliary of the Italian Navy, the steamship *Lago Tana* of 785 tons, with a crew of ninety commanded by Tenente di Vascello C. Corrado Shinko. She had left Trapani two days before, carrying millitary supplies and bound for Tripoli. In addition, she was carrying 127 Italian soldiers, who were to disembark en route at the island of Lampedusa, where they were to reinforce the garrison. It is evident that the Italians hoped that she would slip through unnoticed, but they were unaware of the effectiveness of British Intelligence. The Italian account includes the following:

'She left the island of Pantelleria, where she had berthed from 1500 hours on 19 November to 0800 hours on 20 November, bound for Lampedusa. At 1640 hours one of our reconnaissance aircraft reported sighting a ship, in flames and listing, west of Lampedusa. A motor-torpedo boat and the hospital recovery ship *Capri* were sent immediately from Pantelleria to this position. The latter picked up only two survivors, but the motor-torpedo boat did not find anyone.

'Apart from these two survivors, everyone on board lost their lives. During the following days, fifty-five bodies were recovered from the sea or washed up on the coast of Lampedusa by currents. Only sixteen of these were recognisable, including the body of Tenente di Vascello Shinko.

'The survivors stated that *Lago Tana* had been sighted by an enemy reconnaissance aircraft two hours after leaving Pantelleria. Between 1205 and 1245 hours she had been attacked with bombs and gunfire by eight four-engined aircraft. Only one defensive machine gun was brought to bear in time. The ship was soon reduced to a desperate state and the captain ordered her to be abandoned. But the lifeboats were holed by enemy gunfire while they were being lowered into the water, and they sank. The personnel, most of whom were wounded, were left to the mercy of the sea. At 1600 hours a new air attack delivered the *coup de grâce* to the ship, which sank after sunset.'

The two survivors were mistaken in their identification of 'four-engined' aircraft as well as the numbers involved. Possibly they saw the bombs outboard of the engines on Freer's Beaufighter and mistook them for engines. It is probable that each Beaufighter made two runs over the target, giving the impression of eight aircraft. But the report illustrates the terrible effect of maritime strike aircraft against a military target which was only weakly defended.

The third attack delivered by 227 Squadron on 20 November was led by Dallas Schmidt. It consisted of another sweep along the Tunisian coast, which the Beaufighter crews had dubbed 'Messerschmitt Alley'. Two aircraft were in the bomber role, including Schmidt, with two as fighter cover. They found a convoy which had left Bizerta four hours previously, bound for Palermo. There were two merchant ships – *Puccini* of 2,422 tons and *Viminale* of 8,657 tons escorted by the torpedo boats *Groppo* and *Perseo*.

One of the pilots in the fighter section was a new sergeant who bore the impressive name of Casimir Marmaduke de Bounevialle, an Englishman of distant French descent. This name was too much for his RAF friends, who abbreviated it to 'Cas'. He was twenty-nine years of age and, in 1941, had trained on Harvards and Ansons in Southern Rhodesia, later flying Oxfords at the Advanced Flying Unit at South Cerney in Gloucestershire. After OTU at Catfoss, where he had converted on to Blenheims and Beaufighters, he travelled on a troop-ship to Lagos, from where he was flown to Cairo in an Armstrong Whitworth Ensign, a four-engined airliner belonging to BOAC. In September 1942 he had been a passenger in a Dakota ordered to fly to Malta, but the aircraft crashed on take-off. When he finally arrived in 227 Squadron his navigator, Sergeant Jim Scott, went down with sandfly fever. He was replaced by Sergeant Ralph E. Webb on this sortie.

Schmidt led the four Beaufighters into the attack. They spotted an enemy aircraft, which did not try to interfere with them, as well as a submarine, but Schmidt concentrated on *Viminale*. His cannon shells exploded along the deck and started a small fire aft of the funnel, but his two bombs were near misses. Cas went in second, noting that the two merchant ships seemed high out of the water and therefore unloaded. His method was to fire a short burst from about 1,000 yards as a ranging shot, then a series of short squirts while at the closing speed of about 100 yards a second. He watched the bullets and shells travel along the superstructure of *Viminale*.

The four cannons in the Beaufighter VIC were belt-fed, whereas in the old Beaufighter IC the ammunition drums contained only about sixty rounds and required replacement during combat by the navigator, if there was sufficient time. The cannons were far more prone to stoppages than the machine guns, for a variety of reasons. The gas escape holes became blocked up and the armourers at Malta did not have the drills to keep them clean. The early belt-fed mechanism was also prone to jamming. The compression return springs in the cannons required very fine adjustment, while the chutes for the empty shell cases were not long enough to accept them cleanly. All the armourers could do was improvise in attempts to rectify the problems.

Following Cas, the other two Beaufighters scored hits with gunfire, but the other pair of bombs also overshot. The Italians seemed to have been taken by surprise – or else their ammunition did not contain tracer – for the pilots did not see any return fire. The records show that *Viminale* suffered damage to her upperworks, but the convoy continued and reached Palermo without further incidents.

The following day, Masterman led twelve Beaufighters of 227 Squadron, including Schmidt and de Bounevialle, on a sortie escorting six Beauforts of 39 Squadron in a sweep off Bizerta. The Beauforts were led by an Australian flight commander, Squadron Leader Colin G. Milson, from Winton in Queensland. For once they saw nothing, although they flew over Tunisia at one stage and even became separated in the valleys. There were no ships and no enemy aircraft, perhaps because the latter were fully engaged over the front lines on that day. It was an eerie experience to fly unchallenged over enemy territory, but the whole formation returned safely to Luqa.

On 22 November the new commanding officer of 272 Squadron, Wing Commander John K. Buchanan, led another Beaufighter flown by a Belgian pilot, Flying Officer C.T.H. Delcour, on a sweep to the Tunisian coast. They came across a Cant Z506B floatplane and shot it down into the sea. Before losing his life in 1944, Buchanan became one of the highest-scoring pilots of the Allied air forces in the Mediterranean. On the same day, Johnson led four Beaufighters of 227 Squadron

111

on a shipping strike, but they found no vessels. Instead, they met two unfortunate Ju 52s and Johnson shot down both of them in less than a minute.

The pace of the sorties did not slacken. The next day, Schmidt led four Beaufighters of 227 Squadron on a fighter escort with four Beaufighters of 39 Squadron, led by Wing Commander Larry Gaine. Their orders were to intercept a convoy off Sousse in Tunisia, which was believed to be travelling south. The weather was extremely bad, with thick clouds and electrical storms. At one stage, Schmidt saw three Me 109s only about twenty yards in front of him, but apparently the German pilots did not spot the RAF formation, for no combat took place. When they came out of the worst of the weather, they came across a merchant vessel and an escort. These were *Numidia* of 5,339 tons escorted by the torpedo boat *Ardito*, which had left Tripoli in the early morning of the previous day, headed for Palermo.

Larry Gaine decided not to attack, for he could see that the convoy was travelling north and he thought that it might be carrying Allied PoWs. But Flight Lieutenant Carl Johnson in one of the Beaufighters headed for the torpedo boat. His gunfire raked along the deck, causing considerable damage as well as killing two sailors and wounding eleven. But return fire hit the American's aircraft, which crashed into the sea. Carl Johnson and his navigator, Sergeant Ralph E. Webb, lost their lives; both were nearing the end of their operational tours.

Meanwhile Schmidt spotted an aircraft which he thought was a Ju 52, flying north. He made a beam attack which ended up as a quarter attack, firing a couple of two-second bursts. The transport broke up in the air and the pieces went down burning. According to *Ardito* this was an Italian aircraft, probably a tri-motored SM75. After this attack, the torpedo boat ordered *Numidia* to take shelter in Sousse, while the warship put on full speed and headed for Trapani in Sicily, where she landed her dead and wounded.

In the early hours of 24 November, five Beaufighters of 227 Squadron made a night bombing raid near Palermo, as a diversion for a heavy bomber raid on the port. Once again the weather proved most unpleasant, the trip made even more difficult for the crews since they were flying at the unaccustomed altitude of about 8,000 feet. There were clouds and electrical storms, causing both engines in Schmidt's Beaufighter to ice up. He glided down and they did not start up again until he was down to 2,000 feet.

The results of the bombing could not be seen, but it was on this night that the South African, Lieutenant J. Clements, failed to return. It was learnt later that he and his navigator, Pilot Officer K. Pollard, had been taken prisoner. This event had a curious consequence. Clements had been carrying Masterman's wristwatch, for this was to have been the last operational flight of his tour and he was expected to take it to Egypt for repair. The Italian police took the watch off him, but returned it with his other effects after the war. By this time Masterman was serving in Singapore and Clements sent the watch to him. Unfortunately, this much-travelled wristwatch was stolen from Masterman only a fortnight later.

On 25 November, on the day when 227 Squadron moved from Luqa to Takali, Masterman led eight Beaufighters on an attack against a small but highly important convoy. This consisted of the ammunition ship *Algerino* of 1,371 tons and two F-boats, escorted by the submarine chaser *Eso*. The convoy had left Tripoli the previous evening, sailing east along the coast to the little port of Beurat in Libya, carrying ammuntion and other supplies to Rommel's front line with the Eighth Army. Four of the Beaufighters were carrying two 500 lb bombs apiece, while the others were in the anti-flak role.

The submarine chaser opened up with her main armament as well as flak, but her fire seemed to be partly suppressed by the Beaufighters. Cas de Bounevialle could not see any return fire as he closed to about 200 yards before breaking away. Nevertheless a Beaufighter flown by a Canadian, Flying Officer J.A. 'Red' Rae, was hit by shrapnel, although the pilot managed to fly back and make a forced landing at Takali. Schmidt thought he scored a direct hit with a bomb on the bow of the merchant ship, but the Italian records show that one bomb missed narrowly and exploded underwater. This sprang some of the ship's plates so badly that the pumps could not cope with the inrush of water. The ammunition ship began to settle lower, but *Eso* put a line aboard and began to tow her to the coast. This manoeuvre was very nearly successful, for the two vessels were only about 150 yards from the shore when *Algerino* went down, an hour after the attack. All her sailors were rescued, while all the Beaufighters returned to Takali.

The next day was the turn of 272 Squadron, Beaufighters taking off in pairs for sweeps over the Gulf of Tripoli. Buchanan found a Ju 52 near Pantelleria and got on to its tail. A single long burst put the starboard engine on fire, whereupon it crashed into the sea and blew up.

On 27 November, Buchanan led four Beaufighters of 272 Squadron and found two Me 110s, damaging one. He shot down an SM79 on the following day. On the following day, Schmidt led Tom Freer of 227 Squadron on another patrol along the Tunisian coast, where they found two Fiat CR42s. These single-engined biplanes were slow but highly manoeuvrable, somewhat similar to the RAF's Gloster Gladiators. A dogfight ensued and Schmidt believed that he had shot down one of the Italian machines, but post-war records show that it returned to base in spite of severe damage. The pilot of the CR42 believed that he had damaged a Beaufighter, but both RAF aircraft returned unharmed.

On 29 November, Masterman led three Beaufighters of 227 Squadron, including Schmidt, on another sweep along the Tunisian coast. They found and strafed a small vessel, leaving it smoking. There is no record of this episode in the Italian naval history, but perhaps it was considered insufficiently important to be included.

On the same day, Cas de Bounevialle was one of two pilots who went out on another sweep, strafing trucks on the coast road near Sirte in Libya. As a newcomer to the 227 Squadron, he was often given one of the oldest aircraft, and on this occasion was in a Beaufighter Mark IC. He had used up all the cannon shells in his drums when he found himself unexpectedly over the aerodrome at Sirte. Reluctant to miss the opportunity, he attacked a Ju 52 on the ground with his machine guns. This was very nearly his undoing, for return fire hit his Beaufighter in a wing and the tail, and one wheel of his undercarriage dropped down. On return to Malta in that somewhat forlorn state, he made a successful belly landing at Luqa, which had a longer runway than Takali.

Another anti-shipping attack took place on 5 December when Masterman led four Beaufighters of 227 Squadron, including de Bounevialle, on a sweep near the Kerkennah Islands. They found a convoy which had left Tripoli at 1230 hours the day before, bound for Naples. It consisted of the merchant ship *Col di Lana* of 5,891 tons, escorted by the torpedo boat *Aretusa* and a German motor-torpedo boat. The merchant ship was carrying a mixed cargo of material being evacuated from Tripoli ahead of the advancing Eighth Army. More importantly, she had on board 2,000 British PoWs, who were being taken to Italy before they could be rescued by the Eighth Army. In the early stage of their journey, these vessels were accompanied by another torpedo boat, *San Martino*.

Four hours after leaving Tripoli the captain of *Aretusa*, Capitano di Corvetto Roberto Guidotti, spotted a bright red flare, which he thought might have been a distress signal from some downed airmen. Twenty minutes later, the torpedo boat rescued two British airmen from their rubber dinghy, although the Italian records do not give their names. Shortly after this episode, *San Martino* left the convoy for other duties, and the remaining two vessels sailed on throughout the night.

At 1145 hours the following day, the Italian sailors spotted an RAF reconnaissance aircraft which was shadowing the vessels from a distance. *Aretusa* fired three salvoes in its direction, to alert the Axis air escorts. The RAF aircraft flew off, but the Italians assumed that an air attack would follow. They were correct.

Masterman's formation caught up with the three vessels at 1440 hours. The pilots deliberately avoided the merchant ship and pressed home an attack against the torpedo boat. Cas de Bounevialle saw two escorting aircraft, which appeared to be a Ju 88 and a Me 110, drop their overload tanks and prudently fly off. He hit the bridge of the torpedo boat with cannon shells and bullets, starting a fire and causing a small explosion.

The report of *Aretusa* states that the Beaufighters came in 'at the height of a boa constrictor', making ten passes in all in the face of intense flak. About twenty cannon shells from the attackers caused considerable damage. The bridge was hit, the steering gear was put out of action, the R/T was knocked out, a supply of ammunition exploded, and the crew suffered eighteen casualties. Doubtless the two RAF men were imprisoned below, but they are likely to have guessed the reason for the racket. The four Beaufighters returned safely from the attack.

After about an hour, *Aretusa* managed to repair her steering gear and got under way once more, anticipating further trouble. This came in an unexpected form. When it was dusk, at 1745 hours, a twin-engined aircraft was seen approaching from dead ahead, and a burst of gunfire was directed towards it. The aircraft continued to fly towards the torpedo boat and met a well-directed barrage, which sent it down into the sea. The torpedo boat picked up the pilot, to discover that he was a dying German airman. The captain reported that the German aircraft had not approached the convoy in the recognised manner.

The torpedo boat stopped briefly at Pantelleria before dawn to disembark nine men who were seriously wounded. She then continued with *Col di Lana* to Trapani, where she left two dead, seven less seriously wounded, and the two RAF men. After six hours, *Aretusa* and *Col di Lana* continued to Naples, without further incident. It is not known whether the 2,000 British PoWs were able to witness the attack on the torpedo boat but, if they did, it must have afforded them grim satisfaction.

In the early morning of 8 December, Schmidt led three Beaufighters of 227 Squadron on an anti-shipping patrol, the other two aircraft being flown by Cas de Bounevialle and a Kenyan in the RAF, Pilot Officer J.R. 'Red' Modera. To the south of Lampedusa, the Beau-fighters ran head-on into a formation of about fifty tri-motored transports, flying low. Schmidt jettisoned his bombs immediately and led the other two into the attack. He shot down a Ju 52 from about 1,000 yards and then damaged another as the gap closed. The German aircraft seemed to be trying to force him into the sea but he flew underneath them at about fifty feet, to be met by five Me 110s and a Ju 88 on the other side. Nevertheless, he turned and shot down another Ju 52, but an Me 110 got on to his tail and put his starboard engine out of action. One of the shells knocked the rearward-firing Vickers K gun off its mount, but Sergeant Andy Campbell picked it up and began firing it like a rifle at the Me 110, which broke away from the combat.

Cas de Bounevialle picked on three enemy machines which he thought were transport stragglers, but they proved to be two of the Me 110s with only one Ju 52. He attacked the transport from head-on and sent it down with his second burst. He did not see the result but his navigator, Sergeant L. Jim Scott, called out: 'He's hit the sea. He's burning!' Cas then attacked the Me 110 which was on Schmidt's tail. His cannon shells were exhausted but he could see tracer from his machine guns all round the German aircraft. Modera was able to claim one Ju 52 as a 'probable' while his navigator, Pilot Officer N.K. Hodge, damaged two more with his Vickers gun. It was a most satisfactory result against such heavy odds but, once again, Schmidt limped home to Malta on one engine.

There was a similar encounter the following morning when four Beaufighters of 272 Squadron, led by Buchanan, flew head-on into about thirty-five Ju 52s escorted by two Ju 88s and two Me 110s. Buchanan knocked pieces off one Ju 52 but was attacked by an Me 110 which damaged his Beaufighter. Undeterred, he damaged another Ju 52 and was then hit again, this time by the Ju 88s. Two other Beaufighter pilots sent two Ju 52s down in flames and damaged another. Before the RAF pilots flew off, with cannon shells used up, they saw the two Ju 88s collide in mid-air and crash into the sea.

On 10 December three Beaufighters of 227 Squadron took off to escort a convoy approaching Malta. During the day, three BV222 flying boats were seen. These were large machines, each with six engines and heavily armed, capable of carrying over a hundred troops with full equipment. Flight Lieutenant J.A. 'Red' Rae shot one of these flying boats into the sea and then damaged another, his own machine being damaged by return fire. An Australian pilot, Sergeant A.J. Phillips, also damaged one of these flying boats. He then attacked an F-W200 Kondor, a four-engined bomber used mainly for anti-shipping work, and claimed this as a 'probable'. But the third Beaufighter failed to return. It was flown by Sergeant Pat G.F. Day, with Sergeant Francis W. Featherstone as navigator, and both men lost their lives.

In the early afternoon of 11 December, Buchanan led six Beaufighters of 272 Squadron on a sweep looking for air transports, accompanied by eight Spitfire Vs of 249 Squadron. They found about thirty Ju 52s escorted by three Me 109s and two Ju 88s. The Spitfires shot down all five escorts and then attacked the transports, shooting down one and damaging three more. Meanwhile, the Beaufighters shot down five Ju 52s and damaged several more, for the loss of one of their number. The Australian pilot, Sergeant Charles G.D. Hains lost his life, as did his RAF navigator, Sergeant Dennys C. Lawton.

This intense pace continued, except on those days when unfavourable weather prevented flying. On 12 December two Beaufighters of 272 Squadron went out with two of 227 Squadron. Squadron Leader R. Rankin of 272 Squadron shared in the destruction of a Ju 88 with Pilot Officer Tom Freer of 227 Squadron, the crew being seen to get into their dinghy. On the following day Buchanan shared in the destruction of another Ju 88 with two other pilots of 272 Squadron.

On 15 December, Schmidt led three Beaufighters of 227 Squadron on a sweep to the west, accompanied by five Spitfire Vs of 126 Squadron. They saw nothing for several hours but on their way home, when near Lampedusa, they ran into a formation of about fifteen Ju 52s escorted by about the same number of single-engined fighters. The Spitfires climbed to tackle the enemy fighters, while the Beaufighters tore into the transports at low level. There was a general mêlée and at one stage Schmidt was pouring shells into a Ju 52 while three fighters were on his tail. The Ju 52 went down and then Schmidt damaged two more. Almost inevitably, his port engine was put out of action, this time by the fighters. Pilot Officer Modera also shot down a Ju 52 and damaged two more, while Sergeant Franklin accounted for another and damaged two others. The navigator in Modera's Beaufighter, Pilot Officer Hodges, who always fired his Vickers gun with enthusiasm, shot down another Ju 52. The Spitfires managed to deter the fighters, which were a combination of Me 109s and MC200s. All the RAF aircraft returned home, although Schmidt made his characteristic arrival at Malta on one engine.

Masterman was awarded a DFC on the same day. He led three Beaufighters on another offensive patrol two days later but found no enemy aircraft. However, they spotted an RAF man floating in his Mae West and Masterman dropped a dinghy. The man was picked up by the RAF's air-sea rescue HSL126 and brought into Kalafrana Bay in Malta.

Four Beaufighters of 227 Squadron were sent out in the early morning of 18 December to escort another convoy approaching Malta. The cruiser in command kept the four crews busy for a couple of hours without result but then vectored them on to four SM82s. Schmidt and the New Zealander, Sergeant Ford Franklin, tackled these. Three of the Italian aircraft were hit by Schmidt's fire but none seemed to go down, but then he saw Franklin's machine smoking and descending. The Beaufighter hit the sea and Schmidt saw one man get out. He circled and dropped one of the K-type pilot's dinghies, watching the man clamber into it. Then he saw that one of the SM82s was also in the water, still afloat, and he counted fourteen men sitting on the wings. He watched the RAF men paddle over to them, but they pushed him away. The precise outcome of this drama is not known, but both Franklin and his navigator, Pilot Officer Colin C. MacColl, lost their lives.

On the same day, Buchanan went out with another Beaufighter of 272 Squadron, accompanied by four Spitfires of 249 Squadron. They met a Do 24 and a Ju 88, and the Spitfires made short work of the flying boat. But the other Beaufighter was shot down while attacking the Ju 88. The Belgian pilot, Sergeant Henri F.M. Pien, and his RAF navigator, Flight Sergeant Ronald W. Lane, lost their lives. Buchanan and two of the Spitfire pilots then shared in the destruction of the Ju 88.

The following day, two Beaufighters of 227 Squadron met three He 111s escorting three Ju 52s, flying south. Pilot Officer Tom Freer accounted for one He 111 and shared with Sergeant H.M. Shattky in the destruction of another, but both Beaufighters were damaged and one crashed on landing.

In the afternoon of 23 December, Schmidt landed after an uneventful sortie and was ordered to take off again, leading 'Red' Modera and Cas de Bounevialle on a shipping strike, with two Spitfires of 126 Squadron. Schmidt's Beaufighter was fitted with two 500lb bombs. The formation headed through rain and low cloud to the Tunisian coast, where they had been told they would find an unescorted vessel. Instead, they found a merchant ship of about 1,500 tons escorted by what appeared to be a destroyer, headed towards the port of Sousse and about ten miles away from safety. Five Ju 88s circled overhead.

Cas went in first, firing his cannons and machine guns at the merchant ship. Red Modera tackled the escort vessel but was damaged by return fire. Schmidt also strafed the merchant ship and dropped his bombs, one of which appeared to hit near the funnel. As he cleared the ship he saw that the Ju 88s were waiting to pounce on him. He decided to make another circuit and gave the merchant ship another long squirt. Then the Spitfires dived down from high level, shooting down one of the Ju 88s and damaging two more. All the RAF aircraft returned safely.

There is no record of this attack in the Italian history but it coincides exactly in time and place with the merchant ship *Anna Maria* of 1,250 tons, which had left Palermo at 1630 hours the previous day, escorted by the torpedo boat *Fortunale* and headed for Sousse. The sea was so rough that they were delayed overnight in Pantelleria. They left this port and arrived in Sousse about an hour and a half after the RAF's recorded time of the attack.

The last operational flight made by Dallas Schmidt and Andy Campbell in 227 Squadron took place on Christmas Day 1942, and it proved a fitting end to a very eventful operational tour. Schmidt and Cas de Bounevialle took off at 0710 hours, escorted by four Spitfires of 126 Squadron, to attack a convoy of F-boats off the Tunisian coast. At

0830 hours they spotted two F-boats and two schooners heading south towards the front line of the Axis forces.

After circling for a short while, Cas heard Schmidt call over the R/T: 'OK, Cas, let's have a quick one at them!' Cas followed his leader into the attack and he had a fairly clear run, for both F-boats opened up on Schmidt. He saw his target covered in smoke from the explosions of his cannon shells and then heard a call from Scott in the rear of his Beaufighter: 'Schmidty's sunk his – it's up on end!' Meanwhile the Spitfires remained at higher level, the pilots watching the proceedings with great interest.

Cas called Schmidt on the R/T but could not make out his reply. Then a Spitfire pilot broke in: 'He says he's just about flying, but no more.' In fact Schmidt's Beaufighter had been hit three times, just below his feet. The controls to the elevators, rudder and trims had been severed. Schmidt was heading straight for the Tunisian coast, skimming above the sea at about twenty feet. He flew over several more F-boats while trying to turn on his ailerons and climb. The barges poured fire at him but missed completely. He crossed the coast at about forty feet and eventually managed to turn to starboard by about fifty degrees, heading back towards Malta. All the time, he was trying to climb, for he knew it was impossible to land a machine in that condition and that they would have to bale out. With the throttle wide open, he managed to climb to about 7,000 feet, but then entered cloud. All the instruments were unserviceable and, with almost no controls, he came out of the cloud in an inverted dive. Somehow, he managed to right the machine and point it again in the direction of Malta.

All this time the engines were behaving perfectly. The two men discovered that if Andy Campbell moved position within the fuselage, this helped put the Beaufighter in an attitude for climbing. They went up again, gradually and in a series of jerks. But then the Beaufighter went into another dive. Schmidt thought that it was uncontrollable and ordered Campbell to bale out. The navigator, who had already clipped on his parachute pack, pulled the lanyard of the escape hatch in the bottom of his compartment and dived through. He left behind his K-type dinghy but was wearing his Mae West lifejacket. They were about fifty-five miles from Malta.

After Campbell baled out, the aircraft straightened itself out un-expectedly and Schmidt discovered that it climbed when he opened the throttles fully and dived when he throttled back. With a series of jerks and lurches, he climbed to 17,000 feet and saw the island of Malta. When he was directly over the island, he yanked at the lanyard which opened the escape hatch in the floor behind his seat, and pushed himself backwards through the opening. His parachute opened and he began to float down to safety.

119

Left to its own devices, the Beaufighter began a remarkable display of aerobatics. It looped and rolled, and then circled Schmidt's descending body, skimming dangerously close on three occasions. Several airmen on the ground watched these curious antics. One of these was the Bermudan pilot in 39 Squadron, Hugh Watlington. He and his friends decided that the descending parachutist was a navigator who had wisely decided to bale out after his pilot had gone crazy. But Schmidt landed without injury. His parachute descent had lasted about ten minutes and the Beaufighter crashed at the same time he landed, exploding and burning out. Schmidt pulled out the peaked cap which he kept tucked into his jacket, clapped it on his head, smartened himself up, and made his way back to Takali.

Of course, Schmidt was intensely worried about the fate of Andy Campbell, alone in the sea and far from home. But meanwhile the indefatigable navigator was busy swimming in the direction of Malta. He had a signal light in his Mae West and, when a searching Swordfish approached him after about two and a half hours, fired it to attract attention. The Swordfish dropped a dinghy and High Speed Launch 100 came out from Malta.

Christmas celebrations were in progress in the RAF messes. The atmosphere among the officers of 227 Squadron became even more jubilant when they heard that Campbell had been picked up. They trooped over the Kalafrana Bay, the home of the rescue launch, to welcome him back. As HSL100 appeared in the distance, one of the navigators, Pilot Officer H.J. 'Pop' Lewis, announced to the others: 'I must be the first to wish Andy a Merry Christmas!' Solemnly handing his wallet and cap to a friend, he dived fully clothed off the jetty and began to swim towards the launch. It picked him up and brought both navigators into Kalafrana.

On 29 December, immediate awards were made to Andrew Campbell, who received a DFM, and to Dallas Schmidt, who received a bar to his DFC. It was the end of their operational tour. After the war, Andy Campbell took up teaching and eventually became a headmaster. He died a few years ago. Dallas Schmidt instructed in Southern Rhodesia during 1943 and 1944, and then flew Mosquitos with 404 (RCAF) Squadron, part of the Banff Strike Wing. He trained NATO pilots when the Korean War broke out and continued this for five years. He then became a farmer, for fifteen years. After this he entered politics and, before his retirement, served as Minister of Agriculture for Alberta. Wing Commander Cedric Masterman also finished his tour on the same day and was posted to Egypt, while Anthony Watson was promoted to wing commander and took over 227 Squadron.

The squadron continued to fly on similar operations in the first weeks of the New Year, taking heavy casualties in combat. On 5 January,

Sergeant Brian J. Ward and Sergeant John L. Charlton lost their lives, followed by Sergeant Colin L. Davies and Sergeant Pat N. Goalby on the following day. On 20 January, Warrant Officer G. McG. Thomas and Pilot Officer H.J. 'Pop' Lewis failed to return but ended up as PoWs. On the last day of January, two more crews lost their lives. These were Flying Officer J.A. 'Red' Rae with Flying Officer Leslie H. Hunt, and Sergeant Arthur M. Reynolds with Flight Sergeant Wilfred O. Goff. The squadron was taken off operations on 16 February for training and re-formation.

The Italian submarine *Narvalo* of 1,094 tons when submerged. On 14 January 1943 she was blown to the surface by a Beaufort of 39 Squadron from Malta, flown by Flying Officer John N. Cartwright, and then finished off by two American destroyers. (*Roger Hayward*)

An Me323 under attack off Corsica in August 1943 by a Martin Marauder flown by Wing Commander W. Maydwell of 14 Squadron, part of 328 Wing, 242 Group, Northwest African Coastal Air Force, based at Protville in Tunisia. With three engines put out of action by cannon shells, the Me 323 made a forced landing on the coast. (*The late Squadron Leader J.E. Archbald*)

Aircrews of 144 Squadron at Protville II in Tunisia, discussing the attack on 23 July 1943 in which a convoy off the Italian coast was attacked by their Beaufighters. *Left to right:* Pilot Officer John W. King, DFM, who torpedoed a warship; Flying Officer Harry Woolstencroft, who led the attack and torpedoed a merchant ship, with his navigator, Flying Officer William B. Naples, in the centre; Flying Officer Ronald A. Johnson, who provided anti-flak; and Flight Sergeant Donald E. Hamar, who shot down a Breguet Bizerte flying boat. (*Flying Officer D.E. Hamar*)

Pilot Officer Tom Armstrong (*left*) and Flight Lieutenant A. Derek Frecker, looking remarkably cheerful after their Beaufighter had crashed behind enemy lines on 6 December 1942. This photograph was taken by a passenger, Sergeant A. 'Paddy' Clark. (*Flt Lt T. Armstrong, DFC*)

8

THE END IN TUNISIA

At the beginning of her entry into the war, in June 1940, Italy possessed a little over two million tons of merchant shipping in the Mediterranean. By the end of 1942, approximately half this total had been destroyed by Allied naval and air attack, or by mining.

Of course, new construction in Italian shipyards made good some of this deficiency, while a few sunken vessels were salvaged. In addition a number of ships were requisitioned from conquered countries such as Greece and Yugoslavia. A new source of supply became available after the Anglo-American landings in north-west Africa, for one of the responses of the Axis powers was the invasion of 'unoccupied' France.

On 14 November 1942, German forces entered that part of the defeated country which was still nominally controlled by the Vichy government. The Allies were alarmed at the prospect of the French Fleet, at anchor in Toulon, falling into enemy hands, but when the Axis troops reached that naval port, on 27 November, they found that almost all the French warships had been scuttled or seriously damaged. These included a battleship, seven cruisers, twenty-four destroyers and ten submarines. Three French submarines succeeded in escaping and reaching Allied ports. Only six destroyers and six submarines were left as spoils for the invaders.

However, the Axis acquired many French merchant ships and, after carrying out modifications, was able to press these into service, together with some of their unwilling crews. As a result of such requisitions, together with new construction and salvage, Italy had added about three-quarters of a million tons to her merchant fleet by the end of 1942. There was still plenty of work ahead for the Royal Navy and the bomber and maritime squadrons of the RAF.

Many of these requisitioned French vessels, adapted to carry anti-aircraft guns, were employed on the task of carrying supplies to Tunisia. In addition, the Germans made increasing use of another type of vessel on this run. This was the Kriegstransport or 'KT' boat, as it was known to both the Germans and the British. About thirty of these 'war transports' had been built under licence in Italian and Yugoslavian ports during 1941 and 1942. They were small vessels of only 700 tons and, like the F-boats, were built in sections and then assembled. To reduce dependency on oil, which by then was in seriously short supply, they were fitted with coal bunkers. They were armed with the ubiquitous 'quad gun', consisting of four 20mm cannons synchronised to pour shells at attacking aircraft, and were crewed by seamen of the Kriegsmarine. Their cargoes were normally tanks, artillery and ammunition. At their speed of about fourteen knots, they could make the passage of about 100 miles from Sicily to Tunisia almost entirely at night during the winter months. Although they were usually unescorted, they proved very awkward targets for the anti-shipping squadrons.

Of course, these supply vessels would have been easy targets for the Royal Navy, but the engagements would have brought their warships within easy range of German and Italian bombers. Moreover, the Italian Navy had sown the sea approaches to the supply route with extensive minefields, which restricted the operations of British surface ships.

British Intelligence estimated that during January 1943 as much as 50,000 tons of military cargo reached its destination through this route, not far short of the Axis requirements in North Africa. This was in spite of the sinking throughout the Mediterranean of seventy-two Axis ships in that month.

Another factor which operated in favour of the Axis at this time was the slowness of the Allied air forces in combining into a unified command structure. In north-west Africa at the end of 1942 there were some 1,200 aircraft of the US Twelfth Air Force and about 450 aircraft of the RAF's Eastern Air Command, but the main tasks of these considerable air forces were the support of the Allied armies during their advances and the protection of their supply routes. It was not until mid-January 1943 that part of the US Twelfth Air Force was formed into an anti-shipping unit, and this did not begin operational work until the end of that month. Unified air control, under the new Mediterranean Air Command, was formed towards the end of February under Air Chief Marshal Sir Arthur Tedder.

For the time being, the main burden of destroying the Axis supplies to Tunisia fell on the anti-shipping squadrons at Malta, and there were only a few of these. The main strike force was 39 Squadron, still equipped with torpedo-carrying Beauforts. There were also the Wellingtons of a flight of 69 Squadron, together with detachments of Wellingtons of 221 Squadron and 458 (RAAF) Squadron, sent over from their bases in North Africa. In addition, there were the Albacores of 821 and 828 Squadrons, both Fleet Air Arm.

The commanding officer of 39 Squadron was still Wing Commander Larry Gaine, who had taken over from Wing Commander Pat Gibbs during the previous September. Under his leadership, the squadron was in peak condition. Many of the crews had received advanced training in torpedo attacks at 5 Middle East Training School at Shallufa, near Suez. This had had the effect of improving flying skills and welding each four-man crew into a smooth-running team. The squadron was equipped entirely with Beaufort Mark IIs, with the more powerful Pratt & Whitney engines. Each machine was fitted with ASV radar for identifying vessels at night or through cloud, and as an aid to navigation. Standards of maintenance had improved with supplies of spare parts reaching Malta, while food rations were at last reaching adequate levels. There was no longer the shortage of petrol which had restricted air tests and caused many sorties to be aborted.

Nevertheless, targets during daytime seldom presented themselves, at a time when 39 Squadron was able to count on the escort of the cannon-firing Beaufighters of 272 Squadron, as well as top cover by Spitfires. For the first fortnight of the new year, the Beauforts were occupied in minelaying in the approaches to the Tunisian harbours of Bizerta, Sfax, Sousse and Tunis, as well as the Sicilian harbour of Trapani. The mines they dropped were the same as those carried by the RAF in their 'Gardening' operations off the coasts of north-west Europe, 1,500lb electro-magnetic cylinders with a high blast/weight ratio. These were dropped at low level and floated down with the aid of a small parachute, sinking to the sea bed where they rested until they were activated by the steel hull of a vessel passing overhead.

The mining operations were carried out at night and losses were less severe than those suffered during direct attacks on shipping in daylight hours. Nevertheless, the Beauforts were usually fired upon in their final runs at low level towards the entrances of the ports. Streaks of tracer and bright flashes from bursts of shells at night always seemed more dangerous than the more subdued effect of flak in sunlight. Also, there were the German night-fighters to contend with, and the Beaufort crews could sometimes see the orange light of the air-interception radar which these machines carried in their noses.

The squadron suffered the loss of a Beaufort flown by Flight Sergeant J.T. Seddon during one of these sorties, on the night of 6/7 January. The navigator, Flight Sergeant Christopher Mather, lost his life but the other three crew members survived to become PoWs. On the other hand, these mines were known to have caused serious losses to the Axis supply vessels. Post-war records show that in this area as many as ten Axis vessels were sunk and seven damaged by mines dropped by Beauforts between November 1942 and the following May.

First blood for 39 Squadron in the new year went to Flying Officer John N. Cartwright, the pilot of one of three Beauforts sent out on an anti-submarine patrol in the morning of 14 January. In the early afternoon, when nearly at the end of his patrol, he spotted a conning tower ahead of a British convoy, which was outward bound about 140 miles to the south-east of the island. He dived down and dropped four 250lb depth charges, blowing the bows of the submarine into the air.

At this point the next Beaufort arrived, flown by Flight Sergeant Ewen Gillies. The crews of both Beauforts saw sailors leaving the conning tower, gesticulating and waving white garments, but when Cartwright approached the submarine he was met with a burst of gunfire.

The submarine was the Italian *Narvalo* ('Swordfish' in English), a Bernades type of 1,094 tons when submerged. The day before, she had landed fifty-four tons of ammunition and fuel at Tripoli. She left the port during the evening, bound for Italy and carrying six Italian officers who were being repatriated, as well as eleven British officer PoWs. The explosions from Cartwright's depth charges had put both stern engines out of action, as well as the diving mechanism.

Two destroyers from the convoy, HMS *Packenham* and HMS *Hursley*, closed up at full speed, firing at the submarine on the surface, and the Italian captain ordered his vessel to be scuttled. She sank immediately, but the destroyers picked up thirty-two of the sixty men in her crew, as well as seven of the eleven British prisoners. A signal lamp from one of the destroyers flashed 'Well done, RAF' at the Beauforts.

The next few days were occupied by more minelaying sorties during darkness, but then a period of waxing moon began, sufficiently bright for the Beaufort crews to begin hunting ships at night. British Intelligence was aware that an important convoy had left Palermo in Sicily during the early hours of 17 January, bound for the port of Tunis. This consisted of the Italian *Campania* of 5,287 tons, the French *Jacques Schiaffino* of 1,757 tons and the Danish *Gerda Tofz* of 1,960 tons, the latter two ships having been requisitioned by the Germans. They were escorted by the torpedo boats *Castore*, *Libra* and *Montanari*.

During the evening, two Beauforts found the convoy and both dropped torpedoes. The first, flown by Squadron Leader Les Wordsell, saw no results. The second was flown by Pilot Officer Hugh Watlington. He made a run towards what appeared to be a merchant vessel, but suddenly saw that it was a warship and turned steeply to circle round for another run. At this moment, the torpedo boat bracketed the Beaufort with intense fire, punching holes in the wings and fuselage and slightly wounding the gunner, Sergeant D.F. Gourlay, in the leg. The flak also severed the cable holding the torpedo, which dropped off. However, Watlington brought the damaged aircraft safely home.

The convoy was hidden by low cloud during the daylight hours but six machines went out during the following evening, at a time when the vessels were near the island of Marettimo, off the west coast of Sicily. Two of these were Wellingtons of 69 Squadron. Flight Sergeant A. Milne in a Goofington dropped flares and used his 'Rooster' radio to home in a Fishington flown by Flying Officer J.H. Douglas. Both Wellingtons experienced flak, but Douglas dropped a torpedo and turned for home. Then two Wellingtons of 458(RAAF) Squadron, flown by Flying Officers R.H. Prior and J.M. Pilcher, made further attacks. Finally two Beauforts of 39 Squadron, one flown by Flight Sergeant Ewen Gillies and the other by a Southern Rhodesian, Pilot Officer A.C.W. 'Jimmy' Hewetson, dropped torpedoes. Although some of these crews thought they had scored hits, the Italian records show that the vessels came through unscathed and that they off-loaded their cargoes at Tunis during the following morning.

The next attack by 39 Squadron was successful. During the morning of 20 January, two tankers left Bizerta for Naples, the Italian *Saturno* of 5,022 tons and the French *Sudest*, the latter having been requisitioned by the Germans. They were escorted by the torpedo boats *Ardito* and *Animoso*.

The convoy was attacked during mid-afternoon by twelve B-25 Mitchells of the US Twelfth Air Force and *Saturno* was hit by several bombs. The vessel did not sink but was immobilised. The commandant of the convoy, in *Ardito*, ordered the captain and eight of the crew to remain on board the tanker. The remaining men of the crew were transferred to *Sudest*, while *Ardito* put a line on the crippled tanker and began to tow her. The convoy was diverted to Trapani, the nearest port, and the torpedo boat *Lira* came out to give additional protection.

The vessels were not attacked until the late hours of the evening, when the sound of aircraft engines was heard. *Ardito* cast off the tow, in order to manoeuvre and make smoke. The first aircraft to arrive was a Goofington of 69 Squadron, flown by Flight Sergeant B. McFadden. He tried to make a visual check after the vessels had been picked up on the ASV, but was not successful. Pilot Officer H.A. Dodd in a torpedo-carrying Fishington also arrived. His operator could also see the blips on the ASV, but the torpedo boats were making smoke, firing all the time, and Dodd was also unable to aim at the vessels. Eventually, he brought back his torpedoes.

The last to arrive were two Beauforts of 39 Squadron. One of the pilots, Pilot Officer Jimmy Hewetson, spotted the convoy in the very poor visibility and drifting smoke. He dropped a torpedo but saw no results.

The second Beaufort was flown by Flight Sergeant Ewen Gillies, one of the most experienced torpedo pilots in 39 Squadron. He had joined the RAFVR in August 1940, when he was a nineteen-year-old student in Inverness. After passing through EFTS at Brough, near Kingston-upon-Hull, and SFTS at Cranfield in Bedfordshire, he took his GR course at Squires Gate, near Blackpool. His next courses were at OTU at Chivenor in north Devon and torpedo training at Abbotsinch in Ayrshire. Together with his crew, who were to remain with him throughout his operational flying in Beauforts, he then joined 42 Squadron at Leuchars, from where he flew on a number of operations over the North Sea. The next posting was to 86 Squadron and a flight to Malta, where they arrived on 21 July 1942. By January 1943, they had survived many highly dangerous attacks.

Gillies could make out the outline of the tanker and attacked up-moon. Hewetson's crew, which was still in the area, saw a red flash, followed by a column of water and steam. McFadden's crew, still circling in the Wellington, also saw the explosion. *Saturno* had been hit in the starboard side, and she began to sink. The torpedo boats picked up all the remaining crew on board. Surprisingly, only one Italian sailor lost his life during these attacks, by machine gun fire from one of the Albacores. *Sudest* continued her journey, the convoy having been reinforced by three destroyers which had come out of Trapani, and reached Naples in the morning of 22 January.

On the night of 23/24 January, 39 Squadron shared in the destruction of a convoy which had left Naples the previous morning, bound for Bizerta. There were two merchant vessels, both requisitioned from the French by the Italians. These were *Verona* (formerly *Carimare*) of 4,459 tons, and *Pistoia* (formerly *Oeud Sebou*) of 2,448 tons, and they were escorted by the torpedo boats *Groppo* and *Fortunale*.

The Italians anticipated air attacks at night, for it was the period of full moon. The commandant of the convoy, Capitano di Corvetto B. Farino in *Groppo*, had worked out his tactics in advance. As soon as aircraft engines were heard, he changed direction so that the convoy was sailing directly up-moon. Thus the smaller targets of the ships' sterns were presented to the attackers, while the crews could see the outline of the vessel in front of them. At the same time, the two torpedo boats circled their charges, making smoke and firing furiously. As events were to show, these tactics were to no avail.

The convoy was found by four Beauforts of 39 Squadron, the first to attack being the South African pilot, Captain Don Tilley. He could pick out only one merchant vessel and a warship, and dropped a torpedo which did not score a hit. In fact, this torpedo ran towards *Pistoia*, but it was spotted and the merchant ship made a quick turn to avoid it. Flying Officer John Cartwright dropped four 250lb bombs across the bows of a torpedo boat, but there were no hits. Flight Sergeant Harry Deacon also bombed a torpedo boat, but missed narrowly. Then the last pilot, Pilot Officer Jimmy Hewetson, aimed a torpedo which ran true. There was an explosion and, circling the vessel, he could see that it was down in the water.

Hewetson had hit *Verona*. The vessel came to a halt, while the crew tried to stem the inrush of water. *Fortunale* remained with her, while *Groppo* continued to escort *Pistoia* towards Naples. Three hours later, *Groppo* heard more aircraft noises and then avoided another torpedo. The Wellingtons of both 221 and 458 (RAAF) Squadrons had found this section of the convoy. Wing Commander L.L. Johnson and Sergeant A.B. Dean from the Australian squadron made attacks, but it was a pilot from 221 Squadron who scored a direct hit. Wing Commander E.P. Hutton located and illuminated the target, while Flight Sergeant W. Horning dropped a torpedo. *Pistoia* was hit and set on fire, sinking rapidly while *Groppo* managed to rescue fifty-six of the men who had embarked with her.

In spite of efforts to save her, *Verona* also went down, after dawn the next morning, but *Fortunale* picked up ninety-seven men from her crew of one hundred and twelve. Three more survivors, including the captain, were rescued four hours later by a destroyer which happened to be in transit in the area.

The moon was not bright enough for further attacks at night for the next few weeks, and 39 Squadron reverted to mine laying around the coasts of Tunisia and Sicily, without any particular incident and no losses. On the night of 15/16 February, however, both 39 and 221 Squadrons were out in strength. Their targets were the merchant vessels *Capo Orsa* of 3,149 tons and the German KT13 of 700 tons, escorted by the destroyer *Lampo*. These had left Palermo during the afternoon and were bound for Tunis.

Six Beauforts took off but only two sighted and made attacks. Captain Don Tilley made three runs in very poor visibility, dropping his torpedo on the final run without seeing any results. Flying Officer John Cartwright also attacked, but his aircraft was damaged by very intense flak. The destroyer *Lampo* claimed this aircraft as a certainty, but Cartwright brought it safely back to Luqa.

Then nine Wellingtons of 221 Squadron arrived, some with bombs and others with torpedoes. Both Pilot Officer G. Painter and Sergeant W. Fraser reported direct hits, which were substantiated by the crews of other Wellingtons. According to the report made by the captain of the destroyer *Lampo*, torpedoes were dropped on four occasions, and one of these hit *Capo Orsa*. The report continued:

'At 0245 hours we saw an explosion on the port side of *Capo Orsa*, followed by a sheet of flame. The fire extended over a huge area, as the petrol which the merchant vessel was carrying spread over the surface of the sea. The merchant ship sank gradually and finally disappeared at

'0310 hours... Of the hundred people who had embarked with *Capo Orsa*, the survivors numbered forty-four, of which three were rescued by KT13 and forty-one by the naval hospital ship *Capri*, which was in transit in the area ...'

KT13 and *Lampo* continued their journey and arrived safely at Tunis during the evening of the same day, without further incident.

Although the attacks by the anti-shipping aircraft from Malta were producing results, a substantial portion of the Axis supplies was reaching Tunisia. Tanks and artillery were brought over by the Kriegstransport supply ships, while several tankers made successful runs. On 14 February, in the mountains of Tunisia, the Germans launched their forces against inexperienced American units, threatening to break through at Kasserine five days later and take the whole front from the rear, until they were stemmed by reinforcements of troops and Allied air attacks. After Kasserine, Rommel was put in command of all the Axis forces in Africa.

By far the largest tanker employed on the run to the Tunisian ports was the German *Thorsheimer* of 9,955 tons, a vessel which had been requisitioned from the Norwegians. On 28 January, this tanker had reached Bizerta with almost 10,000 tons of fuel. In the early hours of 20 February, she left Naples for another run to Bizerta, together with the merchant vessel *Fabriano* of 2,493 tons, the latter being the former French *Mayenne*. According to the Italian records, the tanker was overloaded with 13,000 tons of petrol while the merchant vessel had a cargo of 1,700 tons of ammunition and provisions as well as a number of troops. The two vessels were escorted by the torpedo boats *Orione* and *Animoso*.

Of course, British Intelligence was fully aware of the forthcoming journey of *Thorsheimer*, although according to their information she was carrying only 5,400 tons – which was still estimated as over a third of all the fuel shipped to Tunisia during February. The tanker and the merchant vessel were classed as targets of prime importance, and the anti-shipping squadrons at Malta were briefed to attack.

During mid-afternoon, the convoy was reinforced by the torpedo boat *Pegaso*, coming from Palermo, and was also protected by a strong umbrella of fighters during daylight hours. In the early evening, Albacores of 828 (FAA) Squadron began to attack with bombs and torpedoes. In addition, four Beauforts of 39 Squadron went out, but these encountered electrical storms with rain, hail and very poor visibility.

Of the four Beauforts, only one located the targets. This was flown by Flying Officer Stanley R. Muller-Rowland, a torpedo pilot who was eventually to be rated by his peers as one of the most effective of the war. Born in early 1922 in Woking and a product of Uppingham School, he was one of three brothers who had joined the RAFVR. His twin brother, Flying Officer John S.R. Muller-Rowland, was a pilot in Burma, while their elder brother, Flying Officer Eric R. Muller-Rowland, was a pilot with 144 Squadron in England.

There were many brave and determined torpedo pilots in the RAF during the war, but there was something charismatic about Stanley Muller-Rowland. Whereas most pilots flew operationally because this was their duty and they wanted to help win the war, Stanley Muller-Rowland gave the impression that he flew because he loved combat. He courted danger and seemed indifferent to risks. Quietly spoken, slightly built and dark-haired, he had a ready smile and could enter with gusto into the somewhat schoolboyish horseplay in the officers' mess. At the same time, he was intensely meticulous in his approach to flying and the study of tactics. His fellow-officers in 39 Squadron had already recognised his special qualities and looked upon him with considerable respect. In spite of his 'Englishness', however, there was a mysterious side to him. He told his crew that they must never allow him to be taken prisoner, and they assumed that this was because his origins were partly from northern Europe.

Muller-Rowland dropped his torpedo while under an intense barrage of flak, but saw no results. The Italian records state that at that time, after dark in mid-evening, there was no damage to the convoy. But five more Beauforts went out a few hours later, in the early hours of 21 February, and four of these found the convoy in slightly better visibility. Flying Officer John Cartwright, Flight Sergeant L.T. 'Paddy' Garland, and two Canadians, Warrant Officer Richard J.S. Dawson and Flight Sergeant Stanley H. Balkwill, all dropped torpedoes. The crews saw no results in the haze, but it was at this time that *Fabriano* was hit in the boiler room. She remained afloat but was unable to continue her voyage, and turned into Trapani for repairs.

Meanwhile, the Beaufort flown by Flight Sergeant Stan Balkwill was in serious trouble. His navigator was Sergeant E. Fraser Carlisle-Brown, who had transferred to the RAFVR from the army in April 1941. He did not pass his pilot's course at EFTS, but successfully qualified as a navigator at West Freugh in Wigtownshire at the end of that year. Crewing up with Balkwill at OTU in Chivenor, they took further training at Turnberry and, in August 1942, flew out to Gibraltar and finally joined 39 Squadron at Shallufa the following October. Carlisle-Brown's records for the day include the following:

'Sighted one merchant vessel, one tanker and two destroyers. Owing to the nearness of the merchant vessels to the island's cliffs [the island of Marettimo, off the west coast of Sicily], we attacked down-moon and dropped our torpedo in the midst of flak, but we saw no result. The aircraft was hit just before the drop. The damage prevented the use of rudder and elevators and so the aircraft passed directly over the merchant vessel after the drop. The kingpin behind the rudder was hit, resulting in no left rudder and only slight right rudder. The elevators would not respond to descent but there was very slight climb. We sent out an SOS but there was no reply from base ... We tried to maintain height at about 500 feet, with myself moving fore and aft as ballast, as directed by Stan. He also used the trimming tabs.

Arriving at Luqa, we shot off a few reds [from the Very pistol] and with no left rudder made a right-hand circuit. I moved into the nose and then back with the pilot. Since we had no hydraulics, I pumped down the undercart. Stan landed and, at the end of the runway, turned the aircraft.'

Balkwill's courage and skill were recognised by the award of a DFM. Soon afterwards, both he and Carlisle-Brown were commissioned.

Meanwhile, when *Thorsheimer* and the three torpedo boats were getting under way once more for their destination, an aircraft dived down and machine-gunned the bridge of the tanker. This was an Albacore of 828 (FAA) Squadron, which was also active on that night. The captain of the tanker, who was also the pilot, was mortally wounded in this attack. The commandant of the convoy, Capitano di Corvetto Camillo L. Colavolpe in *Orione*, was faced with a problem, for there was no other officer on board qualified to command the tanker. He brought the convoy to a halt once more and took the dying captain to Trapani, where he picked up the captain of *Fabriano* as a qualified replacement and raced back to the convoy.

With her new captain, *Thorsheimer* got under way yet again, escorted by the three torpedo boats, as well as ten German fighters and four anti-submarine floatplanes which arrived at dawn. The convoy continued its journey towards Bizerta until the afternoon, when it was attacked by a force of US B-25 Mitchells escorted by fighters. The Italian report states that three US aircraft were shot down for the loss of a Ju 88 and a floatplane. *Thorsheimer* was hit by two bombs, one of which did not explode, but a fire was caused by the other. The torpedo boats *Pegaso* and *Animoso* went to her assistance, but *Orione* was put out of action by damage to her rudder from three bombs which fell close to her. The damage to *Orione* was repaired in less than an hour, and the next duty of the torpedo boat was to take off from the tanker fifty-nine men who had been wounded. Among these, one of the most serious casualties was her new captain. Once again, the tanker was unable to continue. The commandant of the convoy sent a signal to Trapani, requesting the immediate despatch of a tug, and then put on full speed for that port, in order to land the wounded.

The tug arrived after sunset, but a further air attack began when she was preparing to take the tanker in tow. Six Beauforts had been sent out at dusk, and all found their target. Captain Don Tilley was the first to attack, and his torpedo hit amidships. Flight Sergeant Ewen Gillies* was close behind him, and his torpedo hit slightly astern of amidships. There were two flashes from these hits, with gouts of water and debris thrown upwards, followed by fires. A third torpedo, dropped by Flying Officer Arnold M. Feast, scored a hit between these fires, causing an enormous explosion which enveloped the whole ship in a sheet of flame. Then Flight Sergeant Harry Deacon dropped a torpedo which also hit amidships, causing further explosions. The remaining two aircraft, flown by an Australian flight commander, Squadron Leader R.S.O. 'Moose' Marshall, and Pilot Officer Jimmy Hewetson, brought back their torpedoes. The tanker *Thorsheimer* was completely destroyed.

There was another attack on a convoy during the moonlit nights. Soon after midnight on 24 February, three merchant ships left Bizerta for Naples. Two of these were formerly French – *Alcamo* of 6,987 tons and *Chieti* of 5,457 tons – while the third was the German *Stella* of 655 tons. They were escorted by the torpedo boats *Fortunale, Monsone* and *Animoso*.

The convoy sailed to the north through a calm sea but met a bank of cloud soon after night fell, and signal lamps were lit at twenty minute intervals to avoid collisions. Shortly before midnight, sailors in the torpedo boat *Monsone* spotted two torpedoes running towards them, and these were avoided by a quick turn. The torpedoes were dropped by Wellingtons of 458 (RAAF) Squadron, which were out on that night.

Two hours later, when the moon was high in the sky and the convoy about forty-five miles north-west of Ustica (an island on the western tip of Sicily), there were other torpedo attacks, delivered by the Beauforts of 39 Squadron. These discovered what they reported as a cruiser, two destroyers and one unidentified vessel, sailing north.

Three Beauforts delivered this attack. Squadron Leader Moose Marshall dropped a torpedo at the 'cruiser' but saw no results. The next torpedo was dropped by Flying Officer John Cartwright, who aimed at the merchant vessel. This torpedo hit *Alcamo*, which did not sink but came to a halt, with the torpedo boat *Monsone* in attendance. The third Beaufort failed to return from this attack, although its fate was not seen by the other two crews, nor was it reported by the Italians.

---

* This was the end of Ewen Gillies' tour with 39 Squadron. He was commissioned, awarded a DFC, and posted to Shallufa as an instructor. Later, he joined 254 Squadron at North Coates as a torpedo pilot, and received a bar to his DFC. He remained in the RAF after the war and retired as a squadron leader.

It was flown by one of the Canadian pilots, Warrant Officer Richard J.S. Dawson, and he and his crew lost their lives.

Just over two hours later, three more Beauforts arrived in the area, alerted by a wireless message from Marshall. Flying Officer Stanley Muller-Rowland spotted the two sections of the convoy a few miles apart. In characteristic fashion, he made two dummy runs before deciding that he was in the right position for a torpedo drop. He aimed at the rear vessel, which he noted was low in the water from the previous attack. His torpedo hit *Alcamo* amidships and there was a flash of orange flame. The merchant vessel sank in five minutes, but *Monsone* picked up fifty-four survivors from her crew of sixty-nine.

The second of the three Beauforts did not locate the convoy. The third, flown by Pilot Officer Jimmy Hewetson, failed to return. The fate of this aircraft was recently described by a survivor of the crew, the wireless operator Sergeant A. John Coles, who was twenty years old at the time. Coles had joined the RAFVR in August 1940 and passed through his wireless training at Blackpool and Yatesbury, followed by air gunnery training at Penrhos. Soon after being posted to 86 Squadron in August 1941, he was part of a crew which flew out to the Middle East, where he joined Hewetson's crew during the following month. By 23 February 1943, he had completed twenty-seven operational sorties and was nearing the end of his tour.

Coles picked up the convoy on his ASV and Hewetson flew parallel with the vessels, about a mile away and down-moon, so as to keep in the darker part of the sky. The aircraft was at very low level when he turned to attack up-moon, with the glassy sea glittering in the moonlight. This was in the days before radio altimeters were installed in maritime strike aircraft, and altitude above the sea depended on the pilot's visual judgement while he was concentrating on the target.

There was a sudden and violent crash, with a blinding flash of light immediately in front of Coles. Fortunately for the wireless operator, he had taken his usual precautions before the attack, strapping himself tightly into his seat and pressing his head against his parachute pack, which he held against the Bendix wireless set in front of his forehead. The Beaufort had hit the sea, with the torpedo still in the bomb bay.

The aircraft began to sink rapidly, and water was already lapping round Coles' feet as he unclipped his seat belt. He was uninjured apart from a black eye from the metal release ring of his parachute pack. He jumped up and moved back to the entrance hatch on the port side of the fuselage, from where he could reach out and pull the release handle of the 'H-type' dinghy stowed in the wing. Two other crew members were already in the water, calling on him to get out the dinghy. These were the navigator, Flight Sergeant A.L. 'Jimmy' Brice from Oxfordshire and the gunner, Sergeant R. 'Joe' Bradford from Burton-on-Trent.

To the distress of the crew, they found that the Rhodesian pilot, Jimmy Hewetson, was not in the water and had gone down with the aircraft. But they had other matters to occupy their attention. The circular dinghy came out of the wing and inflated automatically, but it was upside-down. The three men had a great struggle to right it and then hoist themselves on board. Then they found, to their alarm, that it was leaking badly. It is probable that the lanyard connecting the dinghy to the wing had ripped off a piece of rubber when the Beaufort went down. There was a knife attached to the lanyard, but the men had not been able to use it.

Within a few minutes the three Beaufort men spotted a sleek warship gliding silently through the water. They thought it was a destroyer, but in fact it was the torpedo boat *Monsone* searching for survivors of *Alcamo*, using low engine power so that the crew could hear cries for help. John Coles suddenly remembered that they carried whistles fastened to their battle dress blouses, for just such an emergency. The three men began to blow these as hard as they could, and to their relief the warship came up close.

Then the torpedo boat went into reverse and the hearts of the Beaufort men sank, since there was not much air left in their punctured dinghy. But *Monsone* altered course a few degrees to port and came right up to them. A voice called: 'Combien êtes – vous?' The Italians were looking for missing crew members of *Alcamo*, and most of these were French. 'Trois,' replied Coles, and they were helped on board by the Italians, with continual exhortations to hasten, since there was believed to be a British submarine in the area. Once the Italians realised that the three men were British airmen, they were greeted with the inevitable 'For you, the war is over!'

The Italians looked after their prisoners quite well. As the senior NCO, Jimmy Brice was called in front of the captain, Capitano di Corvetto Castelli di Vinci, and given a routine but unsuccessful interrogation in English. Interestingly, di Vinci told him that he felt honour bound to rescue them, in spite of the risk from more torpedoes, since his brother had been the captain of an Italian submarine and had been rescued by the Royal Navy after being depth-charged and forced to the surface.

The three Englishmen were astonished at the speed of the torpedo boat as it raced to Naples, carrying the survivors. They did not enjoy their short stay in the port, for it was subjected to an air attack by RAF Wellingtons. They were imprisoned at Campo PG66 near Naples, but were separated before the collapse of Italy and then met up again at Stalag IVB at Mühlburg in Germany. They were liberated by the Russians on 23 April 1945.

Meanwhile, the other vessels in the convoy also reached Naples, in the early evening of 23 February, in spite of air attacks made on them during the night by Wellingtons of 458 (RAAF) Squadron. During the same day, eleven more men from *Alcamo* were picked up by the Italian air-sea rescue service. Only four men from the crew of the merchant vessel were lost.

After their brief period of success at Kasserine, the Axis forces began to fall back to the coast, harassed by Allied aircraft based in north-west Africa. On 6 March, Rommel launched another attack, this time against the Eighth Army advancing along the coastal plains of Tunisia from the east. This attack, delivered from the 'Mareth Line' on the seaward flank of the Narantha Hills, was bloodily repulsed by the Eighth Army at Medenine. It was to prove Rommel's last effort to restore the situation in North Africa, for he was replaced soon afterwards and returned to Germany as a sick but unbroken man. The Allied armies closed in steadily on their enemy, bottling up forces in a shrinking area of Tunisia.

By this time, the Axis supply system was forced to rely more and more on transport aircraft bringing troops and supplies from Sicily. The targets available to the torpedo-carrying Beauforts, Wellingtons and Albacores based at Malta were diminishing steadily.

One major incident in this period, so far as 39 Squadron was concerned, occurred on 3 March. The very popular Australian flight commander Squadron Leader Moose Marshall lost his life, together with his navigator and wireless operator, when leading a flight of three Beauforts on a daylight strike. Soon after take-off, when flying at low level, his aircraft was seen to hit the water and sink. After about six hours the gunner, Sergeant Lawrence A. Evans, was picked up by a high-speed launch, but he was unable to provide an explanation for the crash. It was generally believed that the engines had cut after oiling up during a long tick-over period before take-off, for there had been a delay on the perimeter track as a result of enemy air activity over Malta.

A convoy left Naples in the early hours of 12 March, bound for Tunis. There were two merchant ships, *Caraibe* of 4,037 tons and *Esterel* of 3,165 tons, both taken over from the French by the Germans. Escorting them were three torpedo boats – *Sirio*, *Ardito* and *Pegaso* – together with the corvette *Cicogna*, although *Ardito* returned with engine trouble after a few hours. The remainder linked up during the afternoon with another convoy, from Messina bound for Bizerta. This consisted of the tanker *Sterope* of 10,496 tons, escorted by the torpedo boats *Cagno*, *Orione*, *Cascino* and *Libra*, as well as the corvettes *Persefone* and *Antilope*. To this powerful force were added two Italian and five German anti-submarine hunters. The tanker was disguised as a merchant ship, with a false funnel erected amidships in addition to her normal funnel towards the stern.

Such an important convoy was certain to become a target for the Beauforts of 39 Squadron, and inevitably the aircraft met a hail of flak when they caught up with it east of Sicily during the evening. Flying Officer Arnold M. Feast was the first to be shot down. He and two of his crew were picked up by the corvette *Persefone* but his navigator, Flight Sergeant Peter G. Exton, lost his life. Ten minutes later, at about 2125 hours, Flight Lieutenant Stanley Muller-Rowland dropped a torpedo which was followed by a flash and a cloud of black smoke from his target. He had hit the tanker in the port bow. Although she did not sink, *Sterope* turned towards Palermo, escorted by the two torpedo boats *Pegaso* and *Cascino*, and reached safety a few hours later. Four other Beauforts harried the convoy, and Sergeant William A. Blackmore and his crew failed to return and lost their lives. One of the other Beauforts, flown by Sergeant J.T. 'Paddy' Garland, was badly damaged but brought safely back to Luqa.

Four minutes after Muller-Rowland scored his success, the merchant ship *Esterel* was hit by a torpedo fired by the submarine HMS *Thunderbolt*. She turned towards Trapani, escorted by the torpedo boat *Orione* and the corvette *Persefone*. Then the Italians learnt that four British destroyers were racing to intercept the remaining vessels. The merchant ship *Caraibe* also made for Trapani, together with most of the warships. But the torpedo boat *Libra* remained behind to hunt for HMS *Thunderbolt*, and was successful in destroying the British submarine.

Another Axis convoy braved the increasingly effective air attacks and made a successful run to Tunisia. This left Taranto in the early hours of 17 March, bound for Bizerta. There were two merchant vessels – *Marco Foscarini II* of 6,406 tons and *Nicolo Tommaseo* of 4,573 tons – escorted by the destroyer *Lubiana*, the torpedo boats *Tifone* and *Antares*, and the submarine chaser *Vas 221*. Nine Beauforts of 39 Squadron were sent out before midday on 17 March, escorted by nine Beaufighters of 272 Squadron. One Beaufighter developed engine trouble five minutes after take-off and the pilot, Sergeant D.W. Frazer, ditched in the sea just off the coast. He and his navigator were picked up within fifteen minutes.

Both commanding officers led their respective squadrons. Wing Commander Larry Gaine was at the head of the Beauforts, while Wing Commander John Buchanan flew the leading Beaufighter. The formation met the enemy convoy off Point Stilo, near the toe of Italy, and attacked. The crews spotted two Ju 88s, ten Me 110s, a Ju 52, a Do 217 and an He 115, circling at about 1,000 feet above the convoy.

The Beaufighters made for these air escorts, but some of the pilots complained later that their cannons failed when they were in scoring positions. Nevertheless, they claimed to have damaged a Do 217, an Me 110, a Ju 52 and an He 115. One Beaufighter was shot down and the crew, Sergeant Lancelot H. Schultz of the RAAF and Sergeant William M. Wainwright of the RAF, lost their lives.

The Beauforts attacked from the direction of the shore and seven aimed their torpedoes at the two merchant vessels. According to the squadron records, hits were scored by Wing Commander Larry Gaine, Flight Sergeant Harry Deacon and Flight Sergeant E.P. Twiname, and there were possible hits by Major Don Tilley, Squadron Leader Colin Milson, Flight Lieutenant Stanley Muller-Rowland, and Flight Sergeant 'Paddy' Garland. Flying Officer Norman Petch lost his torpedo as a result of a faulty selector switch. However, the Italian records show that none of the ships suffered damage and that all carried on safely to Messina.

Normally, the claims made by 39 Squadron were accurate or, if anything, too modest. It can only be guessed that some of these torpedoes, although accurately aimed, struck wreckage, rocks or sandbanks when running from the shoreline, and the explosions gave the impression of hits.

One of the Beauforts, flown by the Australian Flight Lieutenant Donald I. Fraser, was shot down by a German fighter, but the four men were picked up by *Vas 221* and taken prisoner. The remaining Beauforts closed up after the attack, for protection against enemy fighters, and the gunners claimed one Me 110 destroyed, one probable and four damaged. These Beauforts returned safely to Luqa.

The convoy continued and put into Messina for a short while. With some alterations to the escort, it then passed along the north coast of Sicily and put into Trapani. Leaving this port in the early hours of 20 March, the two merchant vessels set course for Bizerta, escorted by the torpedo boats *Fortunale, Sagittario* and *Antares*. Towards mid-day, there was an attack by twenty-one US Liberators escorted by twenty-five Lightnings. Every bomb missed and two US aircraft were shot down for the loss of one German fighter, according to the Italian records. The convoy, which had borne a charmed life, arrived at Bizerta during the evening of the same day.*

Four Beauforts of 39 Squadron were sent out at 2000 hours on 23 March, to hunt off the west coast of Sicily. Three of these sighted nothing, but at 2358 hours Pilot Officer Ralph E. Dodd, a Canadian pilot, spotted a convoy near Trapani. He dropped a torpedo at the largest vessel, and then saw a vivid flash, with showers of sparks and debris, followed by clouds of smoke and steam. The convoy consisted of

---

* *Marco Foscarini II* was sunk by a British submarine on 23 April 1943.

the German merchant vessel *Bernadette* of 302 tons, formerly French, which was under tow by the tug *Tenace* of 250 tons. *Bernadette* had been damaged in an air raid on the port of Tunis and was being taken to Trapani, escorted by four German submarine hunters. Dodd's torpedo hit the tug, which blew up and sank. Another tug was sent out at full speed from Trapani, and towed the merchant vessel into the port.

On the night of 11/12 April, four Beauforts of 39 Squadron and three torpedo-carrying Wellingtons of 458 (RAAF) Squadron were sent out to tackle a convoy which had left Naples for Tunis, consisting of three merchant ships escorted by two torpedo boats and a corvette. One of these merchant ships – *Fabriano* of 2,493 tons – broke down during the evening and was diverted to Palermo, escorted by the corvette *Driade*. She was the vessel which had been damaged by the Beauforts of 39 Squadron in the night of 20/21 February, but she did not survive a second attack. The Canadian pilot Flying Officer Hailstone in one of the Wellingtons found and sank her an hour before midnight. One Beaufort was lost during the night, after having sent an SOS at 0413 hours on 12 April. It was flown by Sergeant Alan F. Eastman; he and his crew lost their lives.

Meanwhile, the Axis forces were being compressed into a smaller and smaller area of Tunisia by the advancing Allied armies. Montgomery broke through the Mareth line on 28 March, after an immense attack on the Axis positions by the Western Desert Air Force. By 13 April, both Sfax and Sousse had fallen to the Eighth Army, leaving only the ports of Tunis and Bizerta for the Axis convoys. The Germans and Italians were then almost wholly dependent on their air transports, which were making as many as 150 sorties a day. These air formations were shot down on such a scale by Allied fighters – primarily Spitfires and Warhawks – that the destruction began to reach the level of a massacre.

On 23 April the Beauforts of 39 Squadron made a torpedo attack which culminated in the last sinking for this type of machine in RAF service. In the evening of 22 April, the merchant vessel *Aquino* left Leghorn in a courageous but forlorn attempt to reach the port of Tunis. She was the former French *El Kantara* of 5,079 tons, taken over by the Italians. When she reached a position to the north of Marettimo Island in the early morning of the following day, under the escort of the torpedo boat *Groppo* and making the hight speed of seventeen knots, she was hit by three bombs dropped by a formation of sixteen Liberators of the US Twelfth Air Force. These bombs started a fire which the Italian crew could not control. Since the vessel was carrying a highly inflammable cargo of fuel in containers, *Groppo* took off 129 survivors of her crew of 135, and set off at high speed for Trapani, leaving the vessel to its fate.

Aquino did not sink, nor did her cargo explode. Beauforts of 39 Squadron were sent out during the night to finish her off. The first to arrive was Flight Lieutenant Stanley Muller-Rowland, who dropped a torpedo which hit amidships, causing a flash and an explosion. Flight Sergeant E.P. Twiname followed him in, making three runs, but each time his torpedo release mechanism failed to operate. Muller-Rowland sent a W/T message 'Still burning' back to Luqa, and two more Beauforts were sent out. Pilot Officer Stan Balkwill found the vessel and also hit her amidships. *Aquino* blew up at last, and sank within five minutes. Seeing this, Pilot Officer Ralph E. Dodd in the other Beaufort did not drop his torpedo.

It seems probable that the Canadian pilot, Stan Balkwill, was the last to score a torpedo hit in an RAF Beaufort. Torpedoes were dropped by 39 Squadron at night during the following month, but no hits are registered in either RAF or Italian records. There were no Beaufort squadrons in the UK. In the eastern Mediterranean, 47 Squadron was still equipped with Beauforts but employed mainly on convoy escort duties. Two Beaufort squadrons, 22 and 217, were based at Ceylon and engaged mainly on anti-submarine duties; they stood ready to attack the Japanese battle fleet, but these warships did not appear in the Indian Ocean, apart from a foray in April 1942.

In this period, the remaining two Tunisian ports were subjected to a tremendous air bombardment, as were the ports in Sicily and the Italian mainland. Dozens of merchant ships were sunk at anchor, as well as some warships. In Tunisia, the resistance of the Axis forces broke at last. All the Axis aircraft which were flyable had left Tunisia, leaving the ground forces with no more than occasional support from Sicily. The last pockets of resistance were mopped up on 14 May. With no means of evacuation, the enemy lost 250,000 men, together with much equipment. The Axis had been cleared out of Africa.

The attack by Beaufighters of 252 Squadron on the Italian seaplane base at Prevesa on the west coast of Greece, showing a CRDA Cant Z501 Gabbione (Seagull) flying boat. (*Wg Cdr D.O. Butler, DFC*)

Wing Commander Dennis O. Butler (*left*), who commanded 252 Squadron from May 1943 to December 1943, photographed with his navigator, Flight Lieutenant Frank A.A. Quinn. (*Wg Cdr D.O. Butler, DFC*)

An attack on 22 August 1943 by three Beaufighters of 252 Squadron against shipping at Prevesa, in which one Beaufighter was shot down. This photograph shows the collier *Bacchus* (formerly French) of 1,810 tons under cannon fire. Renamed *Bertha* by the Germans after the Italian capitulation, she was sunk by a submarine on 3 October 1944. (*Wg Cdr D.O. Butler, DFC*)

The German minelayer *Drache* (formerly Greek) of 1,870 tons, under attack on 26 September 1943 by three Beaufighters of 252 Squadron and one of 227 Squadron, while at harbour in the island of Siros. The vessel was damaged by cannon and machine gun fire but the bombs overshot. She was finally sunk on 22 September 1944 by Beaufighters of 252 and 603 Squadrons at Port Vathi in Samos. (*Wg Cdr D.O. Butler, DFC*)

9

THE SURRENDER OF ITALY

After the fall of Tunisia, three RAF Beaufighter squadrons were formed in 328 Wing, under 242 Group, part of the North-west African Coastal Air Force. Two of these were 39 and 47 Squadrons, both of which had already flown Beauforts in the Mediterranean, with great distinction. The third was 144 Squadron, formerly part of the home-based Coastal Command, a torpedo-bomber squadron which had converted from Hampdens to Beaufighter VICs during the previous January, when based at Tain near Inverness.

During June 1943, these three squadrons were equipped with the new Beaufighter TFX, a variant which had been specially designed for the strike squadrons of Coastal Command and their overseas equivalents. The 'pilot's notes' for this aircraft describe it as 'a long-range low-altitude torpedo-carrying fighter'. It did indeed possess all these attributes, being fitted with more powerful engines than its predecessors – two 1,772hp Bristol Hercules XVIIs rated for flying at sea level. The six machine guns in the wings were usually removed but the four 20mm cannons in the nose were retained, as well as the rearward-firing machine gun in the navigator's cupola. The range was about 1,500 miles, much the same as the old Mark VIC, but the new aircraft was capable of carrying a torpedo of about 2,000lb for that distance and then landing with a small reserve of fuel.

The new base of these squadrons was Protville II, a tented encampment north-west of Tunis. On 1 June the crews of 39 Squadron arrived there from Malta, via Cairo West, and handed over their Beauforts, apart from one machine which was retained as a transport aircraft. No accommodation was ready for them, and the crews spent the first night sleeping in the open.

On 14 June, the crews of 47 Squadron, which had been engaged with Beauforts on naval convoy escorts and anti-submarine work in the central and eastern Mediterranean since the previous autumn, flew from their base of Misurata West in Libya to Shallufa in Egypt. Here they converted on to Beaufighters and then flew over to Protville II.

Their Beauforts were handed over to 16 (SAAF) Squadron, replacing the Bisleys in that squadron.

Fifteen Beaufighter TFXs of 144 Squadron took off from Cornwall on 12 June, headed for Gibraltar, but were diverted by bad weather to airfields in North Africa. One crashed and three others developed airframe troubles, but eleven eventually took off again and arrived at Protville II on 18 June.

Of course, the crew of four in the Beaufort was reduced to two in the Beaufighter. Most pilots in 39 Squadron also had to undergo a conversion course, partly consisting of a practical flying demonstration by an experienced Beaufighter pilot, with a Beaufort pilot standing behind him, following which the 'pupil' pilot was allowed to take over the controls. Many of the Beaufort navigators, who were already capable of handling the rearward-firing machine gun in the Beaufighter, underwent a short course on the wireless set at Protville or were sent to Egypt for this training. The wireless operator/air gunners from the Beaufort squadrons did not form part of the new crews unless they had the opportunity of passing a navigator's course. Some of these men, who were adept in the use of ASV radar, were transferred to 16 (SAAF) Squadron and flew with the South Africans in Beauforts until the squadron was re-equipped with Beaufighter TFXs during the following December.

The ground crews of 39 and 47 Squadrons also arrived at Protville II, to take up their duties with the new Beaufighters. There were in fact two airfields at this base, a mile and and a half apart, each with a 6,000ft runway of silty clay loam, rolled hard. The squadrons of 328 Wing, which had been re-formed in early June 1943, included Marauders, Baltimores and Wellingtons, as well as US Spitfires and Airacobras, all operating from the Protville airfields. The Wing was commanded by Group Captain Geoffrey W. Tuttle OBE DFC, who had previously achieved distinction as the commander of Coastal Command's Photographic Development Unit, later the Photographic Reconnaissance Unit.

These moves were linked with the forthcoming invasion of southern Europe via Sicily, under the codename operation 'Husky'. The primary role of the three torpedo-carrying Beaufighter squadrons was the interception of the Italian Fleet, should the capital ships have the temerity to leave their main base of La Spezia and attempt to interfere with the Allied invasion convoys and their naval escorts. In the event the Italians decided to remain in port, but there was plenty of other operational work to keep the Beaufighter crews busy, in their familiar role of attacking enemy sea convoys. Sicily was supplied by German ferries across the narrow and heavily defended Strait of Messina, but sea convoys still passed from the Italian mainland to the islands of

Sardinia and Corsica, both held by the Axis forces and expected to be defended bastions after the fall of Sicily.*

The three Beaufighter squadrons seldom operated together. Each squadron usually sent out an open formation of eight aircraft in line abreast, with four carrying torpedoes and two more at each end providing anti-flak and fighter protection. The formation extended for about a mile over the sea, on operations which were almost invariably termed 'Armed Rovers'. The distances they had to cover – up to 1,250 miles for the outward and return flight (about five hours flying) – put them beyond the range of escort by any Allied single-engined fighters available at the time.

The first operation was carried out on 21 June by four Beaufighters of 47 Squadron led by Squadron Leader James A. Lee-Evans, who was aged thirty-two and had already completed a tour of operations in the Beauforts of 42 Squadron in the UK. The formation came across a vessel towing about six barges in the Gulf of Aranci, on the north-east tip of Sardinia, escorted by a torpedo boat. They attacked and, according to the squadron records, the merchant vessel was hit on both the port and starboard sides by torpedoes and sank quickly. One Beaufighter, flown by Sergeant A.E. Kemp, lost a propeller from flak, and was escorted home by another Beaufighter, flown by Warrant Officer R. Whitington. On the return journey, Whitington was hit by fire from a B–17 Flying Fortress, which injured him slightly and damaged his control column. But he brought his aircraft back safely, and the other three Beaufighters also landed at Protville II.

The next sortie was made the following day by 144 Squadron, again with four Beaufighters, on an 'Armed Rover'. It was led by Flying Officer Eric R. Muller-Rowland, the elder brother of the Stanley Muller-Rowland who was a flight commander with 39 Squadron at Protville II. After less than an hour, Eric Muller-Rowland's Beaufighter was seen to pull up suddenly from its height of fifty feet and then nose-dive into the water. The reason for this accident is not clear. However, one man was seen to escape from the wreckage, and he seemed to be Muller-Rowland.

In another Beaufighter, Pilot Officer R.A. Johnson sent an SOS back to base and jettisoned his torpedo before making a run-up to drop a pilot's K-type dinghy. Unfortunately, he was then in a collision with another Beaufighter, flown by Pilot Officer J.W. King. Johnson's starboard elevator was cut off, while King's starboard propeller was

---

* Unfortunately for the researcher, the Italian official history of the naval war, consisting of twenty-seven very detailed volumes, does not cover these attacks. It is possible that accurate records were not collected at this stage in the naval war, when Italy was so near to collapse and surrender.

damaged. Both pilots kept control of their aircraft and Johnson dropped the dinghy accurately. Muller-Rowland was seen to get into it and wave to them. The three Beaufighters set course for base and landed successfully.

Meanwhile, an air-sea rescue operation had been put into action, but none of the searching Wellingtons, Baltimores or Beaufighters found any trace of the dinghy. Eric Muller-Rowland and his navigator, Sergeant Ernest W. Alexander, lost their lives. After this sortie, all the Beaufighters of 144 Squadron were grounded for over a week, during which time modifications took place and the crews were occupied in training.

For the time being, only 47 Squadron among the trio of Beaufighter squadrons was able to operate as a strike force. On the next day, 23 June, three Beaufighters of this squadron made torpedo attacks against a couple of vessels which two of the crews reported as tankers, in the Tyrrhenian Sea. One of the vessels blew up with a terrific explosion, and sank. It proved not to be a tanker but the former French *Pescagel* of 1,096 tons, which had been converted by the Germans into the submarine-hunter UJ2212, in transit from Naples to Palermo. But 47 Squadron lost their first Beaufighter and crew on this attack. One aircraft was hit in the port engine, which caught fire and blazed fiercely. It dived into the sea and both the pilot, Pilot Officer Ian H. Robertson, and his navigator, Pilot Officer William D. Joy, lost their lives.

Three more Beaufighters of 47 Squadron went out on 25 June and found a merchant vessel which they attacked with torpedoes and cannon. Squadron Leader Lee-Evans, who led the formation, registered a hit on the stern of the vessel, and then went on to shoot down an escorting He 115 floatplane, which crashed into the sea.

The next attack was on 2 July, when three Beaufighters of 47 Squadron took off in the early morning on an Armed Rover. After half an hour, Flight Sergeant J.E. Carroll was seen to be lagging behind, and then he ditched his machine successfully. The other two crews saw both Carroll and his navigator, Sergeant T.E. Frowen, get into their dinghies. Flight Lieutenant J.R. Hastings flew back to base with information, while Flight Sergeant H. Hare circled the dinghy until he was chased away by three single-engined fighters. Another Beaufighter went out shortly afterwards and found the two dinghies lashed together. Two more dinghies were dropped, and the position reported for rescue by high-speed launch. By August, Carroll was flying once more with his squadron.

There was another ditching the following day when the commanding officer of 47 Squadron, Wing Commander Alistair M. Taylor, led three Beaufighters on a strike against five armed trawlers near Cape Sandalo, on the south-west tip of Sardinia. Two aircraft attacked with cannons, while shore batteries opened up with accurate flak. Flying Officer Charles A. Ogilvie's Beaufighter was hit in the port engine and he turned south, emitting a stream of smoke. He ditched successfully and was seen to get into the dinghy, together with his navigator, Sergeant A.G. Williams. Taylor circled and sent out an SOS. The two men were picked up and a few days later were flying again with the squadron.

In the early hours of 10 July, the Allies invaded Sicily. This massive operation, in which about 2,000 vessels were employed, was preceded by continuous air attacks against enemy airfields and a naval bombardment of the landing places. Four divisions and a Commando brigade of the Eighth Army went ashore at the south-east tip of the island, while three divisions of the US 7th Army assaulted beaches further west. Everywhere the landings were successful. The troops pushed inland and within two days Spitfires from Malta were operating from Sicilian airfields.

The three Beaufighter squadrons at Protville II did not take part in the air cover during the invasion, although Beaufighters of 272 Squadron at Malta were active over Sicily while Beaufighters of 227, 252 and 603 Squadrons provided fighter escort from Libya. For a whole week, the torpedo Beaufighters had stood by to attack the Italian capital ships but, when it became apparent that these were remaining in port, the aircraft were sent against other targets.

At mid-day on 11 July, Wing Commander Taylor led six Beaufighters of 47 Squadron on a strike against two large merchant vessels, escorted by a warship, off the east coast of Sardinia. By this time, the Italians had only eighteen destroyers and nineteen torpedo boats left in service, of which about a third was operationally ready at any one time. These remaining warships were quite inadequate to meet the requirements of the Axis throughout the Mediterranean, even though the Italian Navy had been relieved of its previous task of escorting convoys to North Africa. Nevertheless, the convoy of 11 July put up a barrage of intense flak against the five torpedo bombers, which came out of the sun at about 100 feet. The aircrews reported hits on both vessels, one of which seemed to be sinking by the stern. But Taylor's Beaufighter was hit in the port engine, which burst into flames. The aircraft dived into the water and both the commanding officer and his navigator, Flying Officer Frank Whitlock, lost their lives.

In the early afternoon of the same day, Flying Officer C.V. Brown led six Beaufighters of 144 Squadron against the convoy, which by now was reduced to one merchant vessel and one warship, but reinforced by a flak-ship. Two of the Beaufighters were in the anti-flak role and these raked the warship, enveloping it in grey smoke. Columns of smoke also rose from the merchant vessel after the torpedoes were dropped, and the ship appeared to be down by the stern. In spite of intense flak, all the Beaufighters returned safely.

In the late afternoon, Stanley Muller-Rowland, by now promoted to squadron leader and possessed by an even greater determination after the death of his brother, led six Beaufighters of 39 Squadron on their first strike, also against this convoy. They found the merchant vessel, escorted by two warships and one flak-ship, and attacked with torpedoes and cannon fire. One warship was damaged, while the bow of the merchant vessel was believed to have been hit by a torpedo. The German *Tell* of 1,349 tons was sunk from this convoy. But soon afterwards the Beaufighters were attacked by single-engined fighters. A Canadian pilot, Flight Lieutenant Ian McIntyre, was shot down and lost his life, although his navigator, Sergeant A.E. Fletcher, survived to become a PoW. Muller-Rowland's aircraft was also badly hit, but he brought it back to make a crash-landing at Protville.

The following day, 12 July, the new commanding officer of 39 Squadron, Wing Commander Nelson B. Harvey, led eight Beaufighters against a convoy in the Strait of Bonifacio, between Sardinia and Corsica. Four were armed with torpedoes and four in the anti-flak role. Aged thirty, Harvey was a highly experienced torpedo pilot, one of the handful who had flown Blackburn Baffins, Fairey Swordfish and Vickers Vildebeests before the war. He had already completed an operational tour in the UK, flying Beauforts in 42 Squadron. Although he had been born in Suffolk, his parents lived in Cairo, where his father was chief of police. Harvey took over command of 39 Squadron on 12 June, shortly before the crews began to work up on Beaufighters with the help of 144 Squadron.

The eight Beaufighters found a convoy of two large merchant vessels and two warships in the east of the strait and attacked, but no results were seen apart from a fire on one of the warships. One of the anti-flak section, flown by Pilot Officer Ralph E. Dodd, turned to make an attack against a ferry, but his aircraft was hit by flak and came down in the sea. The Canadian pilot survived to become a PoW but his navigator, Sergeant Ronald A. Fox, lost his life. Another Beaufighter, flown by Flying Officer T.H. Curlee, shot down an escorting SM79.

It was the turn of the other two Beaufighter squadrons during the next day. In the morning, Squadron Leader Lee-Evans led six of 47 Squadron against two merchant vessels and two warships off the north of Sicily. One torpedo hit was claimed against the larger merchant vessel, but Lee–Evans' aircraft was badly hit by the flak and he limped home with difficulty. The commanding officer of 144 Squadron, Wing Commander James McLaughlin, led six Beaufighters against the same target in the afternoon. McLaughlin made two runs and on the second occasion saw a torpedo dropped by Sergeant J.A.W. Howe hit a merchant vessel amidships, following which his own torpedo also scored another hit. In spite of interference by three single-engined fighters and defensive fire from the vessels, all aircraft returned safely.

In the early afternoon of the following day, 14 July, 39 and 47 Squadrons went out against separate targets. Squadron Leader George A. Powell led eight of 47 Squadron against two merchant vessels and an escort off the north-west of Corsica. A few minutes before they arrived at the convoy, two Beaufighters attacked two Ju 52s, one of which was last seen losing height with two engines on fire. Then the aircraft turned to attack the convoy, against intense flak. Two torpedo hits were scored, and Lloyds' records show that it was in this position that the *San Francisco* (formerly French) of 6,013 tons was sunk.

An hour later, Squadron Leader Muller-Rowland led eight of 39 Squadron against two merchant vessels which the aircrews later described as 'tankers escorted by two flak ships and six MC202 single-engined fighters', off the east coast of Corsica. The larger merchant vessel blew up after being hit by torpedoes. Lloyds' records show that this was the German *Capitaine de Diabat* of 3,107 tons. One Beaufighter was shot down by flak, and Flight Lieutenant John N. Cartwright lost his life, together with his navigator, Sergeant William C. Colley. Cartwright was the pilot who had been responsible for the destruction of the Italian submarine *Narvalo* on 14 January.

The pace of these attacks was maintained while the Allied troops were steadily advancing in Sicily against stiff and determined opposition from seasoned German troops. On 19 July, Squadron Leader Kenneth R.P. Painter led eight of 47 Squadron against a small merchant vessel found near the island of Elba. The ship was badly shot up by cannon fire, although all torpedoes missed.

The next day, Flying Officer Gordon L. Reneau from the same squadron led another eight Beaufighters on a strike near the Italian port of Leghorn, where they came across three barges. The types of barges which the Beaufighters found in these waters were not solely the F-boats which the Beauforts and Bisleys had attacked along the coasts of North Africa. There was the naval artillery lighter – or MAL – of 185 tons, equipped with two 88mm guns and six 20mm cannons mounted on a steel-plated deck. In addition, there was the Siebel ferry, a vessel of 143 tons originally designed in 1940 by the aircraft designer Fritz Siebel, a friend of Hermann Goering, for the invasion of Britain. This manoeuvrable vessel could transport about 450 men or ten vehicles; although the wide deck was not steel-plated, it was mounted with a 40mm gun and two 20mm cannons. All these barges, low-lying and with shallow draughts of under three feet, were not only extremely difficult to sink but could put up a fearsome defence against low-flying aircraft. Apart from operating between Sardinia, Corsica and the

146

mainland, they were the main means by which the Germans supplied their troops in Sicily across the narrow Strait of Messina.

The three barges were seen to be heavily laden in their bows and flying swastikas from their sterns. One was hit by cannon fire in the bridge and on the bows, causing an explosion and a cloud of white smoke, while the other two were hit in their sterns.

One Beaufighter was forced to ditch but the crew, Flying Officer Selwyn M. Hunt and Flying Officer G.A. Corbin, were seen to get into their dinghy. They were about ten miles from the port and drifted until the early afternoon of the next day, when they were spotted by an enemy aircraft. After being picked up by an Italian minesweeper, they were brought into Leghorn. On 10 September, two days after the Italians announced their capitulation, the New Zealander Selwyn Hunt was put on a train at Bologna, destined for the Brenner Pass and Germany. The following night, he managed to slip through a hole cut in the floor of one of the wagons, when south of Verona. He walked towards the Swiss border and, after some days, was befriended by an Italian family who gave him shelter throughout the winter. He left them on 22 May 1944 and ten days later succeeded in reaching Switzerland.

Meanwhile, on the same day that 47 Squadron attacked the barges off Leghorn, Flying Officer C.V. Brown led eight Beaufighters of 144 Squadron in an Armed Rover towards Elba. Near the Italian port of Civitavecchia they came across two barges and attacked these with cannon fire. Again, a Beaufighter was shot down and ditched. The pilot, Flying Officer W.C. Bond, became a PoW, but his navigator, Sergeant Austin Smith, lost his life.

An attack against a convoy heading south off the east coast of Corsica during the following day, 21 July, was not successful. There were two merchant ships, escorted by four warships and four flak-ships. Squadron Leader Muller-Rowland led the first wave of six Beaufighters of 39 Squadron. There were no hits with torpedoes, and one aircraft was shot down; the New Zealander pilot, Pilot Officer Donald M. Hunter, and his navigator, Sergeant L.W. Booth, survived to become PoWs. Squadron Leader William B.W. Gracey led the second formation – eight Beaufighters of 144 Squadron – and again there were no torpedo hits. The anti-flak section shot up the escorts and all aircraft returned safely.

Eight Beaufighters of 47 Squadron went out on 22 July and found a merchant vessel escorted by a warship and a tug, near Elba. The merchant vessel made a tight turn and 'combed' the tracks of the torpedoes, which missed. The anti-flak section shot up the warship and also set the tug on fire. No aircraft were lost.

On 23 July, eight Beaufighters of 144 Squadron attacked a convoy consisting of two merchant vessels, two warships and three flak-ships, with two enemy aircraft circling overhead. A Canadian, Flying Officer Robert W. Fulton, dropped a torpedo and then was seen to crash in flames. He and his navigator, Flying Officer Sidney W. Anderson, did not survive. One torpedo was believed to have hit one of the warships. In the anti-flak section, Flight Sergeant Donald E. Hamar attacked a Bréguet 521 'Bizerte' flying boat; it jettisoned depth charges and then began to break up before crashing into the sea. Flight Sergeant J.A.W. Howe was hit in the knee when he attacked one of the warships, while his hydraulics were severed and the pitch lever was jammed. He continued his attack and then limped home behind the remaining aircraft, to make a crash-landing back at Protville II.

On 24 July the new commanding officer of 47 Squadron, Wing Commander James A. Lee-Evans, led eight Beaufighters on an strike against a vessel which they found near the island of Ventotene, east of Naples. Only two aircraft were ordered to attack. A torpedo dropped by Warrant Officer A. Thompson scored a hit amidships and the vessel blew up, with a violent explosion, sinking immediately. It was in this position that the passenger ferry *Santa Lucia* of 452 tons was sunk.

The following day, 25 July, the dictator Benito Mussolini was at last ousted by the Fascist Grand Council, his powers transferred to the monarchy and his place taken by Marshal Pietro Badoglio. Although the new head of state announced that the country would continue the war, it was evident that the majority of Italians were disillusioned by three years of military failure and an alliance with a country they had learned to detest. Their will to carry on was to be further eroded by massive bombardments of their cities by Allied heavy bombers and the invasion of their mainland. Mussolini himself was arrested and imprisoned in a resort near the Gran Sasso mountain in the Appennines.

On 26 July, 144 Squadron ended their short tour in this theatre of war in spectacular fashion. Eight Beaufighters went out at 1025 hours on an 'Armed Rover' patrol along the east coasts of Sardinia and Corsica. They were led by Squadron Leader Gracey, four armed with torpedoes and four in the anti-flak role. While off Sardinia, less than two hours later, they encountered two Me 323s, six-engined transports which could carry about 130 soldiers or their equivalent in cargo. Both were from the 3rd Staffel of the 1st Transportgeschwader 5, based in Sardinia. Two Beaufighters, flown by Sergeant J.M. Murray and Flying Officer J.P. Fletcher, attacked immediately and sent one of the giant transports down into the sea, in flames. It was flown by Oberfeldwebel Heinrich Böge, who lost his life, together with four of his crew. The other Me 323 turned towards the coast, chased by two other Beaufighters, flown by Flight Sergeant Don E. Hamar and Flying Officer J.W. King, and was shot down over land. The pilot, Oberfeldwebel Herbert Karallus, was also killed, along with two of his crew. But the Beaufighter flown by John King was shot down by a single-engined fighter. The pilot spent the rest of the war as a PoW but his navigator, Flight Sergeant Robert E. Tinham, lost his life. Meanwhile, the torpedo-carrying aircraft continued and found a convoy about ten minutes later, consisting of two merchant vessels and a small escort. They attacked, and one merchant ship blew up.

Three days after this action, 144 Squadron was able to return to the UK, leaving behind two fully fledged squadrons of the new torpedo-carrying Beaufighters. The pace did not slacken. On the same day that 144 Squadron flew off – 29 July – Squadron Leader Powell led eight Beaufighters of 47 Squadron on an Armed Rover between the Italian coast and Cape Bonifacio in Corsica. They found a large merchant vessel escorted by a warship and two MTBs. Approaching from head-on and then splitting into two sections, they hit the merchant vessel amidships with a torpedo. Pilot Officer Stewart F. Cowan's Beaufighter, in the anti-flak section, ditched with an engine on fire, but he and his navigator, Sergeant Anthony P. Crawford, got into their dinghy and were picked up by an Italian Red Cross floatplane. The following day, Squadron Leader Muller–Rowland led eight Beaufighters of 39 Squadron to the same target and found it being towed by a tug in the Bay of Naples, under the escort of two warships. The merchant ship *Alfieri* of 4,573 tons was hit and sank, and the Beaufighters returned safely.

The next attack was on 2 August, when eight Beaufighters of 47 Squadron led by Wing Commander Lee–Evans went out on another Armed Rover and found a burning ship in the Gulf of Cagliari, on the south of Sardinia. Thick black smoke was rising from the vessel, while one warship and five MTBs were in attendance. The formation attacked, raking the vessels with cannon fire, and met concentrated flak. One Beaufighter was seen to be heading south with an engine smoking, and it was seen to ditch a few minutes later. The crew got into their dinghy and waved, while three aircraft circled them. Two of these Beaufighters dropped more dinghies, but they were chased away by F-W 190s. The downed men were a Canadian pilot, Flying Officer Gordon L. Reneau, and his RAF navigator, Sergeant S.H. Hutton. They drifted for two days before arriving in Cagliari harbour, where they were captured by Italian soldiers. The prisoners were taken to Rome and then Modena, from where they were put on a train heading towards the Brenner Pass. By then, Italy had capitulated. On 13 September, when north of Trento in the Alps, Gordon Reneau was the eighth prisoner to escape through a hole in a railway truck cut by four Australian officers. He headed east, walking over the mountains, and arrived in Switzerland a week later. Hutton did not have this opportunity and spent the remainder of the war in German PoW camps.

The next attack by 47 Squadron, on 3 August, resulted in the first fatalities for three weeks. Squadron Leader Painter led eight Beaufighters on an Armed Rover from the Italian coast across to Corsica. After raking two schooners with cannon fire, the formation continued down the east coast of Corsica until three merchant ships were spotted ahead. The attack was met with concentrated fire, from the shore as well as the ships. In the anti-flak section, one Beaufighter was seen to burst into flames and crash into the sea. Both the pilot, Flight Sergeant Albert C. Temple, and his navigator, Sergeant William K. Ambrose, lost their lives. No hits from the torpedoes were seen.

The next strike, on 10 August, was led by Flight Lieutenant Stan Balkwill, who had scored the last torpedo hit with Beauforts before 39 Squadron converted on to Beaufighters. Eight aircraft of his squadron attacked two merchant ships in the Bay of Bastia, in the north of Corsica. A hit was credited on the larger vessel, and all aircraft returned safely. This was Balkwill's last operational flight with 39 Squadron. He returned home to Canada, but unfortunately was later killed, when his Mosquito crashed on take-off.

On 12 August, Squadron Leader Norman S. Petch led eight Beaufighters of 39 Squadron on an Armed Rover, hunting for a 5,000 ton merchant vessel reported to be sailing unescorted south of Naples. They made no sightings but were attacked by four Me 109s and two F-W 190s in the area. A Beaufighter flown by a Canadian pilot, Flight Sergeant D.N. Spackman, was shot down but made a good ditching. Spackman and his RAF navigator, Sergeant W.W. Lawson, survived to become PoWs. A Beaufighter flown by Warrant Officer W.K. Patterson returned badly shot up; his navigator, Sergeant John S. Cole, was killed in the action.

The following day was the turn of 47 Squadron, when Wing Commander Lee–Evans led eight Beaufighters on an Armed Rover from the Italian coast to the east coast of Sardinia. They found a convoy southwest of Civitavecchia, consisting of a large merchant vessel escorted by what appeared to be a corvette and one E-boat. All torpedoes missed but each vessel was subjected to cannon strikes. The German R6, a minesweeper of 125 tons, which the crews believed was an E-boat, blew up and sank in this attack, and all aircraft returned safely.

Two days later, an attack on a warship off Corsica by six Beaufighters of 47 Squadron led by Squadron Leader Painter resulted in no hits or losses. On the following day, 16 August, a strike by eight Beaufighters of 39 Squadron led by Squadron Leader Muller-Rowland on two merchant vessels and three warships north of Naples resulted in hits on both merchantmen, again for no losses.

By now, the Germans in Sicily had retreated in good order as far as Messina, still fighting tenaciously. From here, they withdrew the bulk of their forces to the mainland, mainly in small parties carried by Siebel ferries, and by 17 August the whole of the island was in Allied hands.

Meanwhile the Axis still held out in Sardinia and Corsica. The German forces on Sardinia were made up of a Panzer Grenadier Division, the Moelders Fighter Wing, and various flak units. In addition, there were Italian units, but the loyalty of these troops was faltering. Up to June 1943, these Axis forces had been provisioned from Naples, by sea to the port of Olbia in the north-east of the island as well as by air. However, so many ships were sunk on this route, by air attack and by submarines, that it was abandoned. Instead, supplies were sent from Leghorn to Bastia in Corsica, and were then brought by road down the length of the island and transported by Siebel ferries and infantry transports across the Strait of Bonifacio to Sardinia. But by the end of July, when it became clear that Sicily would fall to the Allies, the German's began to evacuate Sardinia by withdrawing small forces across the Strait of Bonifacio to Corsica.

The Italians were becoming increasingly tired and dispirited by their continual defeats in the Mediterranean, as well as the assault on their cities by bombers from North Africa and the RAF's heavy bombers based in England. Their General Staff knew only too well that the next attack would be the Allied invasion of their mainland. In July, the Allies had offered terms for surrender, and discussions were taking place in Madrid. It was time for the Italians to change sides, but Marshal Badoglio dithered for the next few days.

The maritime strike squadrons continued to attack the supply routes to the Axis forces on Sardinia and Corsica. On 19 August, Wing Commander Lee-Evans led eight Beaufighters of 47 Squadron on an Armed Rover along the west coast of Italy. They found a schooner near Civitavecchia and set it on fire with their cannons. A few minutes later, they came across a couple of torpedo boats, but were then attacked by three F-W 190s and one MC202. Two Beaufighters were damaged and crash-landed back at Protville II.

On 24 August, Squadron Leader Painter led ten of 47 Squadron on another Armed Rover. Two Beaufighters returned early with oil leaks and engine trouble, but the remainder continued towards Civitavecchia where they attacked two barges and a schooner, leaving them in flames. Flying Officer J.S. Hayden collided with the mast of the schooner and turned back to base, chased by two F-W 190s. He finally ditched about seven miles from the Tunisian coast and was picked up by a high-speed launch, together with his navigator, Sergeant A.R. Cottle. The remaining Beaufighters continued their sortie and, an hour later, attacked two small coastal vessels off the coast of Corsica. One torpedo was seen to score a hit near the stern of one of the vessels, while bits of superstructure flew off both from cannon strikes.

The next attack was on 2 September, when Squadron Leader Powell led ten of 47 Squadron against two merchant ships and two torpedo boats between Bastia and Leghorn. One Beaufighter burst into flames and crashed into the sea, killing the Canadian pilot Flight Lieutenant James R. Hastings and his RAF navigator, Flight Sergeant Francis P. Hill. Another Beaufighter was hit but ditched successfully. The crew, Sergeant R.A. Forbes and Sergeant A.E. Dingwall, were picked up and spent the rest of the war as PoWs. The merchant vessels were left smoking from cannon fire.

The next Armed Rover took place on 6 September, when Flight Lieutenant Charles A. Ogilvie led ten of 47 Squadron from Corsica to Leghorn. They found a tanker and three E-boats, but no torpedoes scored hits. However, three Ju 52 transports were sighted, and one was shot down into the sea by three of the Beaufighters. On the following day, Wing Commander Harvey led ten of 39 Squadron and found a merchant vessel north of Corsica. It was hit by cannon fire and torpedoes and sank, but at the last moment the crews spotted Swiss markings on the ship.

On 8 September, the Italians at last announced their unconditional surrender, having signed the document five days before. At dawn the following day, two British divisions and one from the United States landed on the beaches at Salerno, invading the European mainland. There was much bitter fighting to follow, but the landings had been preceded by immense air bombardments and Allied fighters were able to keep the area almost entirely clear of the Luftwaffe.

The Italian Navy obeyed the order to surrender and their warships in Taranto reached Malta without incident. But the three battleships, six cruisers and eight destroyers which sailed from Spezia were less fortunate, for they were attacked by eleven Do 217s from the south of France, when near the Sardinian port of of Maddelena. The battleship *Roma* was hit by a radio-controlled bomb of about 3,000lb and blew up after catching fire. About 300 aircraft of the Regia Aeronautica flew to join the Allies, and formed squadrons for the rest of the war alongside the North-west African Air Forces. On 12 September, Mussolini was rescued from imprisonment near the Gran Sasso mountain by German parachutists headed by the remarkable Oberst Otto Skorzeny. He was taken to Germany and later formed a puppet 'government' in northern Italy, but towards the end of the war was captured and shot by Italian partisans. The Italian government declared war on Germany on 13 September.

There was a short respite for the two Beaufighter anti-shipping squadrons while these events were taking place, but the attacks were resumed on 15 September when Squadron Leader Muller-Rowland led eleven of 39 Squadron against a tanker and four flak-ships near the island of Elba. Six torpedoes were dropped but all missed and two Beaufighters were shot down. The crew of one of these Flying Officer G.F. Howard and Sergeant A.W.H. Goldie were captured and eventually taken to Germany. In the other, Flying Officer John C. Yorke and Flying Officer Walter B. Matthias were picked out of the water by Italian sailors and taken to the Italian island of Capraia, east of the north-west tip of Corsica. The Italians befriended them, and the group decided to escape to Ponza, an island off Naples, which had been occupied by the Allies. The RAF men took charge and, with an unserviceable compass but navigating by the stars, reached the island. From there, they were taken in a US launch to Capri and from there in a Royal Navy vessel to Malta. They returned to 39 Squadron, but unhappily both lost their lives about six months later on a sweep over southern France.

Yet another Beaufighter ditched after this attack, about twenty miles from the south-east tip of Sardinia, but the two men got into their dinghy; they were Flying Officer A.P. Ambrose and Flying Officer G.J. Higgin. Muller-Rowland went out the following day and located the dinghy. Together with another Beaufighter flown by Warrant Officer J. Power, he then homed a high-speed launch to the two men, who were picked up after twenty-four hours in the water.

This was Stanley Muller–Rowland's last operational flight with 39 Squadron. His commanding officer, Wing Commander Nelson Harvey, recollects that his flight commander was a 'demon for operations and working up squadron efficiency'. During his period of operations on Beaufighters, his eyes 'glowed with enthusiasm' whenever he was detailed to lead the squadron, and he had to be almost forcibly restrained from participating in every sortie. After each attack, he analysed the methods used and examined photographs meticulously, frequently proposing improvements in tactics. His loss would have been a serious blow to morale in the squadron, where he was known as 'the wonder boy from Woking'. Decorated with a DFC and Bar, he was posted to Shallufa, where his job was to train new crews and pick out future leaders of his own calibre. Those who knew him in his new role as an instructor still remember him vividly. But the anti-shipping squadrons in the Mediterranean had not seen the last of this truly remarkable pilot, who was still only twenty-one years of age.

It was the turn of 47 Squadron on 18 September, when Wing Commander Lee-Evans, who had been gazetted with a DFC in the previous month, led ten Beaufighters on an Armed Rover up the east coasts of Sardinia and Corsica towards Leghorn. After an hour and a half, the port engine seized up in the Beaufighter flown by Sergeant N.V. Hoiles, when at seventy-five feet. He turned back to base, and then had the strange experience of passing a Ju 88 which waggled its wings before turning away to the east. After an hour on the return journey, the starboard engine also failed. The aircraft dropped and Hoiles was unable to adjust the trim before the starboard wing hit the water. He was knocked out but came to amid debris and with his dinghy nearby. He was picked up the next day by high-speed launch when about fifty miles from Bizerta. Unfortunately there was no sign of his navigator, Sergeant Patrick P. Cameron, who lost his life. Meanwhile, the remaining nine Beaufighters continued on their sortie and came across a merchant vessel and escort north of Corsica. They attacked and saw two large flashes from the merchant vessel, as well as pieces fly off the bridge from cannon fire. One of the flight commanders, Squadron Leader Kenneth R.P. Painter, was shot down. He and his navigator, Flying Officer H.T.G. Glen-Davison, were seen to get into their dinghy, but the two men were outside the range of air-sea rescue. They were both taken prisoner and sent to Germany.

During the period from 11 to 18 September, the Germans completed their withdrawal from Sardinia to Corsica, in good order and with all their arms and equipment. All their ferries and infantry transports were then transferred to Bastia in the north of Corsica, from where they continued their withdrawal to Leghorn, a distance of only seventy-seven miles. Many of the Corsicans joined the Maquis resistance movement and, supplied with weapons and ammunition by the Allies, harried the Germans as they retreated north. Needless to say, Bastia was subjected to heavy air bombardment and Allied submarines attacked the larger transports. For the most part, the German evacuation from Corsica was then carried out by ferries and air transports, either direct to Leghorn or via the island of Elba to the mainland. For a few eventful days, the roles of the Beaufighter squadrons at Protville were changed to meet this new situation, from anti-shipping strikes to that of long-range fighters against the air transports.

The first of these fighter patrols took place in the afternoon of 23 September, when two of 39 Squadron took off with two of 47 Squadron. One Beaufighter of 39 Squadron turned back with magneto trouble, but the remaining three carried on and intercepted four Ju 52s and two SM82s north of Corsica. An SM82 was attacked from head-on and crashed into the sea after bursting into flames. Two Ju 52s were damaged, with bits flying off each aircraft. A short engagement then took place with two Arado 196 floatplanes which circled the wreckage, but neither appeared to be hit. But a few minutes later, six more Ju 52s appeared. In the resulting combat, the port engine of one was set on fire but the German pilot made a controlled ditching. Another SM82 then arrived on the scene, but managed to evade an attack by one of the Beaufighters, all of which returned safely.

In the late afternoon of the same day, two more Beaufighters of 39 Squadron took off but neither returned. They met a formation of five Ju 52s north of Bastia and shot down two of them, but one Beaufighter was downed by return fire. Flight Lieutenant A.K.S. McCurdy and his navigator Sergeant W.N. Burton survived to become PoWs in Germany. Five more Ju 52s then appeared and were attacked by the remaining Beaufighter, flown by Flying Officer Neil D. Cox. This Beaufighter was also damaged but Cox made a successful ditching near the north coast of Sardinia. The navigator, Flying Officer W.W. Spearey was injured, but Cox managed to get him into the dinghy. The pilot then got back into the sea and, putting his neck through a rung of the dinghy ladder, swam with it to the shore, a distance of about three miles. Cox found the local Italians to be unhelpful and even hostile, but eventually he managed to get a doctor to attend to Spearey. The navigator was taken to a hospital at Sassari, which US forces had occupied shortly before, and recovered from his wounds. Cox received no award for this gallant action, although he ended the war with the ribbon of the DFC and bar.

In the early morning of the next day, Squadron Leader Petch led four of 39 Squadron on another fighter sweep. Again, one Beaufighter returned with engine trouble, but the remaining three attacked three Ju 52s off the island of Pianosa, near Elba, and shot one down into the sea. But then Petch and his navigator, Pilot Officer G.F. Williams, were seen to ditch and to be picked up by a launch. Later the same morning, Wing Commander Harvey led four of 39 Squadron on another sweep and met three Ju 52s south-east of Bastia. They shot down all three and returned safely.

There was a third sweep on that morning, when Flight Lieutenant N.E.J. Butler led out five more of 39 Squadron. Butler was forced to return with engine trouble, and the lead was taken over by Pilot Officer Harry H. Deacon, who had flown with 39 Squadron since the days when it was equipped with Beauforts. The remaining four intercepted twelve Ju 52s near Elba, shooting down two and damaging a third, but two Beaufighters were also shot down. One of these was last seen heading south, with a damaged engine, but the crew – consisting of a Canadian pilot, Pilot Officer Eric P. Twiname and an RAF navigator, Sergeant Ian A. McCleod – lost their lives. The other was seen to make a good ditching; it was flown by Harry Deacon, with a Canadian navigator, Flying Officer C. Lee Heide. A third Beaufighter, flown by Sergeant A.T.P. Paterson, struggled home on one engine and crash-landed ten miles from base, without injury to the crew. The fourth sweep of the day was carried out by three Beaufighters of 47 Squadron, led by Flying Officer T. Smart. They attacked twelve Ju 52s flying at low level between Corsica and Elba, but there was no conclusive result from the combat, which was interrupted by the arrival of three single-engined fighters, identified as Reggiane Re 2001s. The three Beaufighters returned safely.

On the next day, 25 September, two Beaufighters of 39 Squadron went out with parachute containers intended for the airmen downed on the previous day. They were attacked by two Me 109s while hunting near Pianosa Island and one was shot down. Flying Officer Robert W. Powell, lost their lives. The other Beaufighter, flown by Flying Officer T.H. Curlee, returned safely.

Meanwhile, Deacon and Heide were still afloat. Their Beaufighter had been hit in the port oil tank and before long the engine gave out. Deacon made a perfect ditching, and they got into the dinghy just before the aircraft sank. But they were some distance from shore and it was four days before they managed to paddle to Elba. Even then, they were twice dashed against the rocks and might well have been drowned but for the help of some Italians. Unlike Cox and Spearey on Sardinia, they found the local people to be extremely helpful, although there was little to eat except grapes and potatoes. They hid in the mountains, from where they watched German barges arriving from Bastia carrying troops, tanks and trucks. The island swarmed with troops but the enemy patrols did not find them, for they kept on the move and at one stage hid in a deep cave. After another four days, they joined five Italians in a rowing boat fitted with a crude sail made of sacking, with the objective of escaping to Corsica. The men reached safety in a voyage of over fourteen hours across forty-five miles of sea, landing on a barren stretch of coast. From there, they made their way inland for two days, dirty and hungry but in good spirits, until some Frenchmen took care of them. By 8 October, the squadron learnt that they were safe in Ajaccio and an aircraft was sent to collect them two days later.

The Germans had completed their evacuation of Corsica on 3 October, while the port of Bastia was under fire from machine guns and mortars from the advancing Allies. They succeeded in shipping most of their equipment to Elba in Siebel ferries, leaving behind only about fifty motor vehicles. Meanwhile, the Allies had won the fight at Salerno and were moving up the south and south-east of Italy. On 27 September the large group of airfields around Foggia, on the heel of Italy, was occupied by the Eighth Army. These airfields were to become the home of many squadrons of the Allied air forces, including Beaufighters, for the remainder of the war in Europe.

With their immediate tasks accomplished, the two Beaufighter squadrons did not operate for the next few weeks. In a little over three months, they had made a major contribution to the destruction of the Axis supply system to Sardinia and Corsica. Together with 144 Squadron in the early weeks, thirty-one of their aircraft had ditched in the sea during that period, almost entirely as a result of enemy fire. Fatalities of aircrews had been lighter than those suffered by the Beaufort crews when engaged on daylight attacks, however, amounting to twenty-three crew members. Of the remaining downed airmen, a fairly high proportion managed to get into their dinghies and were rescued. Some of these evaded capture or contrived to escape after Italy capitulated. This lower casualty rate occured because the crew was reduced from four in the Beaufort to two in the Beaufighter, and the men were highly trained in faster and more heavily armed machines.

In October, heavy rainfall created swamp-like conditions in Protville. Early in the month, ten aircrews of 39 Squadron were sent to Shallufa for further torpedo training, and on 21 October all the squadron's aircraft flew to Sidi Amor in Tunisia. From here, detachments were sent to Grottaglie, near Taranto, from where they could cover the Adriatic. On 22 October, 47 Squadron moved to El Adem in Libya, in order to operate over the eastern Mediterranean, as will be seen in the next chapter.

10

SIDESHOW

W hen the major part of the conflict in the Mediterranean moved westward, after El Alamein, the role of the remaining strike aircraft of 201 (Naval Co-operation) Group in Egypt became less prominent. The partnership of 252 and 272 Squadrons broke up when the latter moved to Malta in November 1942. Meanwhile, the Beaufighters of 252 Squadron continued to harass the Axis forces retreating in North Africa, strafing columns of trucks and troops as well as convoys of F-boats.

On 6 December, two pairs of Beaufighters took off from Berka, near Benghazi, to strafe the coast road in the region of Sirte. In one pair of aircraft, Wing Commander Peter H. Bragg ditched three miles from the coast. He survived to become a PoW but his navigator, Flight Lieutenant Eric G. Nichols, lost his life. In the other pair, Squadron Leader A. Derek Frecker crash-landed in the desert after attacking the airfield at Tamet. The nose of his Beaufighter had been hit by flak, the starboard engine put out of action, and the air cooler smashed. Pilot Officer Tom Armstrong was his navigator on this sortie, and they were carrying a passenger, Sergeant A. 'Paddy' Clark, who serviced the aircraft and had managed to persuade the CO to let him fly on this occasion. The three men were unharmed but they were a long way from home and had only a few tins of bully beef, salmon and sardines for their rations. They took a can of water and began to walk towards the Allied lines, hiding when enemy transport appeared and huddling together for warmth in parachute silk during the freezingly cold nights. At one stage, they watched Italian troops mining the coast road. On the seventh day they fell in with some Senussi Arabs, who gave them food, water and shelter. Fifteen days after their forced landing, they were rescued by an armoured car of the 1st King's Dragoon Guards, and the Arabs were rewarded. During their evasion, they had carried an emblem from their Beaufighter, an eagle wearing a top hat and mounted on cannons. In Cairo, the three men became members of the 'Late Arrivals Club', airmen who had returned after being shot down in the Western Desert.

The squadron was also engaged in escorting naval convoys during this period, and Sergeant Stan Kernaghan shot down a Ju 88 on 8 December. Three days later, Wing Commander Patrick B.B. Ogilvie DSO DFC arrived to command the squadron. Apart from a few attacks against F-boats, the squadron was then engaged primarily on more convoy escorts until the following May. It moved to Magrun in Libya on 21 February, from where it was better placed for this work. Kernaghan was gazetted with a DFM on 26 February and left the squadron in May.*

Meanwhile, 227 Squadron was undergoing a slow process of rebuilding after its heavy losses from Malta in January and early February 1943. During this period it had been commanded by the former CO of 272 Squadron, Wing Commander Anthony Watson DSO DFC, who was posted to AHQ Malta on 22 February. The squadron moved to Idku on 1 March and began to receive new Beaufighter VIs, fitted with bomb racks. A New Zealander in the RAF, Wing Commander Russell M. Mackenzie DFC AFC, took over command of the squadron in early April. Four aircraft went out on an offensive patrol in the Aegean on the twenty-first of that month, operating from Gambut in Libya. Although the sortie was uneventful, the men knew that the squadron was actively back in the war.

Both 227 and 252 Squadrons were allotted the task of offensive patrols in the Aegean and along the coasts of the Greek mainland, as far as the range of their Beaufighters permitted. The outer rim of the area controlled by the Axis stretched down the west coast of Greece to Kithera (an island off the southern tip of the Peloponnese) and then to Crete and its nearby island of Scarpanto, and finally to Rhodes. The Beaufighters were able to penetrate this line and reach some of the islands of the Cyclades, the southern Sporades and the Dodecanese.

The eyes of the British had turned to this strategic area for a number of reasons. Churchill believed that the Russian advances in Eastern Europe would eventually bring their forces into the Balkans, and he had no wish to see these countries fall under Communist domination. The majority of the troops in the region were Italians, and their loyalty to the Axis cause was wavering. The Germans were so occupied in other theatres of war that only a sprinkling of the Wehrmacht was represented in the area. It seemed possible that the Allies could gain control of some of the Aegean islands with only a moderate expenditure of resources. This could open up a supply line to Russia via the Dardanelles, thus creating an alternative to the costly and difficult sea route via the Arctic Sea to Murmansk or the route through the mountains of Persia. Moreover, a success of Allied arms in the area might encourage Turkey to enter the war on the Allied side.

---

* He was commissioned and was later awarded the AFC.

In addition to providing long-range fighter escort for warships of the Royal Navy, the sorties of the two Beaufighter squadrons consisted of Armed Rovers which could result in attacks against enemy air transports and shipping. At the same time, heavy bomber squadrons intensified their attacks at night against ports and airfields. Most of the supplies for the Axis garrisons in the Aegean were carried by sea, and it was hoped that these vessels would be vulnerable to attack at a time when the main naval and air strength was concentrated in the central Mediterranean. The most common of these supply vessels were small caiques, former fishing vessels which were fitted with engines as well as sails. Those which were only lightly armed could be fairly easy prey for cannon-firing Beaufighters. Larger merchant vessels or ferries could be bombed, although the Beaufighters of 252 Squadron were not yet fitted with bomb racks. There were only a few Axis destroyers and torpedo boats to act as escorts to convoys, although there were smaller escort vessels with formidable armament, such as UJ-boats (submarine hunters) and R-boats (small minesweepers).

The Beaufighter crews set about their task with enthusiasm but, as usual in war, matters did not turn out exactly as planned. The caiques began to moor up in defended harbours during daylight and to travel only at night. Some of them seemed to be heavily armed, and the aircrews believed that a few of the larger vessels were operating as 'Q-ships' with concealed guns, to spring unpleasant surprises on the attackers. They were correct in this assumption, for the Germans had armed five of these vessels – *GA41* to *GA45* (GA standing for Griechenland Attika) – with an 88mm gun, a 37mm gun and a 20mm 'quad' gun. They also carried depth charges and were fitted with radar and sonar. The crews wore civilian clothes and flew the Greek flag until their armament was uncovered, when they hoisted the German flag. Moreover, the Beaufighters were forced to operate at the extremity of their range from Libya or Egypt and were vulnerable to attack by single-engined fighters based at airfields on the Greek mainland or on Crete and Rhodes. However, if damaged and forced to ditch, they could expect help from friendly Greek islanders. Also, an escape route lay through Turkey, which was turning a blind eye to certain Allied activities along its southern and western seaboards.

The two squadrons continued these operations, with some successes and losses, throughout the spring and summer of 1943. On 26 April, Wing Commander MacKenzie led three Beaufighters of 227 Squadron from Gambut on a strike against a large schooner off the eastern coast of the Greek mainland, setting it on fire. But an aircraft flown by Sergeant Ronald A. Harvey struck the mast of the vessel and plunged into the sea. Harvey and his navigator, Pilot Officer Walter H. Fisher, lost their lives. Another aircraft failed to return from this sortie but the crew,

Flying Officer A.G. 'Tommy' Deck and Pilot Officer G.W. Ridley, managed to make their way to Turkey. They returned to the squadron on 8 June, after a brief period of internment. There was another loss on 28 April, when Sergeant G.H. Harrison and Sergeant J.R. Sloper came down in the sea off the north-east coast of Kithera. They got into their dinghy and became PoWs.

On the last day of April arrangements were made for 227 Squadron to receive all the ground personnel of 272 Squadron remaining in Egypt, thus strengthening the squadron. On 1 May, MacKenzie led four Beaufighters from Gambut on a sweep along the Dodecanese, where they attacked a small steamer, the *Capri* of 154 tons. Flight Lieutenant Tom Freer's aircraft was hit in the port engine by flak but he was able to head for Turkey. He and his navigator, Flying Officer Charles P. Holman, were interned but returned to the squadron on 26 June. On 5 May the main base of the squadron was transferred from Idku to Derna in Libya.

252 Squadron lost a Beaufighter and crew on 9 May, when the Canadian pilot Sergeant Keneth W. Clarke and his RAF navigator, Sergeant Jack Talbot, failed to return from a convoy escort. The crew did not survive. Wing Commander Dennis O. Butler arrived to take over command of the squadron on 11 May and this day was also marked by the shooting down of a Ju 52. Butler had commanded the RAF station at Ismailia in Egypt for the previous eighteen months.

Another loss occurred three days later when Squadron Leader David C. Pritchard led three aircraft in a sweep over the Ionian Sea. One Beaufighter was seen to dive into the sea, and Flight Sergeant Maurice F. Hewitt and Sergeant Eric A.W.J. Mead lost their lives. The remaining two found the auxiliary dredger *Anna Maria II* off the west coast of Greece. The dredger was sunk, with the loss of four killed and one wounded.

On 25 May, six Beaufighters of 252 Squadron strafed the seaplane base at Prevesa, on the west coast of Greece. They found fourteen floatplanes at anchor, destroyed four, badly damaged seven, and blew up a petrol dump. Three floatplanes with Red Cross markings were left unharmed. Five days later, three Beaufighters led by Wing Commander Butler attacked the merchant ship *Tenacia Gennari* of 1,046 tons, which was carrying a cargo of hay from Prevesa to the Gulf of Patras. The hay on deck was left blazing but the ship's crew managed to get the fire under control with the aid of the tug *Littoria*, and the vessel reached her destination.

By now, the pattern of these attacks was established, with 227 Squadron flying from Derna over the Aegean islands and 252 Squadron at Magrun concentrating on the west coastline of the mainland, although the operations of the latter were interspersed with convoy escorts. May was a busy month for 227 Squadron, attacking caiques and small merchant vessels in the open sea or harbours. Some of the caiques could be seen flying German flags and several were sunk by bombs. Crews could be seen to abandon vessels which were left on fire.

On 11 May, Pilot Officer Cas de Bouneviale (who had been commissioned in the previous January) and Sergeant William C. Budd intercepted and attacked a floatplane version of the Ju 52, setting the starboard engine on fire. The German aircraft plunged into the sea with no trace of survivors. The squadron adopted the unofficial motto of 'On, on' and produced a gazette of that name. The official crest of 252 Squadron eventually became a shield with the motto 'With or on'. This was based on the exhortation of Spartan women to their men: 'Either return with your shield or on it'.

The squadrons received congratulations from 201 Group for their successes, after the RAF received intelligence reports to the effect that the Axis was being forced to rely more and more on air transport for supplying the Aegean garrisons. But there were a number of losses in 227 Squadron. A pilot from Southern Rhodesia, Sergeant Eric J. Havnar, failed to return on 16 May; he ended the war as a PoW in Germany but his navigator, Sergeant Denis Galley, was killed. On 21 May three Beaufighters met five Ju 52s and five Arado 196 floatplanes near the island of Melos. One Arado was shot down, but a Beaufighter was hit and dived into the sea; Flight Lieutenant James E. Atkins and Flying Officer Robert L. Wellington lost their lives.

On 2 June, 252 Squadron turned its attention to the railway line on the west coast of Greece, strafing trains and wagons. This was followed by several attacks on caiques, tugs, dredgers and coasters in the same area, as well as a daylight raid on the harbour of Killini, opposite the island of Zante in the Ionian Sea. Bomb racks were fitted to the squadron's Beaufighters during June. A notable success was scored on 27 June, when four Beaufighters led by Squadron Leader Ernest R. Meads bombed an Italian convoy in the Levkas Canal, to the south of Prevesa. This consisted of three merchant ships escorted by two auxiliary naval vessels, which were protected by shore batteries as well as their own armament. The bombs hit the merchant ship *Quirinale* of 3,779 tons, which was then beached. A further bombing attack against the stranded vessel a week later finished her off.

During June, 227 Squadron continued to concentrate on the Aegean, sinking several caiques and setting others on fire. The return fire was surprisingly intense and several aircraft were hit. An attack on 4 June against these vessels in the harbour of Stampalia, an island to the west of Cos in the Dodecanese, resulted in the deaths of Sergeant John A. Lewis and his navigator Sergeant James A. Roff. On 26 June, Cas de Bouneviale and his navigator Flight Sergeant Jim Scott, who were nearing the end of their operational tour, were told to go to Algiers. To their surprise, they were appointed as a personal crew to Air Chief Marshal Sir Arthur Tedder, the C-in-C of Mediterranean Air Command. Tedder sometimes preferred to fly in a Beaufighter since a Dakota required a fighter escort, and he thought that this was a waste of the RAF's resources.

During July, 252 Squadron carried out more convoy escorts and also continued attacks off the Greek mainland. Killini harbour and nearby trains were bombed on the seventeeth, and Prevesa seaplane base was attacked two days later. The aerodrome at Kalamata, in the south of the Peloponnese, was attacked on 24 July. Flight Lieutenant John H. Manley and Sergeant James F. King failed to return on 29 July, during another attack on Killini, and both lost their lives.

On 1 July, four Beaufighters of 227 Squadron flew from Magrun to attack dredgers in the Levkas Canal. One aircraft was shot down and the pilot, Flight Sergeant John Hawkesreed, was killed; his Australian navigator, Sergeant L.R. De Maniel, survived to become a PoW. A week later, the squadron flew to Gardabia West in Libya to give fighter protection to the Allied invasion fleet heading for Sicily. While there, an aircraft crashed taking off on 9 July, killing the pilot, Flight Lieutenant Michael B. Curtis. The Australian navigator, Flying Officer John J. Brennan, died the following day. The squadron returned to Derna on the seventeenth. Escorted by Hurricanes, the crews made a number of sorties on 23 July, strafing radio stations, gun posts and caiques in Crete. A successful attack was made five days later, when Wing Commander Mackenzie led four aircraft against two vessels near the island of Alimnia, off Rhodes. They scored direct hits on one of these, which gave out orange flames and black smoke before listing to starboard. The wreckage of this vessel was seen, with masts and funnel sticking out of the water, when another attack was made on 30 July.

These operations continued for the next fortnight, but on 16 August 227 Squadron was sent to Limassol in Cyprus. Unknown to the crews, they were about to embark on an enterprise which, over the next ten weeks, would cost them the equivalent of their normal front-line strength. They began operations almost immediately, hunting along the Dodecanese for coasters and caiques. The first loss from this new base occurred on 2 September, when four aircraft attacked a caique and one struck the mast with its port wing, exploding on hitting the water. The New Zealander pilot, Flight Lieutenant Walter Y. McGregor, was killed, but his RAF navigator, Flying Officer Cyril E. Turner, ended the war as a PoW in Germany.

Meanwhile, 252 Squadron continued to operate off the west coast of Greece. On 22 August, three Beaufighters bombed a tanker at Prevesa and lost two of their number. The crew of one aircraft, Flight Sergeant

Norman Cresswell and Sergeant Frank S. Wright, became PoWs. In the other aircraft both the Canadian pilot, Sergeant Donald H. Pearson, and the RAF navigator, Flight Sergeant Douglas H.F. Sherburn, were killed. A merchant vessel was attacked near Prevesa on 2 September and hit by cannon fire. On 9 September, the Beaufighters flew to Limassol to join in the sorties being carried out by 227 Squadron. Together with the air-sea rescue 294 Squadron, the two Beaufighter squadrons formed 237 Wing, also based at Limassol. Detachments of Beaufighters from 46 and 89 Squadrons also arrived in Cyprus, the former being stationed at Nicosia and the latter at nearby Lakatamia. These were specialised night-fighter squadrons, equipped with Beaufighter VIs fitted with air interception radar.

This was the period when the Allies were firmly in control of Sicily, the invasion of the Italian mainland had just begun, and the Italian government had surrendered. It seemed a propitious time to exploit the favourable situation in the Aegean. The key to a successful assault in this region was the Axis-held island of Rhodes, which possessed three important airfields: Maritza in the north; Calato in the middle; and Cattavia in the south. Together with the Dodecanese – the twelve islands which stretch in a chain along the south-west coast of Turkey – Rhodes had been seized by the Italians in the spring of 1912, after having been under Turkish rule for 390 years. The inhabitants, primarily of Greek extraction, were promised liberty, but the Italians had managed to hold on to the islands until World War Two.

The Americans did not approve of a venture in the Aegean. They contended that a combined operation against Rhodes would draw Allied resources away from other campaigns such as the landings on the Italian mainland, the invasion of the Japanese-held Arakan in Burma and even the proposed invasion of north-west Europe. It was not enough for Churchill to point out that the operation would also pull German forces away from other theatres of war. The Americans suspected that the British were more concerned with post-war political objectives than the successful prosecution of the campaigns. Their view prevailed and the invasion of Rhodes was postponed. Most of the troops and warships allocated for this purpose, under the codename of operation 'Accolade', were sent to other areas.

Hitler viewed the Aegean in much the same way as the British. Foreseeing the imminent collapse of Italy and the possible loss of mineral resources in the Balkans, he had ordered that plans should be made to seal off the Italian peninsula and to transfer elements of the Wehrmacht to the Aegean. By August 1943, a whole German division of 7,000 men was stationed in Rhodes, together with about 1,500 men on the nearby island of Scarpanto. These Germans were under orders to disarm any Italians who chose not to continue fighting with them.

British Intelligence was well aware of the build-up of German forces in the Aegean, by decrypting signals, but it was still hoped that these forces could be disarmed or overcome with the help of the far more numerous Italians. On the day of the armistice 8 September – the Italian garrison on the small island of Casteloriso, tucked under the southern coast of Turkey, surrendered to a British contingent. Over the next few days, British motor launches and destroyers sailing to this island were escorted by relays of Beaufighters of 227 Squadron. However, two British officers who parachuted into Rhodes during the night of 9/10 September failed to persuade the Italian governor to try to disarm the Germans. Instead, the Germans moved swiftly to overcome the Italians and to occupy the harbours and the three airfields.

The British did not give up hope when the Germans secured their hold on Rhodes. They proposed instead to bypass the island and seize the chain of islands of the Dodecanese, of which the most important were Cos and Leros, as well as the island of Samos to the north. There was only one airfield on these islands – Antimachia, on Cos. It was believed that, if these islands could be secured, Rhodes would be cut off and picked off later. Churchill approved of this proposal. Invoking the spirits of the British generals who had captured Quebec and Gibraltar, he urged the C-in-C in the Middle East, General Sir Henry Maitland-Wilson, to 'improvise and dare' with the limited forces at his disposal.

Accordingly, the plan went ahead. On 14 September a handful of the British Special Forces landed on Cos, an island about twenty-six miles long which is separated from the Turkish mainland by a narrow channel (it is probably best known to the British from the lettuce which bears its name). The men were welcomed by the Greek islanders and most of the Italian garrison. The following day, Spitfire Vs of 7 (SAAF) Squadron flew from Cyprus and landed at Antimachia, supported by supplies flown in by the Dakotas of 216 Squadron. British parachutists were dropped by the Dakotas, which later landed men of the RAF Regiment and the Durham Light Infantry. But these men were only lightly armed and it was soon found that the Italian defences were inadequate. On 14 September, British Special Forces also landed on Leros and, three days later, on Samos. These two islands had no airfields and it was necessary to bring in troops by destroyers and landing ships. Other islands in the Dodecanese were also occupied. Everywhere, the Italian garrisons threw in their lots with the British 'invaders', in the belief that substantial reinforcements would be arriving and that, apart from garrison duties, the war was over for them.

During these combined operations, the duties of 227 and 252 Squadrons were concentrated on fighter escorts to the Dakotas and the naval units carrying troops and supplies to the islands. On one of these escort duties, on 13 September, three Beaufighters of 252 Squadron shot down a Ju 88 which was shadowing three British destroyers west of Cyprus; four German survivors were picked up by high-speed launch and taken to Limassol.

On 17 September, four Beaufighters of 252 Squadron led by Squadron Leader Keith A. Faulkner, together with four from 227 Squadron, attacked two merchant vessels and an escort near the island of Naxos. Faulkner shot down one of two patrolling Ar 96 floatplanes and then strafed the warship and the smaller merchant ship, but his aircraft was hit by intense flak which put the starboard engine out of action. The other Beaufighters bombed the vessels, causing grey smoke to rise to 100 feet from one of them, but several were also hit by flak. An aircraft of 252 Squadron, flown by the Belgian pilot Flight Lieutenant D. Delcour, was hit repeatedly and the navigator, Flight Sergeant Thomas R. Lumsden, was killed. All aircraft landed at Limassol, although one of 227 Squadron made a belly landing. The merchant ship was later reported as sunk.

Meanwhile, it became apparent to British Intelligence that the Germans were reacting violently to the occupation of the Dodecanese. The Germans wrested control of the most important of the other Greek islands from the Italians, including Crete. They also began to draw in long-range bombers from southern Russia and northern France, as well as single-engined fighters from Vienna. It became known that, by the end of September, the Luftwaffe could muster 350 aircraft in Greece and Crete, including ninety Me 109Gs, 130 He 111s and Ju 88s, and about ninety Stuka dive-bombers. The RAF had about 280 aircraft to combat this force, but the Germans possessed the considerable advantage of operating on interior lines, since the distance to Cos was only seventy miles from Rhodes and 150 miles from Crete. On the other hand, the distance to Cos from the RAF's bases in either Cyprus or Libya was about 370 miles, and thus beyond the normal range of single-engined fighters.

Before its build-up was complete, the Luftwaffe began its air assault on Cos. On the morning of 18 September, Me 109s strafed the airfield of Antimachia while Ju 88s made bombing attacks. Although attacks had been anticipated, the defenders were not well equipped. The runway was badly cratered and Spitfires and Dakotas were destroyed. The two Beaufighter squadrons on Cyprus did their best to provide long-distance support for the defenders on Cos, but their effectiveness was necessarily limited.

The German air attacks on Cos continued almost daily and the handful of Spitfires was steadily whittled down. The RAF and the USAAF responded by bombing the enemy air bases, but these attacks did not stop the German aircraft. It seemed possible to the British that these raids were the prelude to an attempt to reoccupy Cos. The Beaufighters went out each day, seeking enemy convoys on the approaches to the island. On 20 September six aircraft from the two squadrons bombed barges and a coaster at Vronti Bay in the island of Scarpanto, but one of 227 Squadron was shot down. The New Zealander pilot, Flight Sergeant Wilfred D. Webster, and his RAF navigator, Flight Sergeant Edward S. Taylor, were killed. In the early hours of the following day, five of 227 and six of 252 Squadron took off for night attacks on Maritza airfield on Rhodes. They dived down, bombing and strafing aircraft and installations, and causing fires and explosions. An aircraft of 227 Squadron failed to return and the RAAF crew, Flight Sergeant Robert S. Neighbour and Flight Sergeant Christopher G. Hoskin, lost their lives.

The Royal Navy was as active as possible in the Aegean. Submarines cruised the area, finding few targets large enough for torpedo attacks, although they sometimes surfaced and sank small vessels by gunfire. Several Italian warships had been captured by the Germans and recommissioned into the Kriegsmarine, but were rarely located. British destroyers searched for enemy vessels, escorted by Beaufighters on frequent occasions, but their range was too short for sustained operations. To extend the periods of their sweeps, they sometimes laid up in concealed anchorages in the islands or made use of Turkish territorial waters, claiming mechanical defects if challenged and boarded. In the early hours of 18 September, the destroyers *Faulknor* and *Eclipse,* together with the Greek destroyer *Vasilissa Olga*, intercepted a German convoy near the island of Stampalia, headed for Rhodes with personnel and supplies. They sank the two merchant vessels, *Paula* (formerly French) of 3,754 tons and *Pluto* (formerly Dutch) of 1,156 tons. The German escort *UJ2104* beached on Stampalia and her crew was later captured by the British.

On 23 September, both 227 and 252 Squadrons began moving from Limassol to Lakatamia, just south of Nicosia. This airfield had the advantage of three dirt strips instead of a single strip but, for the airmen, the living conditions were somewhat similar to those in the Western Desert. There was a tragedy for 227 Squadron on the following day when a Beaufighter taking off from Limassol swung on take-off and crashed into a stationary Beaufighter, killing both crews as well as a pilot who was a passenger.

The first major operation from this new base took place on 25 September, when four aircraft from each squadron took part in an attack against the German torpedo boat *TA10*, which had been beached near Cape Prasonisi on the southern tip of Rhodes. This vessel, the former French *La Pomone* of 610 tons, had been seized by the

Germans from the Italians after the armistice. She had been attacked by the destroyer *Eclipse* in the early hours of 23 September, when escorting the merchant ship *Donizetti* of 2,428 tons. The British destroyer damaged the torpedo boat and sank *Donizetti*, which was carrying about 1,600 Italian personnel from Rhodes to imprisonment in Greece. Unfortunately, all on board lost their lives. The Beaufighters caused further damage to *TA10*, scoring cannon and bomb hits in the face of light flak, and the Germans scuttled the warship the following day.

On 25 September the Germans intensified their air assault on Cos, destroying Spitfires on Antimachia, although the South African pilots fought gallantly against heavy odds. Eight Spitfires of 74 Squadron flew from Cyprus the following day to reinforce the defences, and went into action immediately. Although these Spitfire pilots shot down a number of German aircraft, the airfield at Antimachia was again made unserviceable and the aircraft were transferred to a strip which had been hastily constructed near the west coast of the island.

There was a serious setback for the Royal Navy on 26 September when the destroyer *Intrepid* and the Greek destroyer *Vasilissa Olga* were sunk in Leros harbour by German air attack. On 1 October the Luftwaffe scored another success by putting out of action the Italian destroyer *Euro* at Leros. This warship, which had gone over to the Allies, was abandoned when it sank in shallow water. These naval losses came at a very difficult time for the Allied enterprise in the Aegean.

During the course of 2 October, a German convoy was spotted from the air, first off Paros and then off Naxos, steering east. It was already known from air reconnaissance that a convoy had left Crete by 1025 hours on this day. This consisted of five armed merchant vessels, including *Sinfra* of 4,470 tons and the passenger liner *Città di Savona* of 2,500 tons. In addition, there were six F-boats and the seaplane tender *Zmaj* of 1,870 tons. It was believed at first that this convoy was headed for Rhodes. A force of destroyers from Alexandria, already at sea and escorted by Beaufighters from Cyprus, sailed to intercept but hunted in the wrong area and was forced to head back to Egypt when fuel ran low. Two submarines were ordered to attack the convoy but did not arrive in time.

The German convoy – protected by destroyers, torpedo boats, UJ-boats and R-boats – arrived off Cos in the early hours of 3 October. One contingent of troops landed on the west coast, one in the south, and one near the town of Cos in the north. By first light, about 1,200 well-armed men had been put ashore by ferries and other landing craft, together with artillery and armoured cars. They were soon supported by waves of Stukas and Ju 88s, acting as a form of artillery in the classic Blitzkrieg style. The airfields on Cos were put out of action and German parachutists were dropped to occupy them. The British defenders numbered about 1,600 men, including 250 of the RAF Regiment. Only about 1,100 were combatants, and these were lightly armed. They suffered from the problems of insufficient transport and a very poor road system. The British were supported by about 4,000 Italian soldiers, but most of these were demoralised and thoroughly resentful at the failure to build up sufficient troops and equipment on the island.

The only hope of bringing help to the defenders rested with the Beaufighters on Cyprus, and an all-out effort took place on the day of the landings. By then, 227 and 252 Squadrons at Lakatamia had been joined by a detachment of 46 Squadron, which had exchanged its night-fighter aircraft for Coastal Beaufighters only a week before, in anticipation of employment on anti-shipping attacks. The squadron had already lost one of these aircraft on the night of 27 September, during an intruder raid over the airfields on Rhodes.

Four Beaufighters of 46 Squadron were the first to take off, at 0400 hours, although the crews had little idea of the strength of the German convoy and landing forces. Led by Squadron Leader Thomas P.K. Scade, they bombed and strafed the enemy vessels off Cos. Flak was intense but all returned, one with a wounded navigator. Four Beaufighters of 227 Squadron took off at 0510 hours, but one crashed on take-off. It was flown by Pilot Officer Cas de Bounevialle, who had contrived to return to the squadron to complete his operational tour. He and his navigator, Sergeant Jim Scott, were slightly injured. The remaining three aircraft, led by the Canadian pilot, Flying Officer Percy F. Glynn, found the enemy merchant vessels at anchor, with a long line of barges containing troops being towed to the beaches. They attacked in the face of intense flak, and Glynn's Beaufighter was seen to burst into flames before rolling over and diving into the sea. Glynn and his RAF navigator, Sergeant Timothy J. Barrett, lost their lives. The remaining two aircraft returned to Lakatamia, one with a navigator who had been wounded in the legs by flak.

Wing Commander Dennis Butler led seven Beaufighters of 252 Squadron, taking off at 0610 hours. They could see troops on the decks of the merchant vessels and made strafing and bombing attacks through a wall of accurate flak. The bombs were near misses, and four aircraft were hit by shrapnel, wounding one pilot and two navigators. All seven were lucky to return to Lakatamia.

At 0700 hours the commanding officer of 46 Squadron, Wing Commander George A. Reid, took off accompanied by two night-fighter aircraft of 89 Squadron. They also attacked the convoy and all three were hit by flak or in combat with Ar 196s. This German floatplane was highly manoeuvrable and, with two 20mm cannons firing forward and twin 7.9mm machine guns in the rear cockpit, could give a good account of itself. Reid's aircraft spun into the sea and he was killed. His navigator, Flying Officer W.R. Peasley, made an almost miraculous escape from the aircraft when it was under the water, and was then picked up by a boat and taken to hospital at Bodrum in Turkey. The two Beaufighters of 89 Squadron returned to Lakatamia, one with a wounded navigator.

Squadron Leader J.R.H. 'Ronnie' Lewis took off at 1030 hours, at the head of three Beaufighters of 227 Squadron and one of 46 Squadron. The aircraft were fired at from the shore when approaching Cos, but then the pilots saw six Stukas dive-bombing Antimachia. Jettisoning their bombs, they tore into the Germans. Lewis accounted for one, knocking bits off the wings and causing black smoke to stream from the fuselage before it dived into the sea. Flying Officer Tommy Deck silenced the rear gunner of another and saw pieces fly off the starboard wing. The Stuka crashed in a cloud of dust on a small island offshore. A South African pilot, Lieutenant A.E. Hounsom, attacked a third, but it did not go down and eventually evaded him by making a very tight turn. All four aircraft then attacked another Stuka, shooting bits off the tail. Emitting black smoke, the German aircraft dived to sea level and then suddenly climbed. The Beaufighter pilots lost sight of it, and all returned safely to Lakatamia.

Soon after mid-day, Squadron Leader Horace G. Hubbard led three Beaufighters of 252 Squadron to the target area. They chased an Ar 196 and scored cannon strikes, but the floatplane headed for the concentration of ships, which put up such a tremendous barrage that it would have been foolish to enter. The Beaufighters returned to Cyprus.

Next, it was the turn of 46 Squadron, when Squadron Leader William A. Cuddie took off at 1325 hours with three other Beaufighters. Cuddie was a highly experienced night-fighter pilot who had had the odd experience of chasing the Me 110 flown over Scotland by Rudolf Hess on 10 May 1940. Flying a Defiant of 141 Squadron from Ayr, Cuddie had been closing on the German aircraft when the Deputy Führer baled out near Glasgow. But the flight on 3 October 1943 was Cuddie's last. His aircraft was seen to explode when flying low over the sea through the flak barrage put up by the ships off Cos. He and his navigator, Flying Officer Leonard E.M. Coote, did not survive. In another Beaufighter, Warrant Officer F.W. Ledwidge bombed one of the merchant vessels and was then hit in the port wing. With his engine on fire, he headed for the Turkish coast and ditched at the precise moment when the wing burnt through and fell off. He and his navigator, Flight Sergeant J.T. Rowley, got into their dinghy and paddled for eight hours before landing near a Turkish lighthouse. A third Beaufighter, flown by Flight Sergeant Leslie G. Holmes, was also hit. The pilot ditched successfully and he and his navigator, Flight Sergeant Mark Bell, were picked up from their dinghy by a Turkish caique, taken to the hospital at Bodrum, and returned to their squadron on 30 November. The only surviving Beaufighter was flown by an Australian, Flight Sergeant M.W. Jackson. It was badly holed, but Jackson brought it back to a safe landing at Lakatamia.

The final effort of the day was made when three Beaufighters of 227 Squadron and one of 46 Squadron took off at 1510 hours. They found the landing area and the ships covered with a grey smoke-screen, while three Me 109s approached them from above. Evading the German fighters, they made an attempt to attack some ships they could discern through the smoke, but turned away from the intense flak barrage. Another attempt was made, this time from the west, out of the low sun. The Kenyan pilot, Flying Officer J.R.S. 'Red' Modera, fired a cannon burst from 1,000 yards, but the barrage was so tremendous that they turned away again and headed back to Lakatamia.

The efforts made by the Beaufighter squadrons proved inadequate for the defenders on Cos. The German assault troops, covered by their aircraft, moved remorselessly across the island, crushing the resistance. The inadequately armed British troops, the RAF Regiment, and some of the Italians fought bravely, but their position was hopeless. By the end of the day of the landings, the Germans numbered 2,000 men and were in control of most of the island. Some of the defenders were taken off by the Special Boat Squadron or escaped in other small boats. Others hid in the hills and either escaped at a later date or were captured. The commandant of the German forces was able to report on 4 October that 600 British troops had been taken prisoner, together with 2,500 Italians, forty guns and twenty-two partly destroyed aircraft. His own casualties amounted to only 65 men and two landing craft. Over the next two days, German firing squads executed ninety Italian officers, including the garrison commander.

At 0730 hours on 6 October, Lieutenant A.E. Hounson led four Beaufighters of 227 Squadron on an offensive sweep west of Cos, carrying 250lb bombs. They found some barges near Naxos, which opened fire, but they did not attack and returned safely. Flying Officer B.R.E. Amos took off at 0855 hours at the head of four more of 227 Squadron and made a complete circuit of Cos. The occupants of a small vessel making for Turkey waved to them, but there was no sign of enemy shipping. Amos attacked some enemy troops and transport about halfway along the northern coastline, but then two Me 109s pounced on the aircraft from astern. The Beaufighters jettisoned their bombs and took evasive action, while the navigators opened fire with the rearward-firing Vickers K guns and saw hits on the enemy fighters. One Me 109 gave out streams of black smoke and both broke off the engagement after ten minutes. The four Beaufighters reached Lakatamia and Amos and crashed on landing, without injury to the crew.

171

The Germans had not been confident about their chances of success on Cos and, quite naturally, were pleased with the outcome. They had turned the tables on the British, having relieved their own situation at Rhodes and cut off the British forces on Leros and Samos, further north. The British, who had underestimated the speed and strength of the German reaction, were dismayed, and also worried about the fate of their remaining forces in the Dodecanese. Naval reinforcements, including a cruiser squadron and eight destroyers, had already been ordered from the central Mediterranean but these did not arrive until after the loss of Cos. It was recognised that the lack of long-range fighters had been a major defect in the enterprise, but General Eisenhower had refused to allow any aircraft to be drawn away from the campaign in Italy. However, in early October he allowed the transfer of six squadrons of Lockheed P-38G Lightnings of the 1st and 14th Groups of the US Twelfth Air Force, part of the North-west African Strategic Air Force. These began operating from Gambut on 6 October in support of the Royal Navy, and for a brief period proved very successful in repelling attacks by the Luftwaffe.

The Beaufighters of 227 and 252 Squadrons in Cyprus also flew as fighter escorts to the warships. On 6 October, two of four Beaufighters of 227 Squadron ditched while circling their two cruisers and two destroyers on a sweep west of Cos. One crew, Flying Officer B.J. 'Burgie' Beare of the RCAF and Sergeant R.C. Humphreys of the RAF, was picked up by a destroyer. A dinghy was dropped to the other crew, Sergeants R.H. Carter and M.J. Harris, and the men were picked up later by a high-speed launch. Early the following morning, these warships intercepted a German convoy off Stampalia, headed for Cos. This included the merchant ship *Olympos* of 852 tons, carrying ammunition, six F-boats which were transporting garrison troops to replace the assault troops on the island, and a UJ-boat escort. The convoy had been attacked during the night by a Wellington of 38 Squadron but the torpedo missed. Then the submarine *Unruly* fired torpedoes but these also missed. The surface warships arrived after the submarine had surfaced and opened fire, and they continued the attack. Every ship save one F-boat was sunk, and 400 German troops were killed. On the following day, *Unruly* sank the minelayer *Bulgaria* of 1,894 tons in another convoy, and about 200 German troops lost their lives.

The Germans were not slow in taking their revenge. On 9 October, the anti-aircraft cruiser *Carlisle* and four destroyers were on a similar sweep when they were attacked by Stukas from Rhodes. The destroyer *Panther* was sunk and the cruiser very badly damaged. Seven Lightnings then arrived on the scene and chased the attackers; the pilots claimed sixteen Stukas shot down, but in fact only eight were lost – a serious enough blow to the Luftwaffe. Earlier in the day, another section of Lightnings had attacked three Beaufighters of 252 Squadron which were on patrol over these warships. A machine flown by Flight Sergeant A.W. Pierce was hit in several places, including both engines and the hydraulic system, but the pilot flew it back for a crash-landing at Lakatamia. On 10 October, the Lightning squadrons were recalled to their Tunisian bases, having operated in the Aegean for only a few days, during which time they had carried out 219 sorties.

However, on 16 October a squadron of North American B-25G Mitchells of the 310th Bombardment Group, USAAF, arrived at Gambut. This version of the famous aircraft was fitted with a 75mm gun in the nose, firing 15lb shells. With two .50in machine guns alongside it, the gun was a formidable anti-shipping weapon. These aircraft made their first attack on 10 October, escorted by two Beaufighters of 252 Squadron and one of 227 Squadron. They found and attacked an R-boat and a caique near Cos, scoring hits on both.

Meanwhile, the British plan to attack Rhodes was finally abandoned, but it was decided to attempt to hold Leros and Samos. The Royal Navy made a number of forays into the Aegean and additional supplies were transported to the British garrisons on the islands, as well as reinforcements of troops. The naval units were escorted by Beaufighters of 46, 227 and 252 Squadrons, operating from Lakatamia, but 89 Squadron was ordered to leave for Ceylon. On 12 October, a Beaufighter of 227 Squadron flown by Lieutenant A.E. Hounsom was forced to ditch, but he and his navigator, Sergeant W.H. Duncan, were picked up and returned to the squadron.

Wing Commander Mackenzie finished his tour of duty on 17 October and handed over command of 227 Squadron to Wing Commander John K. Buchanan DSO DFC and bar, who had led 272 Squadron at Malta with great panache from November 1942 to June 1943. On the day of the changeover, two Beaufighters of 252 and one of 227 Squadron escorted Mitchells on an attack against craft in Cos harbour, scoring strikes on barges. One Mitchell was hit by flak but was escorted safely back by the Beaufighters. The day was also occupied with convoy escort duties. While over the cruiser *Sirius* and three destroyers, four Beaufighters of 252 Squadron sighted and chased six Ju 88s. Only Sergeant W. Davenport managed to close with one of them, scoring hits on the port wing and tail before the Beaufighters were recalled to the convoy. Another aircraft of 227 Squadron ditched when on these escort duties. The pilot, Flight Sergeant Robert S. Reid, was picked up by a Supermarine Walrus amphibian but the navigator, Sergeant Harold C. Seymour, lost his life.

The Germans were acutely short of shipping in the Aegean, but in mid-September Hitler had ordered the transfer of as many vessels as possible from the Adriatic. Ten vessels set out, sailing separately and without escort, but only two reached Piraeus, for British Intelligence was well aware of their movements. One was destroyed by Yugoslav partisans, one by aircraft, five were sunk or captured by Allied ships, and one disappeared without trace.

The Royal Navy also scored a number of other successes. In the early hours of 11 October, a submarine sank the merchant ship *Ingeborg* (formerly Danish) of 1,200 tons, off Amorgos. On 16 October, a submarine hit the merchant ship *Kari* (formerly the French *Sainte Colette*) of 1,925 tons east of Naxos, which sank with the loss of over 500 German troops of the 1,500 she was carrying. British destroyers sank by gunfire *UJ2109* on the night of 17/18 October, in the harbour of Kalymnos; she was the former minesweeper HMS *Widnes* of 710 tons, which had been captured by the Germans at Suda Bay on 20 May 1941, after having been damaged and beached. Another loss for the Germans occurred on the night of 18/19 October when the merchant ship *Sinfra* of 4,470 tons, which had carried troops during the assault on Cos, was sunk by torpedo-carrying Wellingtons of 38 Squadron. The vessel had left Suda Bay in Crete, bound for Piraeus with about 2,600 Italians, Germans and Greeks on board. When between Crete and the island of Kithera she was located by ASV and attacked by two Wellingtons, but the torpedoes missed. In the next Wellington, Squadron Leader John M. Milburn dropped a torpedo which hit amidships, bringing the vessel to a halt and causing a fire which could be seen from a distance of thirty miles. A further attack by Flight Sergeant H.F. Van der Pol resulted in a hit which lifted the bows out of the water and caused two explosions. The flak ceased immediately and she sank, taking with her about 2,000 men. Unfortunately, many of these were Italians and Greeks being transported to the mainland as PoWs.

Meanwhile, on 17 October, another Beaufighter squadron completed a move to Gambut to join in the anti-shipping operations. This was 603 (City of Edinburgh) Squadron, one of the famous auxiliary squadrons of the RAF. At the outbreak of war, this squadron had been equipped with Spitfire Is and remained on defensive duties in Scotland until the end of August 1940, when it moved south to take part in the Battle of Britain. The squadron was sent to Malta in April 1942, its Spitfire Vs having been among those which flew from the US aircraft carrier *Wasp* on the twentieth of that month. For over three months, the pilots fought heroically in defence of the island, before the remaining men and aircraft were absorbed by 229 Squadron. Operations began again in February 1943, when the squadron was based at Idku and had received Beaufighters. It was employed mainly on escort duties, but some anti-shipping strikes took place, occasionally in combination with 252 Squadron. After moving west, including a month in Sicily, it was brought back east to Gambut, where one of its main functions became the escorting of the Mitchells. The squadron was commanded by a South African in the RAF, Wing Commander Hugh A. 'Fritz' Chater. The first operation from Gambut took place on 19 October, when two aircraft made a reconnaissance of Cos. Later in the morning, two more Beaufighters combined with two of 227 Squadron and four Mitchells on a sweep north of Crete, when a Do 24 was destroyed on the water and an Ar 196 was claimed as a 'probable'.

The Beaufighter squadrons continued their anti-shipping sweeps and naval escorts for the next two days. On 22 October, Allied destroyers ran into a newly laid minefield north of Cos. The Greek *Adrias* was badly damaged, and HMS *Hurworth* sank. There was another loss in 227 Squadron on the following day, when an aircraft on escort duties crashed near Lakatamia, killing the crew, Flight Sergeant Thomas C. Morfitt and Flight Sergeant Joseph W. Jackson. On 25 October, the destroyer *Eclipse* also struck a mine, sinking with the loss of 140 of the 200 troops she was carrying to Leros. The Beaufighters from Cyprus gave protection to the motor launches attempting to rescue survivors.

The British on Leros and Samos had been obtaining some supplies via Turkey, while others arrived in caiques or in destroyers which made high-speed dashes. The Germans bombed both islands every day, and on 24 October sank the merchant vessel *Taganrog* of 534 tons in Samos harbour. The attitude of the Turks towards the British became far cooler following the German success at Cos. In late October, British Intelligence learnt that the Germans were building up landing forces and airborne troops in Piraeus, as well as moving more units of the Luftwaffe to the Aegean. An attack against Leros seemed imminent, using Cos and neighbouring islands as springboards.

The combination of Beaufighters of 603 Squadron and Mitchells of the US 310th Bombardment Group went out each day from 24 to 29 October. The aircraft usually flew to the area of Cos in formations of about nine, attacking schooners, caiques and barges. On the twenty-seventh they attacked Antimachia airfield, the Mitchells destroying a Ju 52 on the ground while the Beaufighters blasted with cannon fire two groups of soldiers who appeared to have left the aircraft. The squadrons suffered no losses in this period.

The RAF took one other measure to strengthen its anti-shipping forces. On 22 October, the torpedo-carrying Beaufighter Xs of 47 Squadron began to move from Sidi Amor in Tunisia to El Adem in Libya, in order to operate over the Aegean. The commanding officer, Wing Commander James A. Lee-Evans DFC, led eight aircraft on an Armed Rover from Stampalia to other islands in the Cyclades on 28 October, but without finding targets. On the following day, however,

Squadron Leader Charles A. Ogilvie led nine aircraft in an attack on a small vessel with an escort south of Naxos, protected by three Ar 196s. One Beaufighter was shot down and the crew, Flying Officer John Dixon and Flying Officer George A. Terry, were killed. On 30 October, two Beaufighters of 47 Squadron combined with two Mitchells in an attack against Naxos harbour. One Mitchell and one Beaufighter were shot down. The Beaufighter crew, consisting of Flying Officer W.E. Hayter of 47 Squadron and Warrant Officer T.J. Harper of 603 Squadron, managed to evade capture and eventually returned to the squadron.

The Royal Navy continued its operations, but the surface warships were exposed to danger. On 30 October the cruiser *Aurora* and three destroyers entered the Aegean to search for enemy shipping, escorted by Beaufighters from Cyprus. In the early afternoon, the crews of two aircraft from 227 Squadron and two more from 252 Squadron saw about fourteen Ju 88s in vic formations approaching at 12,000 feet, escorted by six single-engined fighters 1,000 feet above. Then about seventeen more Ju 88s appeared, escorted by three MC202s. An Australian pilot in 252 Squadron, Sergeant E.H. Jones, tackled an Me 109 from head on, but the enemy aircraft turned on its back and disappeared from view. The two pilots from 227 Squadron, Flying Officer A.P. Mazur and Flying Officer J.M. Kendall, attacked a Ju 88, scoring numerous hits and silencing the rear gunner before the German aircraft dived straight into the sea. The other pilot of 252 Squadron, Flight Sergeant F.A. Stanger, also an Australian, was attacked from astern by a MC202, which shot away all his rudder fabric. Jones came to his help and attacked the Italian aircraft, which was probably flown by a German, and it went down in a slow spiral. The warships put up an anti-aircraft barrage, but this did not deter the attackers. A bomb hit the cruiser on the stern, causing serious damage and heavy casualties, and another bomb hit a destroyer but did not explode. The cruiser set course for Alexandria, escorted by one destroyer, while the other two destroyers continued their sweep.

On the same day, four Beaufighters of 227 Squadron attacked eight Ju 88s flying at 12,000 feet. Flying Officer Burgie Beare closed with one, which jettisoned its bombs before exploding. He then attacked a second from head-on, and this burst into flames and also crashed. Another Canadian pilot, Flying Officer William Yurchinson, sent a third Ju 88 down in flames, and a fourth German aircraft was seen to be in difficulties. One Ju 88 attacked a Beaufighter flown by a New Zealander, Flight Lieutenant William R. Kemp, shooting away the hydraulics and rudder controls; Kemp flew the aircraft very skilfully back to Lakatamia.

On 3 November some of the German invasion craft were spotted exercising at sea preparatory to moving eastwards for the invasion of Leros and Samos. The Germans had given the codename 'Leopard' to this operation (changed to 'Taifun' on 6 November). Coincidentally, both the British and the Germans were gloomy about their prospects of success in the forthcoming operation. The Royal Navy was worried about the exposure of its warships to German air attacks, mostly because only the Beaufighters were available to supply long-distance fighter escort during daylight, at the extremity of their range, while the Germans feared substantial losses to their ship-borne troops from British warships and aircraft. From this time to the day of the landings on Leros, the movements of the German invasion craft across the Aegean, including their deviations of route and concealments, were faithfully recorded by Spitfires and Baltimores of the photographic reconnaissance squadrons. The vessels sailed in a series of short runs, first from Piraeus to Paros, then to Amorgos, then to Stampalia, and finally to Kalymnos or Cos. There were some variations in the intermediate runs, and the convoys sailed in small sections, usually at night. It thus proved extremely difficult for the Allied air squadrons to intercept and destroy these escorted craft at the times they were in the open sea, and the Royal Navy could try to bring them to battle only in the final stage.

Escorts and sweeps by the Beaufighters in the first few days of November resulted in few sightings. On 5 November six Beaufighters of 227 Squadron were despatched from Cyprus on a daylight sweep around Rhodes, although the invasion fleet was nowhere near these waters. One aircraft returned early and the outcome for the remaining five was disastrous. Four Me 109s appeared north of the island and immediately attacked an aircraft flown by Flight Lieutenant John P. Tremlett, which went down with the port engine in flames. Tremlett and his navigator, Flight Sergeant Robert E. Jobling, lost their lives. Then Pilot Officer John A. Swift and his navigator Flight Sergeant George F. Austin also went down with the fuselage in flames, and both men were killed. A Beaufighter flown by Flying Officer William Yurchinson was attacked several times and then crashed into the sea in flames. Yurchinson and his RAF navigator, Flying Officer Percival M. Wroath, did not survive. A Beaufighter flown by another Canadian, Flying Officer Apollon P. Mazur, was last seen heading south, being chased by the German fighters. Mazur and his RAF navigator, Flying Officer Kenneth Stakes, were also killed. The remaining Beaufighter, flown by Pilot Officer A.C. Gibbard, was attacked twice but managed to draw away. This aircraft was the only one of the five to return, on this black day for 227 Squadron.

Two aircraft were also lost by 47 Squadron on this day, but with less tragic results. Three torpedo Beaufighters led by Wing Commander

Lee-Evans were accompanied by a fighter escort of four Beaufighters of 603 Squadron led by Squadron Leader Gordon B. Atkinson, on a strike against the invasion ships in Lavrion Bay, about thirty-five miles southeast of Piraeus. Two of the escorts turned back with engine trouble, but the remainder reached their objective. They found three merchant vessels and attacked in the face of intense and accurate flak. Lee-Evans dropped his torpedo from about 1,000 yards but his starboard engine was hit and set on fire. Thinking his last moments had come, he gave the enemy vessels a few squirts with his cannons and machine guns, but then ditched successfully. He and his navigator, Flight Lieutenant David A. Heden, became PoWs. Another torpedo Beaufighter, crewed by Flight Lieutenant Thomas C. Graham and Flying Officer John H.K. Langdon, was also seen to be on fire before it ditched. The two men were also taken prisoner. One torpedo was seen to be running accurately and a column of smoke rose from one of the ships. No enemy fighters were present, but other Beaufighters were hit by flak and made the the long return journey with difficulty.

A further strike took place on the following day, when Squadron Leader Ogilvie led four more Beaufighters of 47 Squadron on a cannon strafe of shipping off Paros in the Cyclades. Accompanied by four Beaufighters of 603 Squadron, they swept in from the west and scored strikes on two large barges moored in Yanni Bay. Ogilvie was chased by Me 109s and did not return. The remainder of the formation then tackled four caiques in the small port of Naussa. They silenced gun posts in the harbour and combats took place with eight Ar 196s. A Beaufighter of 47 Squadron was seen to be in combat with an Arado before crashing in flames on a hillside. The crew, Flying Officer Lewis Rossner and Sergeant Henry K. Levy, were killed. The Australian crew of a Beaufighter of 603 Squadron, Pilot Officer K.I.E. Hopkins and Warrant Officer K.V. Roget, shot down an Ar 196 and then ditched. Fortunately, they were picked up by a submarine and taken to Malta, returning to the squadron a week later. The remaining five aircraft returned home but one pilot of 603 Squadron, Flight Sergeant T. Truesdale, was slightly wounded and made a belly landing at Gambut. Ogilvie and his navigator, Flying Officer Michael O'Connor, were reported as 'safe' on 10 December, and Ogilvie returned to the squadron on Christmas Eve.

On 7 November Squadron Leader Atkinson led eight of 603 Squadron to a position off Naxos, where they sighted seventeen invasion barges and other vessels. They made two attempts to attack with cannons but both were broken up by approaching Me 109s and Ar 196s. There were no losses on either side. Six Beaufighters went out the following day, together with three torpedo aircraft and three anti-flak of 47 Squadron. They found a convoy of four small merchant vessels and about fifteen barges escorted by six Ar 196s near the island of Amorgos, in the Cyclades west of Cos. The torpedoes were dropped, without obvious results. Cannon strikes were seen on many vessels and one Ar 196 was shot down into the sea. All 47 Squadron's aircraft were damaged by flak, but the entire formation returned safely.

The attempts to cripple the German invasion fleet continued daily. On 9 November there were two combined Armed Rovers. In the morning, four of 603 Squadron escorted two torpedo Beaufighters of 47 Squadron to Amorgos. One torpedo aircraft turned back when a hatch blew off and damaged the tail, but the remainder found ten barges and two schooners escorted by Ju 88s, Ar 196s and single-engined fighters. The German aircraft attacked and the Beaufighters took evasive action, returning safely to Gambut. In the early afternoon, more of 603 Squadron escorted two of 47 Squadron to Stampalia and attacked a merchant vessel and escort. No results were seen from the torpedoes, but two Ar 196s were shot down into the sea and one sank. All the Beaufighters returned safely.

By 10 November the German invasion fleet had assembled at Cos and the neighbouring island of Kalymnos, the vessels having suffered few casualties in their passages from Piraeus. It is known from German records that this fleet included twenty-five landing craft and one steamship, escorted by two destroyers and two torpedo boats (all formerly Italian), three UJ-boats, six auxiliary vessels, and a large fleet of R-boats and other smaller craft. The air cover was provided by about 300 fighters and bombers, including Do 217s armed with radio-controlled glider bombs. There were two battalions of British troops on Leros, the Royal Irish Fusiliers and the King's Own Royal Rifles, as well as a company of the Royal West Kents. These were supported by other units including the Italian garrison. The defences were considerably more powerful than those on Cos, but the island was even further away from effective air cover. Moreover, the nearest British destroyers also operated at the limit of their range and were forced to shelter in Turkish waters.

Four torpedo Beaufighters of 47 Squadron went out on an Armed Rover in the afternoon of 10 November, escorted by nine of 603 Squadron led by Squadron Leader Atkinson. They sighted a small vessel to the south of Cos and one aircraft dropped a torpedo without results, but the other pilot thought that the target was too small. An Ar 196 in the water was hit by cannon fire but then the formation was attacked by Me 109s. A Beaufighter of 603 Squadron ditched with its starboard engine on fire but the crew, Pilot Officer W.A. Eacott and Pilot Officer W.B.F. Pritchard, survived to become PoWs. The remaining aircraft returned safely.

During the following night, one Polish and two British destroyers bombarded the port of the island of Kalymnos, between Cos and Leros, setting a merchant ship on fire. But the destroyer HMS *Rockwood* was hit by a glider bomb soon after midnight. The bomb did not explode, but it was necessary to tow the destroyer to a Turkish anchorage. Three more destroyers bombarded Cos during the same night and then retired to Turkish waters during the day, to avoid air attack. On 11 November, three Beaufighters of 603 Squadron, led by Squadron Leader Atkinson, accompanied three of 47 Squadron and two Mitchells on a strafing patrol over the seas around the islands, but saw no shipping. The German invasion fleet was nearing Leros on the following night, and fortune favoured the force. The three destroyers which had bombarded Cos missed the interception at the time they made their foray. By then seriously short of fuel, they had to withdraw. The landings began at Alinda Bay in the east of Leros, soon after dawn.

During the morning, Squadron Leader William P. Kemp led two Beaufighters of 227 Squadron on a sweep round the island, accompanied by four of 46 Squadron led by Squadron Leader Dudley T. Arundel. They saw the landing craft with Me 109s circling above but were unable to tackle the single-engined fighters and returned to Cyprus. As the records of 46 Squadron for this date comment, 'Beaufighters operating over Leros are doing so at extreme range and could not possibly provide effective cover'.

Soon after mid-day on the same day, part of the invasion fleet was spotted by four Beaufighters of 603 Squadron and four of 47 Squadron, east of Leros. The aircraft were fired upon, but the crews thought that the warships were British destroyers, which were known to be near these waters, and did not attack. A second strike force, consisting of two torpedo Beaufighters of 47 Squadron and two Mitchells escorted by six Beaufighters of 603 Squadron, was despatched to a convoy off the north-west of Crete. They found a merchant vessel of about 3,000 tons, with one large and five small escorts. The Mitchells went in first, followed by the torpedo aircraft. Both dropped torpedoes but no hits were seen. One Beaufighter, flown by a New Zealander, Flying Officer Athol G. Greentree, with an RAF navigator, Sergeant George H. Freeman, was shot down, and both men lost their lives. The anti-flak Beaufighters raked the vessels and also damaged two Ar 196s.

The Germans found that Leros was a far more difficult proposition than Cos. The island, about ten miles long, consists of three mountainous regions connected by two narrow necks of land, with a coastline so indented that no point is more than a mile from the sea. It was defended by well-trained and determined British troops, although they were short of field artillery. Italian shore batteries drove off some of the landing craft, before being silenced by Stukas. Several landing craft were sunk but others reached the shores. Paratroops were dropped, but some were killed in the air or on landing. The British made counter-attacks and recaptured some positions, causing German losses and taking prisoners, but suffering severe casualties themselves. By the end of the first day, the outcome of the landings was still in the balance. Unfortunately, however, no reinforcements could be brought to the British, while the Germans succeeded in landing fresh troops during the night. Three Royal Navy destroyers bombarded German positions during the night of 12/13 November, but one of three more destroyers which were racing to assist was hit by a glider bomb when east of Cos. This was HMS *Dulverton*, which was scuttled after the other destroyers had rescued the survivors.

Once again, it was only the RAF which could try to help the defenders during daylight. The Beaufighters of 227 and 252 Squadrons on Cyprus concentrated on fighter escort to destroyers, while the strike force at Gambut attempted anti-shipping attacks or the destruction of the Stukas. Early on 13 November, five torpedo Beaufighters of 47 Squadron swept the area around Scarpanto, accompanied by four Beaufighters of 603 Squadron and two Mitchells. They found no targets to attack, but one Beaufighter of 603 Squadron reported engine trouble and then ditched. The Australian crew, Warrant Officer Frank M. Cox and Warrant Officer Norman S. Ferguson, lost their lives. Another section, consisting of four torpedo aircraft, with five of 603 Squadron and two Mitchells, took off a few minutes later. After strafing some gun posts on Leros, they were dived upon by six Me 109s when they swept round the north-east of the island, and a running fight ensued. The attacks were concentrated on the Mitchells at the rear, but the American gunners managed to beat them off. However, a torpedo Beaufighter of 47 Squadron flown by an American in the RCAF, Flying Officer Edgar L. Clary Jr, was shot down and crashed into the sea with the port engine on fire. Clary and his RAF navigator, Sergeant Walter E. Finbow, were killed.

Within a fortnight, 47 Squadron had lost seven Beaufighter TFXs and their crews, including the commanding officer and a flight commander. The RAF took the unusual step of calling on 5 Middle East Training School at Shallufa to reinforce the squadron with crews and their aircraft, to help at this critical time. Seven crews, headed by Squadron Leader Stanley Muller-Rowland, flew to Gambut on the morning of 13 November. Most of the men were 'tour-expired' instructors, but some were advanced trainees. They went into action immediately, taking off at 1340 hours for a fighter sweep round Leros. When north-west of the island they spotted twelve Ju 88s in groups of four, and headed in pursuit of one section which turned and flew away from the island. These Ju 88s dropped their bombs in the sea when the Beaufighters caught up with them. One German straggler was attacked and hit, but it managed to regain the formation. Muller-Rowland then attacked from astern and below, and his cannon fire hit another Ju 88. But return fire set his starboard engine on fire and he ditched in a bay to the north of the island of Patmos. Two of the other Beaufighters circled and saw Muller-Rowland in a dinghy, together with his navigator, Flight Sergeant J.D. 'Paddy' Anderson.

Command of the remaining six Beaufighters was taken over by Flight Lieutenant Lionel W. Daffurn, who was Muller-Rowland's deputy at Shallufa. He was also a highly experienced operational pilot, having served on both 39 and 47 Squadrons when they were equipped with Beauforts and then Beaufighters. He had been awarded a DFC early in November. Daffurn led the Beaufighters on another attack on a Ju 88, to the east of Patmos, but fuel was running low and they were forced to return to Gambut. Another Beaufighter of 47 Squadron, flown by Flying Officer William W. Thwaites, which had taken off twenty minutes later, saw the attack on the Ju 88s and scored more hits on one of them, knocking off a wheel and bits of the fuselage. He ran out of ammunition and also returned to Gambut.

The defenders on Leros were fighting against heavy odds, while the enemy had the benefit of Stukas to act as artillery. These dive-bombers would have been easy prey for the Beaufighters, if they had been able to tackle them, but in turn they were protected by German single-engined fighters. In the early morning of 14 May, four Beaufighters of 47 Squadron led by Squadron Leader Powell, accompanied by three of 603 Squadron led by Squadron Leader Atkinson, took off with four Mitchells from Gambut. They saw bomb bursts on Leros and were fired at from the ground, but otherwise found no targets and all returned safely.

The Beaufighters from Cyprus were less fortunate. Four of 46 Squadron, led by Flight Lieutenant D.J.A. Crerar, took off in the late morning accompanied by four from 227 Squadron, led by Squadron Leader Kemp, to sweep round the island. They came across an He 111 about ten miles east of Leros and gave chase. Crerar closed to 100 yards and scored hits, and the machine was then finished off by Flying Officer B.F. Wild from his squadron. They saw bomb bursts on Leros, but by then it was time to return to base. Almost immediately they were attacked by several single-engined fighters. An Me 109 attacked an aircraft crewed by Warrant Officer Ronald Lindsey and Flight Sergeant Alfred C.A. Gardener. The Beaufighter was seen to climb vertically, roll over and dive into the sea. Both men lost their lives. The remaining RAF aircraft then headed for Turkey and scattered. Another Beaufighter of 46 Squadron, crewed by the RCAF Flying Officer Joseph A. Horsfall and the RAF Flight Sergeant James R. Colley, replied to a call on the R/T but did not return to base. Both men also lost their lives.

During the the early hours of 15 November, destroyers succeeded in bringing some reinforcements from Samos to Leros. While the British troops mounted counter-attacks later on that day, taking heavy casualties but causing many in return, the Beaufighters continued their impossible task. Six of 227 Squadron and one of 47 Squadron took off from Lakatamia and almost inevitably were attacked by single-engined fighters off Leros. Two of the attackers were identified as MC 202s with German markings. Flight Lieutenant Tommy Deck of 227 Squadron got in a four-second burst against one of these, and saw its undercarriage drop down before it dived to sea level and began evasive action. The Beaufighters headed for sanctuary over the Turkish coast, with the navigators firing their rearward guns, and all returned safely.

Five of 47 Squadron took off from Gambut in the late morning, with three of 603 Squadron and three Mitchells. They sighted two enemy warships about thirty miles west of Cos, escorted by two Ar 96s and four Ju 88s. The Mitchells attacked the warships, causing a cloud of black smoke and steam to rise from one of them, but the air battles were inconclusive. All the Allied aircraft returned to base.

The next day, 16 November, was the last of the battle. Six Beaufighters of 603 Squadron took off in the early morning, but two returned with mechanical trouble. The remaining four attacked two Ar 196s, shooting down one and damaging the other. All returned home. Later in the morning, one more took off, together with seven of 47 Squadron led by Squadron Leader Powell. They found a Siebel ferry and two barges near the island of Kalymnos, escorted by seven Ar 196s and four Me 109s. They attacked with cannons, in spite of the air cover and intense flak, blowing up the Siebel ferry and damaging the barges. Of course, the Me 109s dived on them, and three Beaufighters of 47 Squadron were shot down. The only aircraft seen to go down was crewed by Flying Officer William W. Thwaites and Flying Officer John E. Lovell, and both lost their lives. Flying Officer John B. Fletcher and Sergeant Jack Dale in another aircraft failed to return and were also killed. The pilot of the third aircraft, Flying Officer Anthony D. Bond, lost his life, but the navigator, Sergeant Alfred R. Cottle, was later reported as 'safe'. Powell was awarded a DSO for leading this highly dangerous operation.

The defenders on Leros gave up the unequal battle when they surrendered in the evening of 16 November. Once again, some of the troops managed to slip away on small boats and were brought back to Egypt via Turkey. But the Germans took about 3,200 British prisoners, together with some 5,000 Italians. Some of the Italian officers were executed. The German casualties had been extremely heavy, with over 1,100 of the 3,000 troops who had landed killed in the action. The British evacuated Samos during the next two days, while the garrison of the small island of Casteloriso was considerably reduced.

Thus this unhappy campaign ended. It was calculated that casualties on both sides had been roughly equal, including in the air. However, as the official history records: 'Losses among the combined anti-shipping and night-fighter forces of Beaufighters were at the fearful rate of fifty per cent of all the Beaufighter squadrons.'*

The morale of the Germans was boosted by their success, after their series of reverses in North Africa and Sicily. But the British had failed in their strategic objectives and had to relearn the lesson which should have been apparent at the outset: military objectives could not be attained unless command of the air had been secured beforehand.

After a few more sorties, the two anti-shipping squadrons on Cyprus returned to North Africa, 227 Squadron to Berka on 31 November and 252 Squadron to LG 91 on 13 December. There was still plenty of work ahead for them, as well as for 603 Squadron.

The loss of Stanley Muller-Rowland was keenly felt by the crews at Shallufa, but despondency was lifted when he and Paddy Anderson were reported as 'safe and well' on 24 November. In fact, Muller-Rowland was not entirely well, for he had been wounded by some tiny splinters of metal in a very sensitive part of his anatomy. He had spent some time picking them out, fortunately without permanent injury. A Greek fishing boat arrived and took the two men out of their dinghy, although the rescuers implied that they would have slit their throats if they had been German. They were passed from island to island until they reached Turkey, where they were entertained in style by the British Consular staff. They were then sent via Syria and Palestine to Egypt, and arrived back at Shallufa on 26 November.

Stanley Muller-Rowland never realised his ambition of commanding an RAF squadron. After completing his stint as an instructor, he returned to the UK and joined 236 Squadron, an anti-shipping squadron equipped with Beaufighter TFXs, part of the Strike Wing based at North Coates in Lincolnshire. At 0018 hours on 3 October 1944, Squadron Leader Stanley R. Muller–Rowland took off with his navigator, Flying Officer Alan J. Kendall, for the Dutch coast. They were the first of six which went out on that night with rocket projectiles, on an Armed Rover to hunt an enemy convoy. The weather was poor, with low visibility and thick cloud. Only three aircraft found the convoy, and two of these reported that the flak was so accurate that they had difficulty pressing home their attack. In the third aircraft, Alan Kendall sent a distress signal, reporting that they had been hit in the starboard engine and were preparing to bale out. Nothing was

* Molony, C.J.C., *The Mediterranean and Middle East*, vol. V (London: HMSO, 1973)

heard from them again. A post-war 'casualty enquiry' addressed to the Dutch authorities resulted in no further information apart from 'presumed lost at sea'.

Stanley's twin brother, John, survived the war. He earned his first DFC in January 1943 when flying with 60 Squadron, at a time when it was equipped with Blenheim IVs in the Burma theatre of war. The bar to his DFC was gazetted in April 1944, when he was flying Beaufighter TFXs with 211 Squadron in the same theatre. He commanded 211 Squadron from August to October 1944 and was awarded the DSO. After the war, he remained in the RAF and became a test pilot. On 15 February 1950, Squadron Leader John S.R. Muller-Rowland took off from Farnborough in one of two experimental 'Swallow' DH108s, the so-called 'flying wing'. Geoffrey de Havilland, the thirty-six-year-old son of Sir Geoffrey de Havilland, had been killed in one of these machines over the Thames Estuary on 27 September 1946 during an attempt to beat the world speed record. John Muller-Rowland's machine exploded over Buckinghamshire shortly after take-off and he was killed instantly.

Thus all three brothers of the remarkable Muller-Rowland family – Eric, Stanley and John – lost their lives in the service of their country.

The German armed merchant vessel *Gertrud* of 1,960 tons under rocket attack on 1 June 1944 by a Beaufighter of 252 Squadron flown by Flying Officer William Davenport. She was badly damaged but was towed into Heraklion, where she blew up after being hit by bombs dropped by Baltimores of 15 (SAAF) Squadron. Davenport was shot down and taken prisoner on 19 June 1944. (*Flt Lt G.G. Tuffin*)

The German merchant ship *Carola* (formerly the Italian *Corse Fougier*) of 1,348 tons, under attack on 6 September 1944 south-east of Athens by eight Beaufighters of 252 Squadron and four of 603 Squadron, led by Wing Commander Dennis O. Butler. The vessel was badly damaged but reached Piraeus, where she went into dry dock and was later scuttled as a blockship. (*Wg Cdr D.O. Butler, DFC*)

Squadron Leader Anthony J. Mottram and Flying Officer Walter A.J. Hook of 272 Squadron in Italy. Mottram was a professional tennis player before joining the RAF. (*Flt Lt W.A.G. Hook, DFC*)

Warrant Officer Fred 'Pancho' Manning (*left*) and Warrant Officer Spencer 'Flip' Philpott, photographed as RAAF sergeants when first forming a nightfighter crew at Cranfield in Bedfordshire. (*Warr. Off. S.G. Philpott*)

11

ROCKET SQUADRONS

After the conquest of Sardinia and Corsica, 39 Squadron was based at Sidi Amor in Tunisia for only a month. During this period, the detachment at Grottaglie, near Taranto, made one very effective attack. In the morning of 5 November 1943 a force of six Beaufighters led by a Canadian flight commander, Squadron Leader Thomas H. Curlee, took off to attack a merchant vessel reported sailing between Venice and Trieste. This had been sighted by a Marauder of 14 Squadron, also on detachment at Grottaglie. The Beaufighters came across the vessel twenty miles west of Trieste and all six dropped torpedoes. The ship was *Ramb III* of 3,494 tons, a former Italian vessel which the Germans were using as a minelayer. She sank, and the Beaufighters returned safely.

On 20 November the squadron moved to Reghaia, east of Algiers, to begin a new phase in its operations. Here the crews began to convert on to rocket projectiles. The aircraft underwent servicing and were fitted with rocket rails, four under each wing. The crews began to learn the techniques of using this new weapon, and the first exercise was flown on 28 November. Training continued until the end of the year, when the squadron became fully operational in its new form. The four cannons were retained, but the use of torpedoes was discontinued and these weapons were handed over to the Royal Navy.

The anti-shipping squadrons in the Mediterranean were slower than their counterparts in the UK in adopting the rocket projectile as a means of sinking surface vessels. The weapon had been fitted to Beaufighters of 143 and 236 Squadrons at North Coates as early as June 1943, although the third member of this Strike Wing, 254 Squadron, retained torpedoes until the end of the war. The type of warhead normally used in the rocket was the 25lb solid shot, which could be aimed at the sea a few yards in front of the waterline. If it struck accurately, the trajectory of the warhead then curved upwards and penetrated the hull below the waterline, frequently sinking the ship. Within a couple of months, the use of this weapon had accelerated the rate of sinkings along the enemy coasts of north-west Europe.

In the Mediterranean, the rocket projectile was adopted at the end of

May 1943 by the Hudsons of 608 Squadron, when based at Blida in Algeria, and used for anti-submarine work. But the RAF's higher command had been reluctant to convert torpedo-carrying Beaufighters to rockets until they thought that most of the remaining enemy vessels were too small to justify the continued use of torpedoes. However, in the opinion of the commanding officer of 39 Squadron, Wing Commander Harvey, the introduction of rockets inaugurated a period when the anti-shipping Beaufighters could at last meet the enemy on terms of reasonable equality. Events were to justify this opinion, if only in the 'cost-effectiveness' of the aircraft and crews, in terms of results compared with losses.

On 19 December, the North-west African Coastal Air Force was renamed the Mediterranean Allied Coastal Air Force, a name which was considered more suitable geographically. As it happened, however, the first eleven days of 1944 saw a large detachment of 39 Squadron engaged on a task which was quite different to that of anti-shipping, for the aircraft were sent to Marrakesh to guard Winston Churchill. The Prime Minister had flown to Tunis on 12 December 1943 as the guest of Franklin Roosevelt, before a proposed visit to the Italian front. He had fallen seriously ill in Tunis, and his wife had flown out to join him. Churchill needed rest from the strain of his office, and Marrakesh was selected as a suitable place for recuperation. Fortunately, his recovery proved fairly rapid, being helped by generally favourable news of the progress of the war. During this period, 39 Squadron maintained patrols and worked in co-operation with the ground defences to protect Marrakesh from air attack. The Beaufighters were replaced by Spitfires of 32 Squadron, which arrived from Maison Blanche in Algeria.

Returning to Reghaia, the task of 39 Squadron for the next few weeks was to protect Allied convoys from attack by Ju 88s. At this stage, troopships and supply ships were pouring through the Strait of Gibraltar en route to Italy. The western Mediterranean presented more targets to U-boats and the Luftwaffe than the north Atlantic. Of course, the convoys were heavily protected by Allied aircraft, and it was often possible to anticipate the air attacks by noting the arrival of enemy reconnaissance aircraft. These attacks usually took place at dusk, the enemy bombers taking off from southern France. Working backwards from last light, the likely time of arrival of the bombers over the Balearic Islands could be calculated, for these islands were used by the Germans as landmarks before beginning their runs to the convoys.

The Beaufighters of 39 Squadron patrolled the Balearics at the calculated times and, although there were many 'dry runs', achieved some successes. One such interception took place in the late afternoon of 1 February, when Flying Officer Neil D. Cox led six aircraft on a patrol and spotted about twenty-five enemy bombers near Ibiza. These were followed shortly afterwards by fourteen more bombers. In the subsequent air battles, Flight Sergeants W. Pryce and F.A. Cooper each shot down a Ju 88, while the other four aircraft damaged three more. But Flight Sergeant Cooper was shot down, and another Beaufighter crashlanded back at Reghaia. Cooper and his navigator, Sergeant A.V. Bridle, were picked up by air-sea rescue the following day, together with the pilot of the Ju 88 they had shot down.

On 3 February, 39 Squadron was detailed to move to Alghero in north-west Sardinia. Much of the remainder of the month was taken up with moving to this new base and preparing for a new phase in the operations. When the squadron finally arrived, on 19 February, the crews found that another Beaufighter squadron was waiting for them. This was 272 Squadron, which had arrived at the beginning of the month. For the previous four months, under the command of Wing Commander Wyndham A. Wild, 272 Squadron had operated from Catania in Sicily on convoy escorts and on intruder patrols over the Italian mainland. Wing Commander Donald H. Lowe had taken over the squadron on 6 February. From Alghero, the crews spent the early part of the month on familiarisation with the new terrain, and then began fighter sweeps over southern France. The weather was unfavourable and two Beaufighters crashed in heavy rainstorms when returning to Sardinia on 22 February. Both crews lost their lives, Pilot Officer John N. Greville-Smith and Pilot Officer Herbert Mackay in one aircraft, and Flying Officer Alfred W. Howell and Flying Officer Harry Baker in the other. Immediately afterwards, 272 Squadron resumed its role as a maritime squadron, for the new task of the crews was to provide anti-flak escort for the rocket-firing Beaufighters of 39 Squadron.

The two squadrons began training together on 24 February, and practice flying continued for the next fortnight, until the aircraft formed an anti-shipping Strike Wing. The first attack took place on 10 March, led by a Canadian flight commander of 39 Squadron, Squadron Leader N.R.J. Butler. His four Beaufighters were accompanied by six of 272 Squadron, led by a Belgian, Flight Lieutenant René G. Demoulin. They intercepted a merchant vessel of about 3,000 tons thirty miles west of Marseille, escorted by two motor-torpedo boats. Many hits from cannons and rockets were scored and the merchant vessel appeared to list to starboard, but the final result was not seen, owing to smoke. All aircraft returned undamaged.

The next attack, on 12 March, resulted in the first definite sinking of a vessel by the rocket projectiles of 39 Squadron. The commanding officer, Wing Commander Harvey, led four Beaufighters which took off in the early afternoon, accompanied by four of 272 Squadron led by another Belgian, Squadron Leader Charles L. Roman. They sighted three ships near the mouth of the river Ebro in Spain. Two were identified as Spanish but the third was the target they were looking for, the former French *Kilissi* of 3,723 tons. This had been requisitioned by the Germans to carry Portuguese wolfram, a vital material used for hardening steels in the manufacture of weapons such as anti-tank shells, from Spain to Marseille. The vessel was fitted with four 75mm guns, but three of these were silenced by cannon fire. The rockets also struck home, and *Kilissi* caught fire along her entire length. With ten dead, she headed for the beach, where she became a total loss.

A second formation of four rocket-carrying Beaufighters, led by Flight Lieutenant Ivor D. Charles, followed a few minutes later, also escorted by four of 272 Squadron. They came across one of the Spanish vessels, but Charles' instructions over the R/T were misunderstood by the remainder of the pilots, for they went into the attack. Charles was the only pilot in the formation to deliver an attack against *Kilissi*. The remainder attacked the Spanish vessel, *Cabo San Sebastian* of 1,583 tons, which was badly damaged by three rocket hits on the port side below the waterline, two of which then went through the starboard side. There was also extensive damage to the bridge and upperworks, and the cargo was set on fire. The Spanish stated that the vessel would have sunk if she had been further from the shore, but fortunately it proved possible to tow her into Barcelona after temporary repairs.

German propaganda made much of these attacks, since they had been delivered in Spanish territorial waters. However, the Germans did not mention that *Kilissi* was under their control for the purpose of carrying wolfram. Moreover, British Intelligence knew that Spanish waters were used consistently by German U-boats and merchant vessels and that the Spanish had allowed the Germans to set up radar and W/T stations around their coasts. The Germans were also using international markings, particularly Swiss, on some of their merchant vessels, as a *ruse de guerre* to prevent attack.

At this stage of the war, both the Germans and the British sometimes breached the neutrality of European countries. The Fascists in Spain were sympathetic to Germany, but the government of the country took a neutral stance. On the other side of the Mediterranean, Turkey contemplated entering the war on the Allied side, but refused to do so unless large quantities of aircraft and armament could be made over to her, and these were not available. Both Spain and Turkey turned blind eyes to activities within their territorial waters. By then the probable outcome of the war was clear, but the countries were prudent enough to remain neutral.

In the morning of 16 March, Flight Lieutenant Charles led five of 39 Squadron to a position off the Rhône delta, together with four from 272

Squadron. On this occasion, the Beaufighter crews had the comfort of a Vickers Warwick of 284 Squadron following in their wake. This air-sea rescue squadron had arrived at Alghero two days before, and the aircraft carried airborne lifeboats to drop to any crews who were downed into the sea. From this day, the Beaufighter formations were invariably followed by one of these faithful Warwicks on their sweeps. The Beaufighters found two merchant vessels, *Kabyle* of 1,881 tons and *Maure* (the former French *Polemis*) of 1,457 tons. Both were heavily defended with 75mm and 30mm guns, and they also fired 'parachute and cable' (PAC) rockets. This device consisted of a cable 100 metres long, fitted with explosive charges, which unfolded in the air and descended slowly at the end of a parachute, to ensnare low-flying attackers. But the defences availed little, for both ships were hit by cannon shells and rockets. The smaller sank, while the larger was damaged beyond repair. The attackers also came under fire from flak from the shore, while dust was seen from fighters taking off from a nearby airfield. Three Me 109s pursued the Beaufighters and caught up with one of 272 Squadron's anti-flak section, setting the starboard engine on fire before it dived into the sea. Sergeants Peter F. Bishop and Philip W. Leach lost their lives.

The first casualties suffered by 39 Squadron in this phase of their operations occurred on 27 March, when a Beaufighter turned back to base during a sweep in which no targets were found. The crew, Flying Officer John C. Yorke and Flying Officer Walter B. Mathias, were the pair who had been shot down on 15 September and managed to return to their squadron. On this occasion, both lost their lives.

On 6 April, four rocket Beaufighters and four anti-flak went out on another sweep off the Spanish coast. They spotted a vessel near the border with France, but she was seen to carry Spanish markings and the aircraft did not attack. While this ship was being investigated, a Beaufighter of 272 Squadron flown by Squadron Leader Demoulin broke away and made an attack on a small vessel which appeared to be a fishing boat. His cannon strikes began to lead up to the boat, but suddenly his starboard wing crumpled and flames came from the engine, although no fire was seen to come from the boat. The Beaufighter struck the water about fifty yards behind the boat, and both Demoulin and his navigator, Flight Sergeant John S. Barker, were killed.

By mid-April, the Germans had taken the precaution of sailing their ships only at night. In response, the two Beaufighter squadrons timed their attacks at first or last light, hoping to catch the vessels at the beginning or end of their passages. In the early morning of 19 April, Wing Commander Lowe of 272 Squadron led a formation of six anti-flak and six rocket aircraft to the Gulf of Lyons. By then, the crews had been briefed to attack any vessel in the area, irrespective of nationality. They found a ship of about 2,000 tons carrying international markings, near Cape l'Espiguette, and attacked. Rockets and cannons scored hits, but the vessel was not seen to sink. There was some return fire from the ship and a Beaufighter flown by Flight Sergeant Arthur L. Hewitt went into a high-speed stall after pulling out, and then crashed into the sea. Both Hewitt and his navigator, Flight Sergeant Jack F. Garnett, lost their lives.

In the afternoon of the same day, four of 39 Squadron and four of 272 Squadron found a ship of about 600 tons near Barcelona and attacked, scoring numerous strikes. The vessel, which seemed to bear the name *José Illegua*, was left listing to starboard.

On 22 April another Canadian, Flight Lieutenant T.G. Pearse, led six of 39 Squadron and six of 272 Squadron to a position west of Sète in southern France and found a vessel of about 2,000 tons with 'Switzerland' painted amidships. Needless to say, the crews were very sceptical about this nationality and in any case they had been given 'sink at sight' orders. They attacked and scored hits, leaving the ship on fire but still afloat and steaming hard for shore.

By this time, very few enemy ships were available as targets, and the two squadrons began to take up other roles. Two Beaufighters of 39 Squadron went out on a fighter patrol on 1 May. A pilot on his first operational flight, Flying Officer Dennis A. Derby, chased a Ju 88 at low level over the Spanish coast near Tarragona. After an exchange of fire with the rear gunners, the crew saw one of the German's engines begin to smoke. It then hit the ground and blew up. Derby was wounded in his side and right arm by return fire but managed to keep going and flew the Beaufighter back to Alghero. His DFC came through immediately.

The last anti-shipping attack made by the combined squadrons took place on 6 May, when Squadron Leader Curlee led six of his squadron and six of 272 Squadron against a merchant vessel of about 1,500 tons, escorted by two flak ships, at the entrance to Sète harbour. They were met with an intense barrage of light flak from the ships and the shore, but scored numerous hits on the vessel, which bore neutral markings. All aircraft returned safely. A loss occurred on 11 May, however, when Flight Sergeant Raymond Rowell of 272 Squadron and his navigator, Flight Sergeant Roy Satchell, failed to return from an evening patrol. Both men lost their lives.

The remainder of May was taken up with an entirely new task, for the two squadrons were given the job of destroying the German radar stations along the south coast of France, in preparation for the Allied landings. They carried out this work on four occasions, hitting the stations and nearby buildings at Cap Mele, Cap Camaret and Cap d'Antibes. Each time, the formations consisted of four of 39 Squadron and six of 272 Squadron. In these attacks, double rockets were employed by 39 Squadron. This modification was carried out by the squadron engineer officer, Flight Lieutenant W. Bennett. Two rockets with 25 lb warheads were fitted underneath each rail, held together with brackets, producing a deadly and accurate weapon. In addition, four of the eight Beaufighters of 272 Squadron carried four 250 lb bombs apiece, as well as their cannons. These attacks proved extremely effective, for the radar stations and associated buildings were left on fire and covered with smoke, while no Beaufighters were lost.

By the beginning of June, the combined operations of the two Beaufighter squadrons came to an end. The crews turned to night patrols over the Italian coastline, looking for ships and also venturing slightly further inland, along the coast road. Two tank landing craft were destroyed by the rocket projectiles of 39 Squadron on 5 June. Operating from Catania in Sicily or Borgo in Corsica, 272 Squadron carried bombs on similar patrols, making successful attacks on roads and bridges.

In the eyes of the world, events in Italy and the Mediterranean were overshadowed by the momentous D-Day landings in northern France on 6 June and the subsequent battles, even though the Allies had entered Rome two days before. But the war in southern Europe continued, and 39 Squadron began to suffer losses in their night attacks, as well as on the occasional daylight sortie. Flying Officer John L. Griffith and Flying Officer Brian J. Atkin of 39 Squadron failed to return from a night patrol on 8 June, and both lost their lives. Squadron Leader Curlee was forced to ditch the following night, but he and his navigator, Warrant Officer R. Adam, were picked up from their dinghy by air-sea rescue a couple of days later. Flight Sergeants John A. Spence and Norman E.J. Barnes lost their lives on 16 June, and Flying Officers Peter H. Greenburgh and Arnold Oakes the following day. But 39 Squadron was nearing the end of its career as a wholly maritime squadron. During June, Wing Commander Harvey finished his long operational tour and was awarded a DSO. He was posted to Middle East Staff College, while command of the squadron was taken over by Wing Commander Aubrey R. de L. Inniss DFC. Then, on 13 July, the squadron completed a move to Biferno, near Termoli in Italy, on the Adriatic coast. Here the squadron joined the Balkan Air Force, which was being formed with the purpose of assisting the Yugoslav Partisan Army. This became a variegated force of sixteen squadrons and two flights, equipped with Halifaxes, Dakotas, Spitfires, Baltimores, Hurricanes, Venturas, Beaufighters and Mustangs, together with several Italian fighters and bombers, manned by men of five nations. In addition four squadrons of the US 60th Group were assigned temporarily, equipped with Dakotas.

Meanwhile, 272 Squadron began to convert to rocket projectiles on 19 June, while continuing with night operations. The squadron suffered no losses during June or July, but lost the services of its Belgian flight commander, Squadron Leader Charles L. Roman DFC, who was posted to Algiers on 23 July after an association with the squadron which went back to its formation at Aldergrove in Northern Ireland in November 1940. Night operations with rockets began to take their toll of the crews. Squadron Leader John P. Coates and Flight Sergeant Mervyn H. Rogers lost their lives on an armed reconnaissance on 7 August. Flying Officer D.A. Lampard and Flight Sergeant J.W. Smith were forced to ditch four nights later, although they were picked up by a Catalina.

The invasion of southern France began on the night of 14/15 August, under the code name of operation 'Dragoon', meeting little opposition when the American troops landed between Cannes and St Tropez. Within a few days, the whole of the French coastline was in Allied hands. The Luftwaffe withdrew from the area, and the sea war in the western Mediterranean was largely at an end. Only the Adriatic, Ionian and Aegean Seas remained for the operations of the anti-shipping squadrons.

In the eastern Mediterranean, the Beaufighter squadrons needed to lick their wounds for a few weeks after their heavy losses during the abortive attempts by the British forces to hold on to the Dodecanese Islands and Samos in the latter part of 1943. By January 1944, four anti-shipping Beaufighter squadrons remained in the area. These were 227 Squadron, commanded by Wing Commander John K. Buchanan, at Berka in Libya; 47 Squadron, commanded by Wing Commander William D.L. Filson–Young, at Gambut in Libya; 603 Squadron, commanded by Wing Commander J. Ronaldson H. Lewis, also at Gambut; and 252 Squadron, commanded by a Canadian, Wing Commander Patrick H. Woodruff, at Mersa Matruh in Egypt. Of these, 603 Squadron had converted to rocket projectiles during the latter part of 1943 and 252 Squadron was in the course of converting on to them. 47 Squadron was still equipped with torpedoes, while 227 Squadron continued in the fighter/bomber role.

Their targets were normally too small for combined operations, with some notable exceptions. Although the Germans had secured their hold on the Aegean, they were still acutely short of shipping. They had withdrawn some vessels from the Black Sea, but heavy bombing of ports such as Piraeus by both the RAF and the USAAF caused much destruction and the loss of both warships and merchant vessels. Small caiques remained the most common means of transport, lying up in defended harbours during the daylight hours. These vessels were also quite well-armed, and they were often escorted by Me 109s and Ar 196s operating within short distances from their bases. Thus the Beaufighters still had a tough task on their hands.

The year began with a series of attacks by small formations of Beaufighters, interspersed with less dangerous fighter escorts over Allied convoys. On 3 January, Filson–Young led eight of 47 Squadron on a sweep around the coast of Crete, where they were attacked by three Me 109s. These singled out a Beaufighter crewed by Warrant Officer Roger J. Barrett and Flight Sergeant William H. Fairfield and shot it down, killing both men. In 227 Squadron, Buchanan frequently led formations of four aircraft against a succession of targets in the Greek islands and along the coast of the mainland, sinking several caiques. Flying Officer L.F. Morgan and Sergeant R.A.W. Ferguson ditched on 13 January, but both men got into their dinghy and became PoWs, after an attack in which the patrol vessels *GA62*, *GA67* and *GA72* were sunk. Another attack led by Buchanan on 23 January off southern Greece resulted in the destruction of two caiques, but a Beaufighter crewed by a Canadian pilot, Flying Officer Richard B. Hutchison, and an RAF navigator, Flight Sergeant Leslie Sawle, was shot down. Both men lost their lives. Another of the four Beaufighters crashed on return to Berka and the pilot, Flying Officer Kenneth S. Judd, was killed. During an attack against a caique in the same area three days later, Flying Officer Alexander H. Will of the RAAF, and his RAF navigator, Flying Officer Brian Findley, were also killed.

A Beaufighter of 603 Squadron was shot down on 16 January when Flight Lieutenant Alexander P. Pringle led a formation of four on a very long sortie against the harbour installations at Chios, an island north of Samos. Flight Lieutenant Gordon W. MacDonnell and Flying Officer Stanley W. Piner lost their lives. Pringle led another sweep of four aircraft on 27 January, when three Ar 196 and three Ju 52 floatplanes were destroyed near Kithera. Flight Sergeant Alan Rooks reported engine trouble on the return journey and came down in the sea. Although he and his navigator, Flying Officer Morris J.R. Thom, were seen in their dinghy by the other crews, they did not survive.

Caiques were also attacked by 47 Squadron during January, and several were sunk by cannon fire. On 28 January, four Beaufighters of this squadron sank the German motor lighter *Seerose* at Mykonos. A combined attack took place on 30 January, when Wing Commander Filson–Young led six torpedo aircraft and two anti-flak of 47 Squadron, escorted by six of 603 Squadron, against a merchant vessel of about 2,000 tons leaving the island of Melos. The vessel was found with a UJ-boat leading and two flak ships on either side. All torpedoes were dropped, but the only hits appeared to be from the rockets and cannons. A Beaufighter of 47 Squadron ditched but the crew – Flight

Sergeants Cyril A. Melling and Idris L. Davies – were picked up by the Swedish Red Cross ship *Mongabarra* and taken to Piraeus.

By the end of January, the crews of 252 Squadron had completed their rocket training and also entered the fray. Flight Lieutenant Reginald H.R. Meyer led a sweep of eight aircraft to Stampalia on 31 January, where he attacked and destroyed a Ju 88. But a single-engined aircraft appeared on the scene and shot down one of the Beaufighters; Flying Officer Darrell A.L. Hall and Sergeant Alexander K. Cowie lost their lives. Another Beaufighter also failed to return but the crew – Flight Sergeant F.A. Stevenson and Sergeant C. Thompson – managed to reach Turkey and returned to the squadron in early March. On 1 February, 201 (Naval Co-operation) Group was amalgamated with Air Defence, Eastern Mediterranean (to form 'Air HQ, Eastern Mediterranean') in order to create a maritime air force more on the lines of the Mediterranean Allied Coastal Air Force which operated in the eastern and central sector.

All four squadrons carried out similar attacks during the next two months, with almost daily sweeps around the islands or along the Greek coast. Heavy casualties were suffered by 252 Squadron. Two aircraft were caught in downward turbulence when four attacked a caique off the island of Lipsos on 6 February. One hit the mast and recovered but the other, crewed by Flying Officer C.H. Mason and Sergeant J.R. Smith, came down in the sea. Fortunately the men reached Turkey and eventually returned to the squadron. A sweep of four aircraft on 9 February met with disastrous results when they were attacked by three Me 109s near Leros. Flight Lieutenant Reginald Meyer, who was leading the formation, was shot down and lost his life, together with his navigator, Flight Sergeant Peter Grieve. A similar fate befell Flight Sergeants Alfred W. Squires and Walter H. Boon in another aircraft. A third was also shot down, and both the Australian pilot, Pilot Officer Frank P. Stanger, and the RAF navigator, Flight Sergeant James S.L. Reynolds, were killed. The only Beaufighter which returned was flown by Flight Sergeant A.D. Pitt, who managed to reach cloud cover.

Other Beaufighters were lost in February. Warrant Officer Keith Wright of 227 Squadron was killed on 11 February when his Beaufighter was shot down during an attack led by Buchanan in the western Aegean. However, his navigator, Sergeant G.L. Jones, was reported as 'safe and well'. Two days later, Flying Officer Joseph Unwin and Flight Sergeant Kenneth R. Farmer of 47 Squadron were killed when attacking caiques at Hydra. On 16 February, Wing Commander Buchanan was shot down into the sea when leading four Beaufighters of 227 Squadron against a dredger in the Gulf of Argolis, about sixty miles south-west of Athens. A Bulgarian member of the ground staff who had been allowed to fly on the sortie, Leading Aircraftman

Eliahou Eliav, went down with the machine. Buchanan and his navigator, Warrant Officer Reg Howes, got into a dinghy dropped by another Beaufighter. Although Buchanan seemed to be unharmed, he went quiet after some time and then died. It was a sad end for one of the most determined and skilful commanders of the maritime squadrons. Howes, whose commission came through a few days later, was reported as 'safe in friendly hands'.

In the early afternoon of 22 February, three of the Beaufighter squadrons made a combined attack against a target which justified the use of torpedoes. This was the merchant vessel *Lisa* (formerly the Italian *Livenza*) of 5,343 tons, which was known to have left Piraeus the day before, bound for Heraklion in Crete. She was carrying a mixed cargo which included heavy guns. Wing Commander Filson–Young led six torpedo-carrying and two anti-flak Beaufighters of 47 Squadron, escorted by eight of 227 Squadron and two of 603 Squadron. Six Beaufighters of 252 Squadron were also ordered to escort the torpedo bombers, but they missed the rendezvous. Four Mitchells of the US 340th Bombardment Group participated, each carrying a 75mm cannon. The formation met the enemy vessel, escorted by two torpedo boats, five Ju 88s, four Me 109s and six Ar 196s, near the island of Dia on the north coast of Crete.

The Mitchells drew off the Ju 88s and Me 109s, and shot down two for the loss of one their number. Meanwhile, the Beaufighters passed through heavy flak from Crete and then approached the convoy. The eight Beaufighters of 227 Squadron, led by Squadron Leader Dennis B. Bennett, and the two of 603 Squadron, led by Flight Lieutenant Alexander P. Pringle, attacked the escort vessels and shot down one of the Arados. But three of 227 Squadron were shot down. In one aircraft, Flight Sergeants Sidney B. Appleton and Jack Fenton lost their lives. Flight Sergeant Robert F. Scarlett and Flying Officer Geoffrey S. Hartley were killed in another. The pilot of the third, Flying Officer John C. Corlett, was also killed. His navigator, Flying Officer Gwynfor Williams, was the only crew member to survive, to become a PoW. The two anti-flak aircraft of 47 Squadron also attacked the escort vessels, one of which caught fire. Six torpedoes were then dropped against *Lisa* and a large explosion was seen on her starboard bow. Later reconnaissance and intelligence confirmed that she had sunk without trace.

A Beaufighter of 47 Squadron was lost from flak on 25 February, when four aircraft swept round Scarpanto to attack a caique and a schooner. The crew – Flying Officer R.S. Euler and Flight Sergeant C.A. Boffin – spent four days in their dinghy before they were picked up by a British destroyer. Another Beaufighter of 227 Squadron was shot down two days later, when four aircraft swept along the west coast of

Greece. Flying Officer William M. Davies and Flight Sergeant Geoffrey A. Brown were both killed.

At this stage, 47 Squadron was nearing the end of its service in the Mediterranean, for there were few suitable targets left to justify the use of torpedoes. After a few cannon attacks against small vessels, coupled with night intruder operations, the squadron was sent to Amriya in Egypt on 15 March. Soon afterwards, the crews flew out to India, to operate in the Far East theatre.

The other three Beaufighter squadrons also carried out night intruder operations in March. Flight Lieutenant J.S. Holland of 227 Squadron succeeded in shooting down a Ju 52 near Maleme aerodrome on the night of 4/5 March, and Squadron Leader Bennett of the same squadron accounted for a Ju 88 the following night in that area. Wing Commander J.R. Blackburn arrived to take over command of 227 Squadron on 15 March. The squadron suffered another loss during the late afternoon of 30 March, when Sergeant Philip E. Davies and Flight Sergeant Ronald W. Beach failed to return from escorting a convoy, both losing their lives. On the same day, Squadron Leader Bennett led an attack on Kalamata harbour. Flight Sergeants L. Hibbert and H. Parker did not return, but were picked up the next day by a British destroyer.

Bad weather over Matruh hampered 252 Squadron's operations during the early part of March, but the squadron scored a success on the thirteenth when a Canadian pilot, Flying Officer Edward A.T. Taylor, spotted a formation of three Ju 52s during a weather reconnaissance over Rhodes. He shot down two into the sea, but the third escaped. Taylor was awarded a DFC. The commanding officer of the squadron, Wing Commander Patrick H. Woodruff, finished his tour of duty during March and was replaced by Wing Commander Bryce G. Meharg.

One of the most remarkable sorties in a Beaufighter was made by Flight Lieutenant Pringle of 603 Squadron on 8 March. His aircraft was the first of five to take off in the late afternoon, on night intruder operations over the north coast of Crete. The weather was poor but he spotted two warships in line astern near the island of Dia. The Beaufighter was fitted with eight rocket projectiles with 60 lb explosive warheads, designed to cause damage and fires rather than penetrate hulls. Pringle attacked the leading ship and saw three fires break out immediately. These spread rapidly until the whole ship was ablaze and a large explosion took place. More explosions could be seen from the Beaufighter during the return journey, followed by a glow which was visible from a distance of forty miles. The other four Beaufighters saw nothing in the area, and indeed two of them abandoned their patrols in the bad weather. It was soon verified that Pringle had hit and sunk a destroyer. This was the German *TA15* (formerly the Italian *Francesco Crispi*) of 970 tons, armed with four 120mm guns as well as 20mm flak guns, and with a complement of 152. She was later raised and salvaged but lasted only a few weeks, for she was destroyed in an air raid on Piraeus. Alexander Pringle, who had also distinguished himself in earlier operations, was awarded an immediate DFC.

Attacks against small targets continued during April and May. On 3 April, Flying Officer Robert W. Densham and Flying Officer Kenneth N. Bradford of 252 Squadron lost their lives on an intruder patrol. Two days later, one of four Beaufighters of 227 Squadron which was attacking a caique off the Greek coast hit the mast and crashed in flames against a hillside, killing Flying Officer Robert J. Owen and Flight Sergeant Leonard A. Everett. Casualties were also suffered by 603 Squadron. On 8 April, a Beaufighter was shot down when six attacked Karlovassi harbour, in the north of Samos. The pilot, Sergeant Herbert Lacey, went down with the machine, but the navigator, Sergeant John Foster, managed to reach the shore in his dinghy and evade capture. On 11 April, another Beaufighter was shot down when four of 603 Squadron investigated a landing strip being built on the island of Paros. Both the Australian pilot, Warrant Officer Edward T. Lynch, and the RAF navigator, Flight Sergeant Cyril C. Sykes, lost their lives. This landing strip was attacked with cannon fire by four of 252 Squadron on 20 April. Trucks and a roller were blown up while the work party scattered. The leader of the formation, Squadron Leader Christopher Foxley-Norris, put in a claim for 'one diesel roller 20/30 tons destroyed', to the surprise of RAF headquarters in the Middle East.

During the course of April, some of the operations carried out by 227 Squadron had been in conjunction with 16 (SAAF) Squadron, which had converted from Beauforts to Beaufighters at the end of 1943 and then trained on rocket projectiles. At the end of the month, the RAF crews were advised that their squadron would be taken over by the SAAF, but they continued to fly independently on anti-shipping attacks for the next few weeks, fortunately without casualties during May. Similarly, 603 Squadron carried out several attacks during May and suffered no losses. But 252 Squadron was less fortunate, losing a Beaufighter when four attacked six barges near Cos on 16 May. The four aircraft made three attacks, but then one was seen to pull out with the starboard engine on fire and dive into the sea. Both Pilot Officer Dennis C. Lendrum and Flying Officer Donald C. Rooke were killed. Another Beaufighter was lost in the same area on 25 May when the Canadian, Flying Officer Edward A.T. Taylor, led three Beaufighters on an attack against a barge and a caique. Taylor did not pull out of his dive but struck rising ground and then cartwheeled into the sea. He and his RAF navigator, Flight Sergeant David C. Dick, did not survive.

By May 1944, the German troops in the Aegean were in difficulties, for their supplies were beginning to dry up. Only sixteen merchant ships totalling 15,000 tons remained seaworthy for supplying the Aegean islands, and during the latter part of the month caiques were prevented from leaving harbour owing to bad weather. The German Naval Command decided to make a major effort to stock up Crete, by assembling in Piraeus the most important convoy since the island had been occupied. This consisted of the merchant ships *Tanais* (formerly Greek) of 1,545 tons, *Sabine* (formerly the Italian *Salvatore*) of 2,252 tons, and *Gertrud* (formerly the Danish *Gerda Toft*) of 1,960 tons. These were escorted by four warships captured by the Germans from the Italians, the destroyer *TA14* (formerly *Turbine*) and the torpedo boats *TA16* (formerly *Castelfidardo*), *TA17* (formerly *San Martino*) and *TA19* (formerly *Calatafimi*). In addition, four heavily armed UJ-boats reinforced the torpedo boats, as well as R-boats. The whole convoy set sail on the evening of 31 May, bound for Heraklion. Air cover was provided by Ar 196s and Ju 88s at dawn the following morning.

The RAF was fully aware of the composition and cargo of the convoy, from intelligence decryptions and aerial reconnaissance. The anti-shipping strike force detailed to attack 'the June 1st convoy', as it became known, was the largest of its type gathered by the RAF during the war in the Mediterranean. Two waves set off to launch their attacks when the convoy was approaching its destination. The first consisted of twelve Marauders of 24 (SAAF) Squadron, together with eighteen Baltimores of 15 (SAAF) Squadron and 454 (RAAF) Squadron. They were escorted by thirteen long-range Spitfires of 94 and 213 Squadrons, together with four Mustang IIIs with which 213 Squadron was being equipped. This force caught up with the convoy when it was about thirty miles north of Heraklion, and went into the attack. Bombs from the Baltimores hit the afterdeck of *Sabine*, which was leading the convoy, while others fell around the UJ-boats. The Marauders' bombs fell just ahead of *Sabine*. A Baltimore of 454 (RAAF) Squadron was shot down.

Five minutes later the second strike force, consisting entirely of Beaufighters, came out of the sun to attack with rockets and cannons. The formation was led by Wing Commander Meharg of 252 Squadron at the head of ten of his squadron, two of which were in the anti-flak role. They were accompanied by eight of 603 Squadron and four of 16 (SAAF) Squadron, also in the anti-flak role, with two of 227 Squadron as fighter escorts. Flak hit Meharg's Beaufighter before he reached the convoy, and the aircraft dived in the sea beside one of the ships, with a wing on fire. A Beaufighter of 603 Squadron, crewed by Flight Sergeants Ronald M. Atkinson and Dennis F. Parsons, was also

199

hit, and both men lost their lives. In 16 (SAAF) Squadron, a Beaufighter crewed by Captain E.A. Barrett and Lieutenant A.J. Haupt was seen to head south with the port propeller feathered, but the men made a successful force-landing on Crete and were taken prisoner. The two Beaufighters of 227 Squadron tackled the Arados. Flight Sergeant F.G.W. Sheldrick climbed from 200 feet and shot down one of them. The other, crewed by Flying Officers John W.A. Jones and Ronald A.R. Wilson, came down off the north-east coast of Crete on the return journey. Jones was taken prisoner, but Wilson was reported as 'safe in friendly hands'.

The effect of the attack by the Beaufighters on the convoy was little short of devastating. They hit *Sabine* several times and set her on fire, hit *Gertrud* in the engine room and also set her ablaze, and damaged the upper works of *Tanais* so severely that some of her crew jumped overboard. The escorts also suffered from the rockets and cannon fire. Two UJ-boats were hit. Burning fiercely, *UJ2105* capsized and sank at 1920 hours, and *UJ2101* went down ten minutes later. The torpedo boat *TA16* was so badly hit that she was almost incapable of steering.

The merchant ship *Tanais*, with blackened superstructure, reached the inner harbour of Heraklion at 2210 hours. The shattered *TA16* also reached the harbour. But nine Wellingtons of 38 Squadron attacked the harbour at 2250 hours, causing much destruction and setting fuel dumps on fire, for the loss of one of their number. Meanwhile, the torpedo boat *TA19* had taken *Gertrud* in tow, but was relieved by a tug. This brought the blazing merchant vessel into Heraklion at about 0400 hours the following morning. However, *Sabine* burnt out and was beyond assistance. She was torpedoed by one of the three serviceable German warships, which then departed for Piraeus.

The miseries of this German convoy were not at an end. Aerial reconnaissance during 2 June confirmed that a ship was burning in Heraklion harbour, with other likely targets near her. Another bombing force was despatched during the afternoon, reaching the harbour at 1740 hours. This consisted of eleven Marauders of 24 (SAAF) Squadron, nine Baltimores of 15 (SAAF) Squadron, and two Baltimores of 454 (RAAF) Squadron. Bombs from the Marauders fell on warehouses and gutted them, while some of the bombs from the Baltimores struck the unfortunate *Gertrud* amidships. The merchant ship was still on fire, and she was carrying oil, ammunition and bunker coal. The bombs caused the fires to spread and, about ninety minutes later, the merchant ship exploded. Pieces flew in all directions, causing further damage to the docks and the city. The damaged torpedo boat *TA16*, which was berthed nearby, also caught the force of this explosion and sank in harbour. All the bombers returned safely. The only merchant vessel in this ill-fated convoy to survive the aerial onslaught was *Tanais*, albeit damaged. However, she did not last long, for she was sunk by a British submarine on 9 June when returning to Piraeus.

It had been thought that the commanding officer of 252 Squadron, Wing Commander Meharg, must have been killed, but a few weeks later the squadron was informed that a wing commander resembling him had been seen in Athens, under the escort of German soldiers. Indeed, Meharg ended the war as a PoW, as did his navigator, Flying Officer E.H.G. Thompson.

On 10 June, Wing Commander Dennis O. Butler returned to take over command of 252 Squadron, and Wing Commander John D.T. Revell assumed command of 603 Squadron five days later. At this time the Beaufighter squadrons were hunting the few remaining enemy vessels which were supplying the Dodecanese. The most important of these were *Agatha* (formerly the Italian *Aprilia*) of 1,259 tons, *Anita* (formerly the Italian *Arezzo*) of 1,165 tons, and *Carola* (formerly the Italian *Corse Fougier*) of 1,348 tons. These three vessels – escorted by the warships which had survived the 'June 1st' convoy, the destroyer *TA14* and the torpedo boats *TA17* and *TA19* – succeeded in reaching Port Laki in Leros on 13 June, having kept outside the range of Beaufighters during their journey from Piraeus. On 18 June, a Royal Navy party raided Port Laki and damaged two of these warships, *TA14* and *TA17*.

The remaining warship was the torpedo boat *TA19*, the former Italian *Calatafimi* which had tried in vain to protect the tanker *Proserpina* during the attack by 47 Squadron outside Tobruk on 26 October 1942. She was found by eight Beaufighters of 252 Squadron on 19 June, led by Flight Lieutenant Charles A. Whyatt, when south-west of the island of Kalymnos. The torpedo boat was escorted by two R-boats, with three Ar 196s as air cover. One Beaufighter tackled an Arado, causing smoke to appear from the starboard wing, while the vessels were raked by 25lb rockets and cannon fire. There were many hits on the torpedo boat, and a large explosion was seen amidships. The warship did not sink, but returned to the mainland and went into dock near Athens for repairs. One Beaufighter, crewed by Pilot Officer William Davenport and Flight Sergeant C.P. Grainger, ditched with the starboard engine on fire after this attack, but both men were picked up by the Germans and became PoWs.

Meanwhile, *Anita* and *Agatha* left Leros and arrived at the port of Rhodes, where they unloaded. They survived attacks by Venturas and Wellingtons on this port and then slipped out during the evening of 2 July, escorted by R-boats and other small craft. Eight Beaufighters of 252 Squadron, led by Squadron Leader Ian B. Butler, took off from Gambut at about 2000 hours to hunt in the shipping lane between Rhodes and Cos. At 2252 hours, Butler spotted the two merchant vessels, about two miles apart, north-west of Rhodes. After being fired at, he waited until Flight Lieutenant Whyatt arrived, so that one aircraft could draw the enemy fire while the other attacked. Butler's attack against the leading vessel did not produce any visible results, but Whyatt made several dummy runs over the second vessel before firing eight rockets with 60lb warheads. There was an explosion and bursts of flame, and the vessel caught fire from end to end. She presented a clear target for the following Beaufighters, which were armed with a mixture of 25lb and 60lb rockets. This vessel proved to be *Agatha*, and she sank during the early hours of the following morning. The other merchant vessel, *Anita*, escaped, but was sunk by a British submarine on 14 July.

During June and the early few days of July, 227 Squadron continued to operate from Berka, on attacks against caiques and other small vessels, interspersed with night intruders and convoy escorts. No aircraft were lost in this period. However, preparations were being made to move to Alexandria, and the main party moved off on 15 July. From this port, the squadron ground personnel sailed to Italy, to join the SAAF as part of the new Balkan Air Force at Biferno. The aircrews were posted out and the squadron became 19 (SAAF) Squadron. This ended two very eventful years of the squadron's service in the RAF's maritime air force, during which time the crews had given the enemy some severe knocks but had also suffered heavy casualties.

The remaining two anti-shipping Beaufighter squadrons operating in the Aegean, 252 and 603 Squadrons, continued their work, although they found fewer large targets to attack. Sweeps were carried out, primarily against caiques, with some successes and a few losses. Seven of 603 and one of 252 combined on 21 July in an attack against a couple of small vessels east of Mykonos, during which a Beaufighter of 603 Squadron was shot down by intense flak; Flight Sergeants Donald Joyce and Kenneth F. Thomas lost their lives.

Three aircraft of 603 Squadron were lost on 23 July, when six Beaufighters carried out a sweep in the central Aegean. Led by Flight Lieutenant A.G. 'Tommy' Deck, who had joined the squadron for a second tour, they met several Ar 196s near Mykonos. In the ensuing air battle, the Canadian Warrant Officer L.F. Sykes and his RAF navigator, Sergeant W.H. Foxley, came down on the sea but were picked up by a British submarine. In the second aircraft, the navigator Flight Sergeant Jeffrey J. Rogers lost his life, but the pilot, Flying Officer K. Jenkinson, was picked up by a British destroyer after floating in his dinghy for over six days.

The third aircraft came down in the sea with engine failure, after the pilot had shot down an Ar 196. It was flown by Flying Officer Cas de Bounevialle, who had also returned to operational flying for a second tour. Bounevialle and his navigator, Flight Sergeant A.E. 'Gillie'

Potter, were rescued from their dinghy by a Greek caique, which took them to the mainland south-east of Athens. The RAF men were told to wait for partisans, but after four days nobody had arrived and they began to walk. When they at last made contact, the partisans took them to the island of Euboea, from where a caique carried them to Izmir in Turkey. They were accommodated in the south of this town by a likeable English lady, Mrs 'Ma' Perkins, who ran a hostel for RAF internees somewhat on the lines of a seaside landlady, providing bed and breakfast. Restrictions were not severe during their short stay, and they were even able to visit the Kursaal nightclub. From Izmir, they were taken by rail to Aleppo in Syria and then flown to Cairo, from where they were sent straight back to 603 Squadron at Gambut.

In the evening of 28 July, six of 252 Squadron went out on a night sweep in the central Aegean, where they attacked a convoy of small vessels north of Suda in Crete. Flight Lieutenant Charles A. Whyatt was seen to make two attacks on the second vessel in the convoy but was hit in the port engine. He reported that he was going to ditch, but the Beaufighter was seen to be on fire and then to explode when it hit the water. Whyatt and his navigator, Flight Sergeant Raymond A. Barrett, did not survive.

Two more Beaufighters of 252 Squadron were shot down on 1 August, when four went out at dawn to the west coast of Greece. On reaching the island of Levkas, the four split into pairs to continue the hunt. One pair attacked two small vessels, which fired parachute and cable rockets as well as 20mm cannons. Both aircraft were hit, and one was forced to ditch. The Canadian pilot, Warrant Officer Charles G. Davis, was later reported as 'safe in friendly hands', but the RAF navigator, Sergeant George N. Waller, was taken prisoner. The other pair attacked an F-boat and both were also hit by flak. One Beaufighter, crewed by another Canadian, Pilot Officer John D. Clark, and an RAF navigator, Flight Lieutenant Edwin A.C. Young, reported that it was heading for Italy. It was seen to be smoking and then ditched, with only debris and an inverted dinghy left on the surface. Both men lost their lives.

Much of the remainder of the month was occupied with night intruder patrols. A Beaufighter of 603 Squadron failed to return from an operation on the night of 30 August while over the shipping routes north of Crete. The Canadian pilot, Flying Officer H.W. Soderland, and the RAF navigator, Flight Sergeant I.L. Nicol, were taken prisoner.

During August, the Germans realised that their hold on Greece and the Aegean had become untenable. Not only was it proving impossible to supply their garrisons on the islands by sea but their lines through the Balkans were harried by partisans and from the air. On 30 August, the

Red Army entered the oil centre of Ploesti in Romania and this vital source of fuel was thereafter denied to them. When the advancing Russians reached the border of Yugoslavia, the Germans decided to use their remaining ships to bring back from the Aegean as many of their troops and as much of their material as possible, and then to evacuate southern Greece.

The two maritime Beaufighter squadrons joined in the task of making the evacuation of the Aegean islands a difficult and costly operation. One of the remaining enemy vessels engaged on this task was *Carola*, which had undergone repairs at Port Laki in Leros. The port had been under frequent attack by Wellingtons, but the vessel had escaped damage. On 5 September she left the island for Piraeus, escorted by two flak ships. Wing Commander Dennis O. Butler took off the following morning at the head of eight Beaufighters of 252 Squadron to attack the vessel at extreme range, together with four of 603 Squadron as top cover. They came across the convoy when it was nearing the Greek mainland, south-east of Athens, and attacked with rockets and cannons, in the face of 37mm and 20mm flak as well as parachute rockets. The vessels were all severely hit and left smoking, while the Beaufighters of 603 Squadron chased and damaged an escorting Ar 196. Two Beaufighters were hit but all returned safely. The merchant vessel did not sink and reached Piraeus, but was so badly damaged that she went into dry dock. The Germans scuttled her on 10 October, as a blockship for the port.

In the morning of 9 September, Wing Commander Butler went out again, leading eight of 252 Squadron on an attack against an enemy convoy which had been spotted by 603 Squadron the previous night. This was the submarine hunter *UJ2142* (formerly the Italian *Filio Pi*), accompanied by an armed caique. The Beaufighters caught up with the convoy between Crete and Milos and caused severe damage with rockets and cannon, each aircraft making two runs. No aircraft were hit, in spite of return fire.

A Beaufighter of 603 Squadron ditched when on a sweep of eight aircraft on 13 September, but the crew, Pilot Officer Albert B. Woodier and Sergeant Harold Lee, managed to evade capture. The next attack was on the following day, when eight of 252 Squadron and eight 603 Squadron made an attack on the harbour of Paroekia in the island of Paros. Some of the aircraft were carrying rockets with 25lb warheads, while others carried 60lb warheads. They made a devastating attack and sank the minesweeper *Nordstern* of 260 tons, as well as a smaller craft. One Beaufighter was hit but all returned safely.

On 19 September, Wing Commander Butler led eight of 252 Squadron to the island of Andros in the Cyclades, where they attacked the small tanker *Elli* (formerly Greek) of 272 tons in Gavrion harbour.

The vessel was en route from the island of Siros to Salonika. They scored numerous hits on the vessel, causing an explosion. As they left, a further explosion rose to 2,000 feet, and the tanker sank. All aircraft returned without damage.

In the morning of 22 September a Beaufighter of 252 Squadron flown by Flying Officer D.G.R. 'Paddy' Ward set off on a five-hour reconnaissance flight over Leros and Samos. An important target was located alongside the jetty at Port Vathi in Samos. This was *Drache*, a former Greek merchant ship of 1,870 tons which had been used by the Germans as a minelayer and which had recently made two fast trips in the Aegean as a troop transport. Eight Beaufighters of 252 Squadron, led by Wing Commander Butler, set off for Port Vathi in mid-afternoon, accompanied by four of 603 Squadron. Approaching the port from the landward side, the aircraft of 603 Squadron engaged the ground positions while those of 252 Squadron hit the auxiliary vessel with about a dozen rockets armed with 60lb warheads. Return fire included parachute rockets, but it was inaccurate and all aircraft returned. A series of explosions came from *Drache*, and reconnaissance the next day revealed that she was a burnt-out wreck.

Another target was located by a Baltimore of 459 (RAAF) Squadron operating from Berka. This was *Orion* of 700 tons, which had been sent to the eastern Aegean to help evacuate troops. The Baltimore shadowed the vessel and saw her shelter in the island of Denusa, ten miles east of Naxos. Shortly before mid-day on 23 September, Flight Lieutenant C.W. Fowler led seven of 252 Squadron to the attack, accompanied by five of 603 Squadron led by Flying Officer Cas de Bounevialle. One of 603 Squadron turned back with engine trouble, but the others received a W/T message giving the position of the enemy vessel. They found her in a small cove and hit her with 25lb and 60lb rockets, in the face of accurate 20mm and 40mm flak. Three Beaufighters were hit and one, crewed by Flight Sergeants Stanley C. Skippen and Jack A. Truscott of 252 Squadron, jettisoned its rockets and broke away overland. Both men lost their lives.

When the remaining aircraft were on their return journey, a large explosion and a sheet of flame were seen from the Denusa area. However, the fate of the vessel was uncertain, and a further strike force, consisting of five of 252 Squadron and three of 603 Squadron, was despatched before the others landed. They arrived over Denusa at 1848 hours, to find that *Orion* was beached and still burning. There was no flak, and all aircraft attacked, leaving the vessel with fresh fires. Later reconnaissance showed that she was lying broadside on to the beach, listing badly and burnt out.

On 23 September, Wing Commander Foxley-Norris, who had spent several months as 'Wing Commander Operations' at Gambut, was appointed as commanding officer of 603 Squadron. Another attack against shipping took place on 27 September, when Wing Commander Butler led eight of 252 Squadron to the island of Andros. Butler went ahead and reconnoitred the harbour, before rejoining his formation and leading them into the attack. They attacked the transport *Helly* (formerly the Greek *Ismini*) of 314 tons as well as a caique and the jetty, making two runs. There was no return fire, and all aircraft returned safely. The transport caught fire and sank.

Ten Beaufighters of 603 Squadron, led by Wing Commander Foxley-Norris, took off at mid-day on 3 October, accompanied by two of 252 Squadron, to hunt for the minelayer *Zeus* of 2,423 tons, off the east coast of the mainland of Greece. This vessel, the former Italian merchant ship *Francesco Morosini*, was considered a prime target, for she was playing an important part in the evacuation. One Beaufighter of 603 Squadron turned back with engine trouble. The formation did not find *Zeus* but came across a convoy of five small vessels to the east of Athens, and attacked. Rockets and cannon fire damaged three of the vessels, but return fire was intense and two Beaufighters of 603 Squadron were shot down. The pilot of one aircraft, Sergeant Desmond Harrison, was killed, but the navigator, Sergeant Derek V. Bannister, was later reported to be 'safe in friendly hands'. The other aircraft was crewed by Flying Officer Cas de Bounevialle and Pilot Officer A.E. 'Gillie' Potter. Bounevialle ditched with his starboard engine on fire, not far from the position where he had ditched six weeks earlier. The men were not injured, but were picked up by a UJ-boat and taken to Piraeus. From there they were escorted to Athens for a brief interrogation, and then put on a train for Yugoslavia. The train travelled only by day, since partisans were apt to attack at night. They reached Skopje and were then flown by Ju 52 to Zagreb. Another train took them to Vienna and Budapest, and eventually to Frankfurt. Ending up at Stalag Luft III at Sagan in Upper Silesia, they were marched out in January 1945 and liberated by the Russians near Berlin.

Bounevialle and Potter were unlucky for, only three days after they ditched, British forces began to land on the mainland of Greece. Athens was occupied on 14 October. British landing parties also occupied Samos, and then the islands of Syros, Naxos, Lemnos and Scarpanto. On 24 October, the German garrison in a three-storeyed building in the island of Kalymnos was encouraged to surrender when five Beaufighters of 252 Squadron blasted their home with 60lb rockets and cannon fire. The building was left on fire, with black smoke, debris and dust rolling up the valley when the aircraft departed.

By the end of October, the whole of coast of southern Greece was in British hands, although about 18,500 German troops were left in Crete,

Rhodes, Leros, Cos and Melos, together with about 4,500 Italian Fascists. These offered little danger to the Allies and were being dealt with gradually from the air and by landings. Some of the garrisons were left to stagnate, acutely short of food and harried by the RAF and partisans, until they decided to surrender.

With few targets left to attack, the anti-shipping activities of 603 and 252 Squadrons tailed off. Wing Commander Butler was awarded a DFC after leading his series of successful attacks. At the end of November 603 Squadron was taken off operations, and the following month returned to the UK, where it reassembled at Coltishall as a Spitfire squadron. But 252 Squadron remained in North Africa until February 1945 and then moved to Greece, where it was partly engaged on air-sea rescue duties, still equipped with Beaufighters, until the end of the war.

While these events were taking place in the Aegean, only one other Beaufighter squadron remained in the Mediterranean in the anti-shipping role. This was 272 Squadron, which was based at Alghero in Sardinia, with detachments at Borgo in Corsica. In early September 1944, this squadron continued to concentrate on attempts to destroy the enemy's remaining coastal trade in the Gulf of Genoa, partly using rockets during night attacks. Four aircraft were lost in a few days during these attacks. A Beaufighter flown by a Canadian, Warrant Officer William Henry Billing, failed to return on the night of 30/31 August; both Billing and his RAF navigator, Flight Sergeant Harry Thornton, were killed. In the early hours of 4 September, a Beaufighter was shot down by flak when three attacked a convoy of four ships near Sestri Levante, east of Genoa; Flying Officer Anthony F. Reynolds and Flying Officer Norman F. Young lost their lives. Later in the same night, four more Beaufighters tried to find the same convoy and another was shot down when attacking a barge; Flying Officer Cecil N. West and Flying Officer Francis G. Burgess also lost their lives. Yet another aircraft was lost in the early hours of 6 September when four attacked another convoy off La Spezia; Flight Sergeant John Horsford and Warrant Officer John C. Watson were killed on that occasion.

Then 272 Squadron was presented with the task of executing one of the most spectacular anti-shipping attacks of the war. The beautiful liner *Rex* of 51,062 tons, which at one time had held the Atlantic Blue Riband for Italy, had lain for some time in the heavily defended harbour of Trieste. In early September, British Intelligence learned that the Germans had set scuttling charges in her and that she was to be used as a blockship. On 4 September, she was spotted by photo-reconnaissance aircraft, being towed out of harbour by tugs. Two days later, she was sighted in Capodistria Bay, six miles south of Trieste.

It was decided that the RAF should sink her, and a detachment of 272 Squadron was sent from Borgo. On 7 September the Beaufighters landed at Falconara, near Ancona on the Adriatic coast of Italy, which had been recently occupied by the Allies.

At 1025 hours the next morning, Squadron Leader Roderick H. Rose led eight Beaufighters to the attack, escorted by eight Mustangs. They encountered flak from an F-boat, which was quickly silenced by the Mustangs, as well as heavy flak from the shore. The Beaufighter pilots estimated that they scored 4,000 strikes with 20mm cannon on the liner, as well as fifty-five hits with 25lb rockets below the waterline and four more on the superstructure. All aircraft returned safely, leaving the liner on fire. The squadron was credited with the destruction of the liner, but for good measure another strike was ordered. The choice fell on 39 Squadron, part of the Balkan Air Force, based at Biferno. Led by Flight Lieutenant Robert H. Pitman, six Beaufighters took off at 1700 hours, together with two Beaufighters of 16 (SAAF) Squadron and four Mustangs of 213 Squadron. They approached the stricken liner from the land, through valleys and rainstorms, and finally down a hill. Every Beaufighter claimed hits with 25lb rockets, and *Rex* was left on fire along her entire length, listing to port. Later photographs showed her resting on her side, with only about a third above the water. Squadron Leader Rose was awarded a DSO, as was Flight Lieutenant Pitman.

On 15 September, 272 began moving to Foggia in Italy, with the task of clearing German shipping from the northern Adriatic. The targets were only small vessels, but they were well-armed and highly dangerous. Attacks took place mainly at night, and the first loss occurred on 26 September, when two Beaufighters attacked a schooner in harbour. The aircraft crewed by Flight Lieutenant Frank H. Foden and Flying Officer C. Porter was seen to climb to 300 feet with the port engine on fire and then dive into the sea, killing both men.

At the end of September Wing Commander Geoffrey H. Park took over command of 272 Squadron from Wing Commander Lowe, who was 'tour-expired'. By then, five experienced crews had finished their tours of operations and were posted away. Already suffering from operational losses, the squadron was by then very short of crews. In addition, the ground staff of one flight were still awaiting transport from Borgo, resulting in operational difficulties. However, at this time seven Beaufighter crews were attached from 255 Squadron, a night-fighter squadron also based at Foggia and mainly engaged on night intruder operations over the Balkans. Several other crews were transferred from 153 Squadron, another night-fighter squadron, which was disbanded on 5 September when based at Reghaia. Since these crews were already skilled in flying the Beaufighter, the conversion period to rockets and the circumstances of anti-shipping work were speedily accomplished.

Meanwhile, a series of operations took place along the northern Adriatic. In the late afternoon of 14 October, Wing Commander Park led two Beaufighters on an armed reconnaissance to the coastline of Istria. The other pilot, Flight Lieutenant David A. Lampard, saw his commanding officer fly between the mainland and a small islet. There was a shower of white and red fire, followed by smoke. Lampard climbed to 2,000 feet for a better view but could see only a wisp of white smoke. He continued and attacked two schooners with rockets and cannons, and then returned home. Both Park and his navigator, Flying Officer Dennis L. Edwards, lost their lives. Command of the squadron was taken over temporarily by Squadron Leader Roderick H. Rose.

Ten days later, another Beaufighter was shot down by a flak ship when two made a reconnaissance of Venice. It was crewed by two veterans of 227 Squadron who had returned for a second operational tour with 603 Squadron, Flight Lieutenant Tom St B. Freer DFC, and Flight Lieutenant Charles P. Holman DFC. The pilot of the other aircraft, Flight Lieutenant F.H. Bower, saw Freer attack with cannons and rockets. But then Freer's port engine began to blaze, and the fire increased when they set course for base. Freer ditched off the north-west corner of the Istrian peninsula. He survived to become a PoW but his companion of many operational flights, Charles P. Holman, lost his life.

One of the crews which transferred from 255 Squadron consisted of two Australians, Warrant Officer Fred C. 'Pancho' Manning and Warrant Officer Spencer G. 'Flip' Philpott. Recently, Philpott summarised the duties of his new squadron:

'Our main task in 272 Squadron was hunting ships in the Gulf of Venice between Venice and Trieste, also flying about forty to forty-five kilometres inland where there were many rivers and canals, so this was good hunting ground. We also covered the Gulf of Quarnaro, the Gulf of Fiume and the islands of Cherso. This was all very interesting and beautiful country from the air, except for the fact that the Germans shot at us as we flew by admiring the scenery.'

The first flight made by this new crew was on 4 November, when they were airborne an hour before dawn with a Beaufighter flown by Flight Lieutenant Dudley L. Gaydon. Finding a landing craft off the islands west of Split in Yugoslavia, both attacked with cannons and four rockets apiece. The barge sank immediately, leaving about sixty bodies in the water. They used up their remaining rockets on a small coaster and a two-masted vessel, scoring more hits, before returning home. But a flight made by two more Beaufighters in the afternoon of the same day in the islands further north met with disaster. After making attacks on launches and a schooner, one Beaufighter crashed into cloud-covered hills in Italy when returning to base. Both Flight Sergeant Robert E.E. Mankelow and Flight Sergeant Ivor D. Goodwin were killed.

The squadron carried out night operations for the next few days, attacking more small craft. Some of these operations were carried out with the Wellingtons of 458 (RAAF) Squadron, which had moved to Foggia on 4 September 1994. After its phase of anti-shipping work with torpedoes, this Australian squadron had been employed on anti-submarine work, equipped with powerful Leigh Light searchlights. When the U-boats had been cleared out of the Mediterranean, it reverted to its anti-shipping role, carrying bombs and using Leigh Lights and flares. However, the Beaufighter crews generally found that they could achieve better results on their own during moonlit nights.

Eight Beaufighters took off on a special mission before dawn on 19 November. Their target was a base at Lussin Piccolo, on the island of Cherso south of Fiume in Yugoslavia, which British Intelligence had learned housed 'human torpedoes'. The Beaufighters attacked at first light, firing rockets with 25 lb warheads. Spencer Philpott recorded:

'Lussin Piccolo was on a small inlet and the target was completely covered with camouflage nets, blending into the surroundings. Because of its importance, it was heavily defended ... once again the Germans were at their guns since it was too early for breakfast. When the first couple of Beaufighters went in, all hell was let loose. Gun posts all around the inlet were firing, with Beaufighters like bees around a honey pot, each pouring rockets into the inlet. Then it was open season as we finished off with cannons just for good measure ... When our cine-camera film was later developed it showed Pancho's rockets ripping into the German headquarters building at the docks.'

All the Beaufighters returned safely on that occasion. The following morning, Warrant Officer Manning went out, together with another Beaufighter flown by Flying Officer J.D. Murray, as well as an escort of four Spitfires. They attacked four barges on Lake Marano, to the west of Trieste, sinking three of them, and then set a small coaster on fire.

On 22 November the new commanding officer of 272 Squadron, Wing Commander Robert N. Lambert DFC, led ten Beaufighters on another attack against the torpedo base at Lussin Piccolo in Yugoslavia. Each aircraft fired eight rockets, at various targets in the creeks, and also attacked the flak defences with cannon fire. All aircraft returned, leaving the targets smoking.

Murray and Manning went out just before dawn the following morning, again with a Spitfire escort. They found a tanker of about 2,000 tons in the Gulf of Trieste and attacked, watching the crew jump overboard and leaving the vessel on fire. Then they attacked a group of barges in Lake Marano, as well as a flak position. On its return journey the formation encountered four single-engined enemy fighters, but these were chased north by the Spitfires.

A Beaufighter ditched with engine trouble on 26 November, shortly after four attacked a barge on Lake Marano. Flight Lieutenant Dudley L. Gaydon and Flying Officer Raymond V. Fawkner-Corbett got into their K-type dinghies and appeared unharmed. The remaining aircraft circled the position for fifteen minutes, but there was nothing they could do to help the men. They were both picked up by the Germans and became PoWs.

Wing Commander Lambert led six Beaufighters on a sweep to the area of Lake Marano on 7 December, escorted by four Spitfires of 237 Squadron from Falconara. They attacked a barge, which broke in half and sank. Then they tackled six stationary barges in a canal, sinking two and leaving others on fire. But an aircraft crewed by Flying Officer John R. Rutland and Flight Sergeant Ernest M. Potts reported an oil leak and belly-landed in a field. The other crews saw the two men sitting on the port wing, waving to them, apparently unharmed. Rutland and Potts managed to evade capture, and returned to the UK in March 1945.

Two days later a new flight commander, Squadron Leader Anthony J. Mottram, led six Beaufighters to the Gulf of Trieste, escorted by six Spitfires of 237 Squadron. Mottram had been awarded a DFC when flying Beaufighters with 489 (NZ) Squadron in the UK, while his navigator, Flying Officer Walter A.G. Hook, had received a DFC after completing a tour with the Beauforts and Beaufighters of 39 Squadron in the Mediterranean. When flying at 150 feet, the Beaufighter and Spitfire formation encountered medium and light flak from the shore. This was both intense and accurate, and an aircraft flown by Flying Officer John C. Horlock and Warrant Officer Frank H. Rapley was hit. Horlock attempted a force-landing in a field but the aircraft blew up when it skidded along the ground. Rapley tried to rescue Horlock, but was forced out of the burning machine. The pilot lost his life, and the navigator ended the war as a PoW. The other aircraft scored hits on three barges, two of which sank.

The commanding officer, Wing Commander Lambert, was seriously wounded on 10 December. He led four Beaufighters on a rocket attack against five barges and a tug east of Venice, sinking four of the barges. Three more barges and a warehouse were also attacked, and left burning. Lambert then tackled three more barges but the Beaufighter was hit by light flak after breaking away. He was wounded in the right arm and chest. His navigator, Flying Officer A.E. Easterbee, came forward to render first aid and then took over the control column to bring the aircraft clear of the flak. Lambert was weakened by his injuries, and Easterbee put the aircraft on a course for the nearest airfield, at Fano, between Rimini and Ancona. On arrival, Lambert made a successful belly landing on soft ground alongside the runway, with Easterbee standing astride the well and holding the throttles. The two men were not injured in the landing but Lambert was taken to hospital, where it was discovered that his wounds were extensive but not dangerous. However, it was estimated that he would be out of action for about two months, and Squadron Leader Johnson assumed command of the squadron.

The following day, a Beaufighter crashed near base when returning from a night patrol in poor visibility. The aircraft was found to be burnt out, and both Warrant Officer Derek W. Lane and Flight Sergeant Burlington W.R. Morgans were killed.

Operations in the remainder of December were restricted to some extent by poor weather, although a few attacks took place, mainly between Venice and Trieste. On one occasion, Warrant Officer Manning spotted a rowing boat near Venice, containing a German soldier in a very amorous position with his girl friend. Manning drew Philpott's attention to this interesting sight and then put down the nose of his Beaufighter, pulling out just over the boat but chivalrously refraining from opening fire. The two Australians were rewarded with the spectacle of the German diving over the side into the ice-cold water, still wearing his uniform jacket but minus his trousers.

After a few more operations, Manning and Philpott were posted to the UK at the end of the year.

The first casualty in 1945 occurred on 3 January, when two Beaufighters took off in the late evening for a patrol in combination with a Wellington of 458 (RAAF) Squadron. The crew of one aircraft, flown by Squadron Leader Mottram, called up the other crew half an hour after take-off, but received no reply. Mottram continued and attacked a tanker in the Gulf of Venice, without seeing any results. The other Beaufighter did not return, and both Flying Officer Roy T. Greig and Flying Officer Bernard D. Lilley lost their lives.

The remainder of January continued with a series of small attacks, but on the last day of the month the squadron lost yet another commanding officer. Two Beaufighters took off in the late afternoon and one, flown by Squadron Leader Johnson, made a rocket attack on a motor launch in the Gulf of Trieste. The aircraft touched the sea when pulling out of the dive and blew up, killing both Johnson and his navigator, Pilot Officer Harold Roe. The death of both men was keenly felt by the squadron. The loss of Richard Johnson was made even more poignant on the following day, for news came through of both his promotion to wing commander and his appointment as commanding officer. Squadron Leader Anthony J. Mottram took over temporary command of the squadron.

Operations continued intermittently to the end of the war. The last casualty occurred on 6 March, when Flight Sergeant Erik C. Berg and Warrant Officer Henry F. Kirk failed to return from a daylight sortie, both men losing their lives. The squadron moved to Falconara on 20 March, and the ubiquitous Wing Commander J. Ronaldson H. Lewis DFC, arrived to take over command of the squadron a week later.

The squadron was disbanded at the end of April. The final entries in the Operations Record book of 272 Squadron include a summary of its activities in the Mediterranean, showing 100 aircraft destroyed in combat with forty-nine probably destroyed or damaged. In addition, the record includes 137 enemy aircraft destroyed on the ground, with 124 probably destroyed and damaged. On the ground, 832 trucks and twelve trains were destroyed or damaged. The squadron also claimed sixty-seven enemy vessels sunk and 318 damaged, but most of these were small coastal vessels or barges which were not registered in Lloyds' Lists. The liner *Rex* was additional to this list. Of the merchant ships which were registered in Lloyds' Lists, official figures prepared after the war show 273 vessels sunk by the whole of the RAF and Commonwealth Air Forces in the Mediterranean, totalling 440,040 tons GRT. In addition, seventy-nine ships totalling 108,731 tons were shared with the FAA or the USAAF. Apart from these merchant vessels, many enemy warships were destroyed from the air. The Beauforts and Beaufighters of the maritime air force played a major part in these attacks, the crews achieving many successes, albeit at a heavy price in terms of casualties.

BIBLIOGRAPHY

Barker, R., *The Ship Busters* (London: Chatto & Windus, 1957).

Brown, J.A., *Eagles Strike*, (Cape Town: Purnell, 1974).

Calvocoressi, P., *Top Secret Ultra* (London: Cassell, 1980).

Clark, A., *The Fall of Crete* (London: Anthony Blond, 1962).

Delve, K., *The Winged Bomb* (Leicester: Midland Counties, 1985).

Fielding, X., *Hide and Seek* (London: Secker & Warburg, 1954).

Gröner, E., *Die deutschen Kriegsschiffe, 1815–1945* (Munich: Lehmanns, 1966).

Herington, H.T., *Air War against Germany and Italy 1939–43* (Canberra: Australian War Memorial, 1963).

Hinsley, F.H. et al, *British Intelligence in the Second World War* (London: HMSO, 1979–1990).

Lenton, H.T., *German Warships of the Second World War* (London: MacDonald & Jane's, 1975).

Lewin, R., *The Life and Death of the Afrika Korps* (London: Book Club Associates, 1977).

Lewin, R., *Ultra goes to War* (London: Hutchinson, 1978).

Lloyds War Losses, Second World War, vol. III (Guildhall Library, (unpublished).

Lucas, J., *War in the Desert* (London: Arms & Armour, 1982).

Macksey, K., *Kesselring* (London: Batsford, 1978).

Molony, C.J.C., *The Mediterranean and Middle East*, vol. VI Part I (London: HMSO, 1984).

Moss, W.S., *Ill Met by Moonlight* (London: Harrap, 1950).

Nesbit, R.C., *Torpedo Airmen* (London: Wm Kimber, 1982).

Nesbit, R.C., *The Strike Wings* (London: Wm Kimber, 1984).

Pack, S.W.C., *The Battle for Crete* (London: Ian Allan, 1973).

Pitt, Barrie, *The Crucible of War: Western Desert, 1941* (London: Jonathan Cape, 1980).

Playfair, I.S.O. & Molony, C.I.C., *History of the Second World War: The Mediterranean and Middle East*, vol. IV (London: HMSO, 1966).

Psychoundakis, G., *The Cretan Runner* (London: John Murray, 1955).

Public Record Office:
ADM 199/725   Operation 'Monsoon' – Report by *Furious*
AIR 2/5684   Recommendations for Awards, Escaped PoWs 1941–46
AIR 8/1019   Oil as a Factor in the German War Effort, Mar–Jun 1946
AIR 15/42   Operational Training Units – policy, Jan 1939–Apl 1942

AIR 15/570   Operational Squadrons – training, Jly 1942–Apl 1943
AIR 15/571   ——, Jly 1943–Oct 1943
AIR 15/572   ——, Dec 1940–Jly 1941
AIR 15/573   ——, – training policy, Jly 1941–Feb 1942
AIR 15/574   ——, Feb 1942–Apl 1943
AIR 15/575   ——, Apl 1943–Aug 1944
AIR 15/576   ——, Aug 1944–Aug 1945
AIR 15/589   Bombing training, Nov 1943–Mar 1944
AIR 15/591   Navigational training, Jly 1941–Sep 1945
AIR 20/2859   Aircrew: operational tours, Mar 1941–Sep 1944
AIR 20/8023   SOE Middle East and North Africa, 1941–1943
AIR 22/124   Air Staff Operational Summary, Jan 1942–Mar 1942
AIR 22/130   Air Ministry and War Room Summaries, Jun 1943–Jly 1943
AIR 22/186   Middle East Table of Operations, Feb 1944–Jun 1944
AIR 22/272   State of Aircraft in the Mediterranean, Mar 1941–Dec 1941
AIR 23/6743   Escapes from Cos and Leros, 1943
AIR 23/7426   RAF Station Shallufa, 1942–1943
AIR 24/908   AHQ Malta Operations Record Book, Jun 1940–Aug 1942
AIR 24/909   AHQ ——, Sep 1942–Jun 1943
AIR 25/795   201 Group ——, Sep 1939–Dec 1942
AIR 25/796   201 ——, Jan 1943–Jan 1944
AIR 26/337   247 Wing ——, Apl 1942–Feb 1944
AIR 26/435   328 ——, Oct 1942–Oct 1944
AIR 27/211   15 Squadron Operations Record Book, Jan 1942–Dec 1943
AIR 27/227   16 ——, Jan 1944–Aug 1944
AIR 27/263   21 ——, Nov 1935–Dec 1942
AIR 27/390   37 ——, Jan 1942–Dec 1942
AIR 27/399   38 ——, Jan 1942–Dec 1942
AIR 27/407   39 ——, Apl 1940–Dec 1943
AIR 27/460   46 ——, Apl 1916–Dec 1943
AIR 27/464   47 ——, Jan 1942–Dec 1943
AIR 27/465   47 ——, Jan 1944–Mar 1946
AIR 27/607   69 ——, Jan 1942–Dec 1942
AIR 27/608   69 ——, Jan 1943–Dec 1943
AIR 27/729   89 ——, Oct 1941–Dec 1943
AIR 27/926   126 ——, Jun 1941–Dec 1943
AIR 27/982   144 ——, Jan 1943–Dec 1943
AIR 27/994   148 ——, Jun 1937–Dec 1942
AIR 27/1166   196 ——, Oct 1942–Jun 1944
AIR 27/1368   221 ——, Nov 1940–Dec 1943
AIR 27/1409   227 ——, Aug 1940–Dec 1943
AIR 27/1410   227 ——, Jan 1944–Jly 1944
AIR 27/1449   236 ——, Jan 1944–May 1945
AIR 27/1508   252 ——, Nov 1940–Dec 1943
AIR 27/1509   252 ——, Jan 1944–Sep 1946
AIR 27/1577   272 Squadron Operations Record Book, Nov 1940–Dec 1942
AIR 27/1578   272 ——, Jan 1943–Apl 1945
AIR 27/1579   272 ——, Appendices, Mar 1941–Apl 1945

AIR 27/1902   458 ——, Sep 1941–Dec 1943
AIR 27/1925   466 ——, Oct 1942–Dec 1943
AIR 27/2007   540 ——, Oct 1942–May 1945
AIR 27/2010   540 ——, A Flight Appendices, Mar 1944–Oct 1944
AIR 27/2079   603 ——, Sep 1925–Dec 1943
AIR 27/2080   603 ——, Jan 1944–Aug 1945
AIR 28/409   Kalafrana Operations Record Book May 1916–Oct 1943
AIR 28/503   Luqa ——, Jan 1942–Dec 1942
AIR 28/504   Luqa ——, Jan 1943–Dec 1943
AIR 28/506   Luqa ——, Appendices Mar 1943–Jun 1943
AIR 28/587   Nicosia ——, Feb 1944–May 1945
AIR 28/701   Shallufa ——, Dec 1940–Aug 1945
AIR 41/4   Flying Training – Aircrew Training 1934–1942
AIR 41/25   The Middle East Campaigns, vol. II. Operations in the Western Desert Jun 1941–Jan 1942
AIR 41/19   The RAF in Maritime War, vol. 6; The Mediterranean and Red Sea
AIR 41/54   The RAF in Maritime War, vol. 7 Part I; The Mediterranean Reconquest and Submarine War, May 1943-May 1944
AIR 41/76   The RAF in Maritime War, vol. 7 Part 2; The Mediterranean Reconquest and End of Submarine War, Operations in the Adriatic, Greece and the Aegean, 1944–1945

Rawlings, J.D.R., *Coastal, Support and Special Squadrons of the RAF and their Aircraft* (London: Jane's, 1982).

Richards, D. & Saunders, H. St G., *The Royal Air Force 1939–45* (London: HMSO, 1953–54).

Roskill, S.W., *The War at Sea* (London: HMSO, 1954–61).

Shores, C. & Ring, H., *Fighters over the Desert* (London: Spearman, 1967).

Shores, C., Ring, H. & Hess, W.N., *Fighters over Tunisia* (London: Spearman, 1975).

Shores, C.F., *Pictorial History of the Mediterranean war*, vol. I (London: Ian Allan, 1982).

Smith, P. & Walker, E., *War in the Aegean* (London: Wm Kimber, 1974).

Spooner, T., *Warburton's War* (London: Wm Kimber, 1987). *Ufficio Storica della Marina Militare: la Marina Militare nella Seconda Guerra Mondiale*: vol. VII, *La Difesa del Traffico con l'Africa Settentriole dal 1 Ottobre 1941 al 30 Settembre 1943* (Roma, 1958), vol. VII, *La Difesa del Traffico con l'Africa Settentriole dal 1 Ottobre 1943 al Caduta della Tunisia* (Roma, 1962).

Van Creveld, M., *Rommel's Supply Problem, 1941–42* (London: RUSI Journal, 1974).

Wood, T. & Gunston, B., *Hitler's Luftwaffe* (London: Salamander, 1977).

Index

Mankelow, Flt/Sgt Robert E.E. 210
Manley, Flt/Lt John H. 163
Manning, P/O Ralph V. 94, 95, 96, 97, 99
Manning, W/O Fred C. 209, 210, 212
Mareth line 135, 138
Marlow, Fred 31, 32, 33, 35
Marshall, Sqn/Ldr R.S.O. 132, 135
Martin
  Baltimore 73
  Maryland 22, 29
Mason, W/Cdr Arthur J. 35
Masterman, W/Cdr Cedric A. 85, 86, 105, 106–7, 108, 109, 111, 113, 114, 117, 120
Mather, Flt/Sgt Christopher 124
Matthias, F/O Walter B. 153, 190
Maturba 45, 46
Mayers, W/Cdr H.C. 56
Mazur, F/O Apollon P. 176, 177
McGarry, P/O Terry A. 74, 82–4
McGregor, Flt/Lt Walter Y. 163
McIntyre, Flt/Lt Ian 145
McLaughlin, W/Cdr James 145
McLeod, Sgt Ian A. 155
Mead, Sgt Eric A.W.J. 161
Meads, Sqn/Ldr Ernest R. 162
Mediterranean Air Command 123
Mediterranean Allied Coastal Air Force 187
Medley, Sgt John 28, 35
Meharg, W/Cdr Bryce G. 197, 199, 201
Meyer, Flt/Lt Reginald H.R. 195
Miller, Flt/Sgt Ivor R. 86
Miller, Sgt J.G. 83, 84
Milson, Sqn/Ldr Colin G. 111, 137
mining operations 124
Modera, P/O J.R.S. 115, 116, 117, 118, 171
Moffatt, P/O John D. 81
Montgomery, General Bernard 90, 103, 138
Morfitt, Flt/Sgt Thomas C. 175
Morgans, Flt/Sgt Burlington W.R. 212
Morris, F/O Graham W. 47
Mottram, Sqn/Ldr Anthony 211, 212
Muller-Rowland, F/O Eric R. 130, 142, 143
Muller-Rowland, Sqn/Ldr John S.R. 130, 185
Muller-Rowland, Sqn/Ldr Stanley R. 129–30, 133, 136, 137, 139, 145, 146,

147, 149, 150, 152, 153, 181, 182, 184–5
Murray, Sgt J.M. 148
Mussolini, Benito 59, 89, 148, 152

Nash, W/O Gordon D. 69–70
Neighbour, Flt/Sgt Robert S. 167
Nichols, Sgt Colin B.A. 61
Nichols, Flt/Lt Eric G. 158
Nicosia 18, 164
Nisbet, F/O T.F. 54, 55, 56–7
No. 5 Middle East Training School 19, 181
Noome, Lt Frederick O. 80
North American B-25G Mitchell 173
North-West African Coastal Air Force 140, 187

Oakes, F/O Arnold 192
Ogilvie, Sqn/Ldr Charles A. 144, 152, 176, 178
Ogilvie, W/Cdr Patrick B.B. 159
O'Hara, Flt/Sgt Eric 76
Olive, Sgt John E. 47
Operation Agreement 67
Operation Crusader 39, 43, 49, 51
Operation Dragoon 193
Operation Hercules 53–4
Operation Husky 141
Operation 'M-43' 51
Operation Plug 22
Operation Torch 104
operational casualties 13
Orr, P/O Kenneth B. 48
Owen, F/O Robert J. 198

Painter, Sqn/Ldr Kenneth R.P. 146, 150, 151, 154
Park, W/Cdr Geoffrey H. 208, 209
Parsons, Flt/Sgt Dennis F. 199–200
Partridge, P/O Dennis de M. 80
Patricia Bay, British Columbia 18
Patterson, Sgt John E. 52
Pearse, Flt/Lt T.G. 191
Pearson, Sgt Donald H. 164
Pearson, P/O Robert B. 108
Petch, Sqn/Ldr Norman S. 137, 150, 155
Phillips, Sgt A.J. 83, 116
Philpott, W/O Spencer G. 209, 210, 212
Pidsley, Major Douglas W. 95, 96, 99
Pien, Sgt Henri F.M. 118
Piner, F/O Stanley W. 194
Pitman, Flt/Lt Robert H. 208